## ATLA Monograph Series
## edited by Dr. Kenneth E. Rowe

1. Ronald L. Grimes. *The Divine Imagination: William Blake's Major Prophetic Visions.* 1972.
2. George D. Kelsey. *Social Ethics among Southern Baptists, 1917-1969.* 1973.
3. Hilda Adam Kring. *The Harmonists: A Folk-Cultural Approach.* 1973.
4. J. Steven O'Malley. *Pilgrimage of Faith: The Legacy of the Otterbeins.* 1973.
5. Charles Edwin Jones. *Perfectionist Persuasion: The Holiness Movement and American Methodism, 1867–1936.* 1974.
6. Donald E. Byrne, Jr. *No Foot of Land: Folklore of American Methodist Itinerants.* 1975.
7. Milton C. Sernett. *Black Religion and American Evangelicalism: White Protestants, Plantation Missions, and the Flowering of Negro Christianity, 1787–1865.* 1975.
8. Eva Fleischner. *Judaism in German Christian Theology Since 1945: Christianity and Israel Considered in Terms of Mission.* 1975.
9. Walter James Lowe. *Mystery & the Unconscious: A Study in the Thought of Paul Ricoeur.* 1977.
10. Norris Magnuson. *Salvation in the Slums: Evangelical Social Work, 1865–1920.* 1977.
11. William Sherman Minor. *Creativity in Henry Nelson Wieman.* 1977.
12. Thomas Virgil Peterson. *Ham and Japheth: The Mythic World of Whites in the Antebellum South.* 1978.
13. Randall K. Burkett. *Garveyism as a Religious Movement: The Institutionalization of a Black Civil Religion.* 1978.
14. Roger G. Betsworth. *The Radical Movement of the 1960's.* 1980.
15. Alice Cowan Cochran. *Miners, Merchants, and Missionaries: The Roles of Missionaries and Pioneer Churches in the Colorado Gold Rush and Its Aftermath, 1858–1870.* 1980.
16. Irene Lawrence. *Linguistics and Theology: The Significance of Noam Chomsky for Theological Construction.* 1980.
17. Richard E. Williams. *Called and Chosen: The Story of Mother Rebecca Jackson and the Philadelphia Shakers.* 1981.
18. Arthur C. Repp, Sr. *Luther's Catechism Comes to America: Theological Effects on the Issues of the Small Catechism Prepared in or for America prior to 1850.* 1982.
19. Lewis V. Baldwin. *"Invisible" Strands in African Methodism.* 1983.
20. David W. Gill. *The Word of God in the Ethics of Jacques Ellul.* 1984.
21. Robert Booth Fowler. *Religion and Politics in America.* 1985.

22. Page Putnam Miller. *A Claim to New Roles.* 1985.
23. C. Howard Smith. *Scandinavian Hymnody from the Reformation to the Present.* 1987.
24. Bernard T. Adeney. *Just War, Political Realism, and Faith.* 1988.
25. Paul Wesley Chilcote. *John Wesley and the Women Preachers of Early Methodism.* 1991.
26. Samuel J. Rogal. *A General Introduction of Hymnody and Congregational Song.* 1991.
27. Howard A. Barnes. *Horace Bushnell and the Virtuous Republic.* 1991.
28. Sondra A. O'Neale. *Jupiter Hammon and the Biblical Beginnings of African-American Literature.* 1993.
29. Kathleen P. Deignan. *Christ Spirit: The Eschatology of Shaker Christianity.* 1992.
30. D. Elwood Dunn. *A History of the Episcopal Church in Liberia, 1821–1980.* 1992.
31. Terrance L. Tiessen. *Irenaeus on the Salvation of the Unevangelized.* 1993.
32. James E. McGoldrick. *Baptist Successionism: A Crucial Question in Baptist History.* 1994.
33. Murray A. Rubinstein. *The Origins of the Anglo-American Missionary Enterprise in China, 1807–1840.* 1996.
34. Thomas M. Tanner. *What Ministers Know: A Qualitative Study of Pastors as Information Professionals.* 1994.
35. Jack A. Johnson-Hill. *I-Sight: The World of Rastafari: An Interpretive Sociological Account of Rastafarian Ethics.* 1995.
36. Richard James Severson. *Time, Death, and Eternity: Reflections on Augustine's "Confessions" in Light of Heidegger's "Being and Time."* 1995.
37. Robert F. Scholz. *Press toward the Mark: History of the United Lutheran Synod of New York and New England, 1830–1930.* 1995.
38. Sam Hamstra Jr. and Arie J. Griffioen. *Reformed Confessionalism in Nineteenth-Century America: Essays on the Thought of John Williamson Nevin.* 1996.
39. Robert A. Hecht. *An Unordinary Man: A Life of Father John LaFarge, S.J.* 1996.
40. Moses Moore. *Orishatukeh Faduma: Liberal Theology and Evangelical Pan-Africanism, 1857–1946.* 1996.
41. William Lawrence. *Sundays in New York: Pulpit Theology at the Crest of the Protestant Mainstream.* 1996.
42. Bruce M. Stephens. *The Prism of Time and Eternity: Images of Christ in American Protestant Thought from Jonathan Edwards to Horace Bushnell.* 1996.

# The Prism of Time and Eternity

## Images of Christ in American Protestant Thought from Jonathan Edwards to Horace Bushnell

Bruce M. Stephens

*ATLA Monograph Series, No. 42*

The American Theological Library Association
and
The Scarecrow Press, Inc.
Lanham, Md., & London
1996

SCARECROW PRESS, INC.

Published in the United States of America
by Scarecrow Press, Inc.
4720 Boston Way
Lanham, Maryland 20706

4 Pleydell Gardens, Folkestone
Kent CT20 2DN, England



British Cataloguing-in-Publication Information Available

**Library of Congress Cataloging-in-Publication Data**

Stephens, Bruce M.
The prism of time and eternity : images of Christ in American Protestant thought, from Jonathan Edwards to Horace Bushnell / by Bruce M. Stephens.
p. cm. —(ATLA monograph series ; no 42)
Includes bibliographical references and index.
1. Jesus Christ—History of doctrines—18th century. 2. Jesus Christ—History of doctrines—19th century. 3. Theology, Doctrinal—United States—History—18th century. 4. Theology, Doctrinal—United States—History—19th century. I. Title. II. Series.
BT198.S73 1996 232'.0973—dc20 96-17618 CIP

ISBN 0-8108-3172-4 (cloth : alk.paper)

⊖™ The paper used in this publication meets the minimum requirements of American National Standard for Information Sciences—Permanence of Paper for Printed Library Materials, ANSI Z39.48–1984.
Manufactured in the United States of America.

# CONTENTS

# SERIES EDITOR'S FOREWORD

Since 1972 the American Theological Library Association has undertaken responsibility for a modest monograph series in the field of religious studies. Titles are selected from studies in a wide range of religious and theological disciplines. We are pleased to publish *The Prism of Time and Eternity: Images of Christ in American Protestant Thought from Jonathan Edwards to Horace Bushnell* by Bruce M. Stephens as number 42 in the ATLA Monograph Series.

# INTRODUCTION

The author of the *Epistle to the Hebrews* admonishes his readers that "Jesus Christ is the same yesterday and today and forever." (Heb. 13:8). However, the answers to Christ's haunting question, "Who do you say that I am?" reflect not sameness but variety from the time that the question was asked to the present. While this variety of answers has received widespread attention from the historians of doctrine and much has been written on the topic of Christology it is not clear that Christology has received the systematic attention that it deserves, specifically within American Christianity. The present study focuses on changing conceptions of Christ in American Protestantism from Jonathan Edwards to Horace Bushnell. While it may be argued that in the American context Christology and the Second Person of the Trinity generally have been neglected in favor of the doctrines of original sin, the atonement and regeneration, nevertheless there were major figures within the period under consideration for whom the study and the formulation of the doctrine of the person of Christ were of enormous importance. The struggle to formulate a Christology that was both faithful to the wider stream of historical Christianity and reflective of the specific experience of Christianity in America helped to create a tradition of lively theological debate in the century following Jonathan Edwards. It would seem therefore to be a worthwhile undertaking to reconstruct at least in part the Christological debates within American Protestantism from the mid-eighteenth to the mid-nineteenth century as a modest contribution to a wider understanding of the religious experience of the American people.

The person of Christ is a significant doctrine on which to focus not only because of its centrality within the history of Christian doctrine but also because this doctrine serves as a touchstone to understanding better the Christian faith within a particular historical and cultural context. Indeed, the answers to the question, "Who do you say that I am?" cannot be surveyed without taking into account the historical, cultural and theological context within which the question is asked and the answers are given. The history of doctrine is just such an effort to get at, in this case, how the person of Christ is understood within these various contexts and how this understanding has been brought to intellectual expression. Every effort will be made here to be faithful to the seriousness of these doctrinal formulations and their contexts, recognizing at the same time that the person of Christ cannot be captured or exhausted in doctrines alone. In addition to and alongside the more formal Christologies formulated in the history of doctrine there are popular portraits or images of Christ that emerge and to which some attention also must be given. The assemblage of these doctrines and portraits as formulated and drawn in the sermons, treatises, tracts and memoirs of major figures between Edwards and Bushnell should expand our understanding and appreciation of American Protestantism, as we search for the several Christs who emerge from the pages of their works. The objective is a theologically informed historical account of a particular doctrine that will provide a distinctive but not exhaustive vista on the period under study and on major religious figures within it.

1

The troublesomeness of Christology was not unique in the history of doctrine to the religious thinkers who will come under consideration in our study. From the days of the early church fathers the figure of Christ refused to stand still, and the formulation of the person of Christ put forth by one divine as the absolute scriptural truth on the matter was rejected by another as an absolute absurdity. What was mystery for one thinker turned out to be nonsense to another, and the clear image of Christ set forth by one was rejected by another as a blurred and unrecognizable figure. Yet Christology, as the reflective and systematic study of the person of Christ, is at the center of Christianity, and it is the task of Christology to work out as precisely as possible the theological claim that in Christ the human and the divine are united. The challenge is to unpack each doctrine and portrait of Christ to see how it was arrived at in the first place, recognizing that it has proved to be no easy task through the centuries to hold the divinity and the humanity of Christ together. There should be no reason then to expect that the major figures we encounter in this study will be exempt from this difficulty of aligning the two natures of Christ. There is a wide doctrinal spectrum running the gamut from outright denials of Christ's divinity to serious questions about the genuineness of his humanity, and yet somehow in the midst of this confusion a recognizable figure emerges who represents continuity in the midst of change and sameness in the midst of variety.

This problem of continuity and change is clearly evident in the christological controversies of the fourth and fifth centuries, and many of the same issues that came to a head in the Council of Chalcedon in A.D. 451 are present in the christological debates in American Protestantism among the major figures from Edwards to Bushnell. The portraits of Christ in the early church are many, including that of Docetism, which tends to construe the incarnation as a theophany, and while not totally denying the humanity of Christ, tends to divinize him in such a way as to remove him from all contact with our humanity. Likewise, Ebionitism tends to neglect Christ's divinity by construing it as a superadded dignity conferred on him because of his moral and religious stature. Similarly Apollinarianism extolled the divinity of Christ at the expense of his humanity by replacing his human mind with the divine Logos, under the conviction that Christ otherwise is subject to sin and that his death would then be that of a mere man, which is certainly insufficient for the salvation of humankind; therefore, the Apollinarians gave up on the idea of uniting the humanity and the divinity of Christ in one person.

Of the several portraits of Christ set forth in the fourth and fifth centuries, perhaps none created more havoc then or in late eighteenth- and early nineteenth-century American Protestantism than did Arianism. Strictly speaking, Arianism has more to do with trinitarian than with christological issues because the controversy is over the relationship between the first two persons of the trinity and not over the relationship between the divinity and the humanity of Christ. But trinitarian and christological issues are not neatly sorted out from each other, as Arianism demonstrates, because Arius's primary interest was finally in the person of Christ. Arius arrived at the conclusion that Christ was a secondary divine being who at the same time was a created being, serving as an intermediary between God and the world and therefore inferior to God. Because the Son had a beginning "there was a time when he was not," and therefore he is a creature; a perfect creature to be sure, but not divine because he is "alien and dissimilar in all things from the Father." To the Arians it was absolutely essential, if Christ was to effect the salvation of humankind, that he be human in every way, a reminder that who Christ is cannot be separated from what Christ does. This link between the person of Christ or the relation between the human and the divine and the work of Christ or the atonement would emerge as a particularly troublesome issue in American Protestant theology between Edwards and Bushnell, so much so that some were driven to despair and to publicly confess that "they have taken our Lord and laid him we know not where."

It would be too much to claim that the issues separating the rival schools of ancient Antioch and Alexandria were replayed in their entirety in American Protestantism between the last half of the eighteenth and the first half of the nineteenth century; still the issues over which the Antiochenes and the Alexandrians quarreled were not absent from the American scene. The Antiochenes, with their devotion to the humanity of Christ and their denial of the possibility of the union of the two natures in the one person of Christ, had their counterparts in New England and elsewhere. Likewise, the Alexandrians, with their emphasis on the deity of Christ and their insistence on the union of the two natures in Christ, had their counterparts among the disputants within the American context.

To this growing list of christological options may be added the Nestorians, who perceived the incarnation as an extrinsic but not an essential union of the human and the divine in Christ. They rejected the term *Theotokos,* or "Mother of God" as inappropriate because Mary was the mother of the man Jesus but not of the divine Logos, leading to a charge against them of a duality of Sons. In opposition to the Nestorians stood the Eutychians, who taught that before the incarnation there were two natures but after the incarnation only one nature in Christ. The distinction of the two nature is thereby compromised to such an extent that the human nature of Christ is absorbed by the divine. Again, it is too much to claim that the issues separating the Nestorians and the Eutychians were replayed *in toto* during the course of the christological debates in American Protestantism between Edwards and Bushnell, but there were themes from each of these two ancient rival schools that emerged on the American scene in the period under consideration.

An attempt to bring the rivalries and conflicts of these several schools under some control was made at the Council of Chalcedon with its definition of the person of Christ, according to which Christ is

> truly God and truly man, the same of a reasonable soul and body; consubstantial with the Father in Godhead, and the same consubstantial with us in manhood, like us in all things except sin; begotten before ages of the Father in Godhead, the same in the last days for us and for our salvation [born] of Mary the virgin *theotokos* in manhood, one and the same Christ, Son, Lord, unique: acknowledged in two natures, without separation—the difference of the natures being by no means taken away because of the union, but rather the distinctive character of each nature being preserved, and [each]combining in one Person and hypostasis—not divided or separated into two Persons, but one and the same Son and only-begotten God, Word, Lord, Jesus Christ.

Just as it satisfied completely neither the Antiochenes nor the Alexandrians, neither the Nestorians nor the Eutychians, so too the christological "definition" of Chalcedon had both supporters and detractors in American Protestantism's struggles toward its own christological definition. The question of just how the two natures are united in the one person of Christ is left unresolved by the Chalcedonian Decree, giving rise to further division and debates. For example, the Monophysites argued that in Christ there is only one dominant nature after the incarnation and that is the divine nature, in opposition to Chalcedon, which specified two complete natures in one person. Later there were further difficulties that arose in conjunction with the question of whether the divine or the human nature of Christ suffered, as well as the problem of whether there are two wills in Christ, one divine and the other human. The Monothelites, in an attempt to conciliate the Monophysites, adopted the formula of two natures but one "divine-human operation" instead of two distinct but cooperating wills. And so, despite its best effort to offer a creedal standard of christological orthodoxy, Chalcedon by no means succeeded in solving the issues, much less ending the debates, on the person of Christ. What it did accomplish was a rather admirable job of setting the parameters within which constructive christological debates could take place.

The christological controversies of the fourth and fifth centuries in some ways offer a useful background against which to trace the christological controversies in American Protestantism between Edwards and Bushnell. Not only do many of the same issues appear and reappear, but repeated references also are made by all sides to the patristic sources to buttress one position or to tear down another; second only to the the Bible, the church fathers were cited most frequently for authoritative support. For some of the participants the controversy over the person of Christ was a matter that had long since been settled, if not by the formulation of Chalcedon then certainly by the Westminster Confession. For others the controversy over the person of Christ signaled that christological doctrine could not contain the meaning of Christ in its fullness, and that beyond doctrinal formulations there are images or portraits of Christ that must be discerned and studied. It is to this constellation of doctrines and images that we now turn.

# Chapter I

## JONATHAN EDWARDS AND THE NEW DIVINITY: THE EXCELLENCY OF CHRIST

In the interstices between earning his Yale degree, preaching to his congregation in Northampton, Massachusetts, which ultimately dismissed him, leading a revival, counseling the Indians among whom he lived at Stockbridge, and caring for the needs of his large family, Jonathan Edwards (1703–58) was able to write a number of polished treatises, to bring to near completion several other works, and to leave behind an enormous volume of notes and fragments in manuscript form.[1] Among these numerous published and unpublished works there is not an extant extended treatise from Edwards on Christology, and unlike "Edwards on the will," there is no formative or watershed document for Edwards on Christology.[2] We are therefore forced to reconstruct his views on Christology from both these published and unpublished sources, taking Edwards's doctrine of the Trinity as the point of departure

---

1 For biographical information on Edwards see Sereno E. Dwight, "Memoir of Jonathan Edwards, A.M." in *Works of President Edwards*, vol. 1, ed. Sereno E. Dwight (New York: S. Converse, 1829-30). See also Alexander V. G. Allen, *Jonathan Edwards* (Boston: Houghton Mifflin, 1889); Ola Winslow, *Jonathan Edwards 1703-1758* (New York: Macmillan Publishing Co., 1961); Perry Miller, *Jonathan Edwards* (New York: World Publishing Co., 1959); Patricia J. Tracy, *Jonathan Edwards, Pastor: Religion and Society in Eighteenth-Century Northampton* (New York: Hill and Wang, 1981).

2 See Franklin B. Dexter, "The Manuscripts of Jonathan Edwards," in *Proceedings of the Massachusetts Historical Society*, Ser. 2, 15 (March 1904): 2–18; see also Thomas A. Schafer, "Manuscript Problems in the Yale Edition of Jonathan Edwards," in *Early American Literature* 3 "Winter 1968-69): 159–171; see also in this connection Daniel B. Shea, "Jonathan Edwards: The First Two Hundred Years," in *Journal of American Studies* 14 (April 1980): 181-197.

because of the general trinitarian structure of his thought and the specific relation that his Christology has to the Trinity.

Beginning with the premise that God knows all that there is to be known, it follows that the knowledge of God includes self-knowledge. The idea that God has of himself is perfect, as is to be expected because all things with God are perfect. But unlike in the minds of humans, in the mind of God the perfect idea that God has of himself is the substantial and not merely the ideal image of God, and as such is therefore one with the essence of God. Unlike human ideas, which are but shadows or images of the thing itself, the perfect idea that God has of himself is truly and properly God, the Logos or the Second Person of the Trinity. "The Son is the deity generated by God's understanding, or having an idea of himself and subsisting in that Idea."[3]

From all eternity, again because he is perfect, God not only of necessity has thought but also has loved, and the infinite mutual love or consent between the Father and the Son is the Third Person of the Trinity: "The Holy Gh. is the Deity subsisting in act, or the divine essence flowing out and Breathed forth in God's infinite love to and delight in himself."[4] And so from the perfect idea and the perfect love that God has of and for himself it follows that "the whole divine Essence does truly & distinctly subsist both in the divine Idea & divine Love, and that each of them are properly distinct Persons. It confirms me in it that this is the True Trinity because Reason is sufficient to tell us that there must be these distinctions in the deity, viz., of G. (absolutely considered) & the idea of G., & Love and delight, & there are no other Real distinctions in G. that can be

---

3 George Park Fisher, ed, *An Unpublished Essay of Edwards on the Trinity* (New York: Scribner & Sons, 1903), 110. This essay, along with Edwards's *Treatise on Grace* and his *Observations Concerning the Trinity and the Covenant of Redemption* (London: James Clarke Co. Ltd., 1971), has been edited and introduced by Paul Helm .

4 Fisher, *An Unpublished Essay of Edwards on the Trinity*, 110. See also *Miscellany # 94*, in *The Philosophy of Jonathan Edwards From His Private Notebooks*, ed. Harvey G. Townsend (Eugene: University of Oregon Press, 1955), 252f. This *Miscellany* was first published by Egbert C. Smyth in *Exercises Commemorating the Two Hundredth Anniversary of the Birth of Jonathan Edwards* (Andover, 1904), Appendix I, 8–16.

thought."[5] So much then for the eternal *ad intra* relations of the Godhead that result from divine thought and love.

God's knowing and loving himself has not only *ad intra* but also and no less important *ad extra* relations because it is the very nature of God to be self-communicative, to exhibit the divine glory to his creatures through both creation and redemption and to take delight in these *ad extra* activities. "This communication is of two sorts: the communication that consists in understanding an idea, which is summed up in the knowledge of God; and the other is in the will consisting in love and joy, which may be summed up in the love and enjoyment of God. Thus, that which proceeds from God *ad extra* is agreeable to the twofold subsistencies which proceed from Him *ad intra,* which is the Son and the Holy Spirit,—the Son being the idea of God, or the knowledge of God, and the Holy Ghost which is the love of God and joy in God."[6] In other words, there is "an order of acting fit to the order of subsisting" that is a particularly excellent method of gratifying the divine inclination to self-communication.

It is the Trinity that gives structure to both the essence and the action of God, providing coherence and richness to the being and the activity of God in time and eternity. The persons of the Godhead "have as it were formed themselves into a society for carrying on the great design of glorifying the deity and communicating its fulness, in which is established a certain oeconomy and order of acting [and] there is a natural decency

---

5 Fisher, *An Unpublished Essay of Edwards on the Trinity,* 110. See also *Miscellany #259* in Townsend, *The Philosophy of Jonathan Edwards from His Private Notebooks,* 254. The influence of Andrew Michael Ramsay, commonly called the Chevalier Ramsay (1686–1743), on Edwards's doctrines of the trinity and the person of Christ was documented in two rather lengthy articles entitled "Remarks of Jonathan Edwards on the Trinity," by Edwards A. Park in *Bibliotheca Sacra* 38 (January 1881): 147–87, and 38 (April 1881): 333–69. Both Horace Bushnell in his *Christ in Theology* (Hartford, Conn.: Brown and Parsons, 1851), vi, and Oliver Wendell Holmes in his *Pages from an Old Volume of Life* in *Writings,* vol. 3 (London, 1891), 396, suggested that Edwards had written a treatise on the trinity that fell short of orthodox views and that the treatise was therefore being witheld. Park was writing to soothe the fears of the orthodox and to assure them that Edwards's views on the trinity were well within the bounds of orthodoxy. See also Richard D. Pierce, "A Suppressed Edwards Manuscript on the Trinity" in *Crane Review,* vol. 1, no. 2 (Winter 1959): 66–80.

6 *Miscellany* #94 in Townsend, *The Philosophy of Jonathan Edwards From His Private Notebooks,* 257.

and fitness in that order and oeconomy that is established."[7] In his office as redeemer in the drama of redemption Christ consents to suffering and humiliation, obviously treatment far different from that enjoyed by Christ in the *ad intra* relations of the Trinity. It would appear that the *ad extra* relations of Christ make of him a subordinate or inferior being, a product of the divine will who is sent to suffer and die. But against this Arian tendency Edwards is affirming that the Second Person of the Trinity is not a product of divine will but of divine knowledge, even as the Spirit is the product of divine love. Christ and the Spirit as the Second and Third Persons of the Trinity are the very essence of God and therefore share equality with the First Person of the Trinity because it is the very nature of God both to know and to love. And since the Trinity is not a product of time, as the Sabellians assert, Christ does not become Son at the moment of the incarnation any more than the Spirit becomes the Paraclete at the moment of Pentecost; the Second Person of the Trinity is the eternal Logos even as the Third Person of the Trinity is the eternal Spirit. For Edwards the Trinity ultimately has to do with relations, the relations within the Godhead in eternity and the relations between the Godhead and humanity in time. It is this trinitarian foundation that then will undergird and inform Edwards's Christology throughout.

In his early notes on "The Mind," Edwards observes that "one alone, without reference to any more, cannot be excellent; for in such a case there can be no manner of relation no way, and therefore, no such thing as consent. . . . In a being that is absolutely without plurality there cannot be excellency, for there can be no such thing as consent or agreement."[8] Edwards goes on to suggest that excellency consists in equality, which may otherwise be called "simple beauty," as for example two

---

7 Jonathan Edwards, *Observations Concerning the Scripture Oeconomy of the Trinity and Covenant of Redemption*, ed. Egbert C. Smyth (New York: Scribner's, 1880), 24. Essentially this is *Miscellany #1062*, which Smyth published believing that it was "the unpublished essay on the trinity" referred to by Horace Bushnell and Oliver W. Holmes.

8 Jonathan Edwards, *The Mind*, in *Works of Jonathan Edwards: Scientific and Philosophical Writings*, vol. 6, ed. Wallace E. Anderson (New Haven: Yale University Press, 1980), 337. See also *Miscellany # 117* in Townsend, *The Philosophy of Jonathan Edwards from His Private Notebooks*, 258.

perfectly equal globes placed side by side possess simple beauty in their equality. There is however a higher type of beauty, which is "complex beauty" or proportion, the harmony among several beings who viewed in themselves are unequal, but who taken in the whole perspective agree with or consent to each other and therefore partake of this complex beauty. Since "all beauty consists in similarness, or identity of relation," what is more beautiful and excellent than the trinity, the *ad intra* relations of three persons among whom there is consent of being to being, which in turn produces equality and identity? What then if something of the simple beauty and excellence of these *ad intra* relations could be communicated *ad extra* to the creature who through the capacities to know and to love was created for communion with God?

To the other side then, "if there are two bodies of different shapes, having no similarness of relation between the parts of the extremities, this, considered by itself, is a deformity, because being disagrees with being; which must undoubtedly be disagreeable to perceiving being, because what disagrees with being must necessarily be disagreeable to being in general, to everything that partakes of entity, and of course to perceiving being."[9] To go from dissent or contrariety to being to consent or love not only of beings but also of "being in general" is the goal of salvation, and in this transformation from deformity to conformity with being, "excellency" plays a leading role, especially "the excellency of Christ."

For it is excellency that consists in "the consent of being to being, or being's consent to entity. The more consent is, and the more extensive, the greater is the excellency."[10] Consent here is roughly synonymous with consistency or agreement, and the consent of being with being that culminates in the consent of being to being in general or entity is the grand design toward which all things are directed. "The greater a being is, and the more it has of entity, the more will consent to being in general please it. But God is proper entity in itself, and these two therefore in him become the same; for so far as a thing consents to being in general, so far it consents to him. And the more perfect created spirit are, the nearer they come to their creator

9 Ibid., 335. See also Wallace Anderson, introduction to vol. 6, *Scientific and Philosophical Writings,* 111ff.

10 Ibid., 336.

in this regard."[11] Christ is therefore the model of excellency because of his perfect consent not only to being to being but also to being in general. There is no greater excellence than that of Christ, in whom the excellency of God appears in its fullness. Excellence is something to behold, and Christ as the visibility of God stands forth as the concrete embodiment of the divine impulse to self-communication: "Excellence, to put it in other words, is that which is beautiful and lovely."[12] There is no more beautiful and lovely being than Christ, in whom the union of the human and the divine overcomes the natural disagreement or lack of consent between these two very dissimilar orders of being.

Consent however is properly predicated only of minds in relationship to other minds, the relation of stones for example is not one of consent. "There is no other proper consent but that of minds, even of their will; which, when it is of minds toward other things it is choice. Wherefore, all the primary and original beauty or excellence that is among minds is love."[13] Relationship implies consent of being to being and beyond that especially to being in general; on the other hand to dissent from beings and especially from being in general is to narrow the range of relationships, which disrupts excellency, which in short is sin. Relationship revolves around beauty and deformity: "It is beautiful as it is a manifestation of love to spirit or being in general. And the want of this proportion is a deformity because it is a manifestation of a defect of such a love. It shows that it is not being in general, but something else that is loved, when love is not in proportion to the extensiveness and excellency of being."[14] It is the restriction of love to that which is less than totally deserving of love that throws things out of proportion, and Christ is the one who restores the balance by loving only "in proportion to the

---

11 Ibid., 337. See also Elizabeth Flower and Murray G. Murphey, *A History of Philosophy in America*, vol. 1 (New York: G. P. Putnam & Sons, 1977): 137–99, especially 152ff.

12 Ibid., 344. See also Roland Delattre, *Beauty and Sensibility in the Thought of Jonathan Edwards* ( New Haven: Yale University Press, 1968), especially 148–61.

13 Ibid., 362.

14 Ibid., 362. See also the fine discussion of "The Unified Mind of Jonathan Edwards" by Leonard R. Riforgiato, in *Thought* 47 (1972): 599–610.

extensiveness and excellency of being." The sinner needs to be called back by Christ from his or her dissent from beings and from being in general, which is bad enough, but "another deformity, that is more odious than mere dissent from being, is for a being to dissent from, or not to consent with, a being who consents with his being."[15] The excellence of Christ is the visible evidence that God is a being who consents with our being. Who then are we to dissent from such a being as that by carving out a piece of the whole and mistaking that part for being in general?

To seize upon a part and identify it with the whole is the worst possible error, but one commonly made by natural men who do not know the nature of true virtue. The beauty of the whole consists in the proportion of the parts mutually consenting to or agreeing with each other, regulated by the law of love or consent. It is for this reason that "true virtue most essentially consists in benevolence to being in general. Or perhaps, to speak more accurately, it is that consent, propensity and union of heart to being in general, which is immediately exercised in general good will."[16] In the moral order of things consent translates into virtue, and Christ is the model of virtue because of his perfect consent to the whole realm of consenting beings and to being in general. The consent to beings and especially to being in general is not within human powers because human beings are bent on a course of dissent from both; nevertheless a way has been opened through the excellency or virtue of Christ whereby the change from dissent to consent is now possible. Christ bridges the dissimilarities of the human and the divine and brings the two together in a perfect union.

One of Edwards's most memorable sermons is entitled "The Excellency of Christ," based on the text of Rev. 5: 5, 6, in which his attention is captured particularly by the conjoining in Christ of the diverse "excellencies" of the lion and the lamb. In Christ are conjoined such diversities as infinite highness and

---

15 Ibid., 363. See also William A. Clebsch, *American Religious Thought: A History* (Chicago: University of Chicago Press, 1973): 11-56.

16 Jonathan Edwards, *The Nature of True Virtue,* ed. William Frankena (Ann Arbor: University of Michigan Press, 1960), 3. See also John E. Smith, "Jonathan Edwards as Philosophical Theologian," *The Review of Metaphysics* 30, no. 2 (December 1976): 306–24.

infinite condescension, infinite justice and infinite grace, infinite majesty and transcendent meekness. Only because Christ was both God and man, both divine and human was he able to conjoin these diverse excellencies along with the deepest reverence toward God and equality with God. On earth Christ showed reverence toward the Father, yet in his divine nature "God the Father hath no attribute or perfection that the son hath not in equal degree and equal glory."[17] The obedience that Christ rendered to God while on earth is not an occasion, as the Arians make it, to transform Christ into "an under God." Again, contrary to the Arians, Christ is self-sufficient and not a dependent being, whose "proceeding from the Father, in his eternal generation or filiation, argues no proper dependence on the will of the Father; for that proceeding was natural and necessary, and not arbitrary."[18] The Second Person of the Trinity proceeds both *ad intra* and *ad extra* not as an arbitrary exercise of divine will but as the natural necessity of divine knowledge.

The conjunction of diverse excellencies is reflected not only in the person but also in the work of Christ, in his acts from infancy to manhood. For example, his taking on flesh and assuming human nature and the manner of this condescension: clearly this act joins the lion of divinity with the lamb of humanity. As the lamb, Christ had no place to lay his head, but as a lion he worked miracles of raising the dead, walking on water and healing the sick. The final suffering of Christ is a clear exhibition of the conjoining of humiliation and glory, of uniting the excellency of humanity with the excellency of divinity. Christ shows us of what consent to beings and to being in general consists, of what relationships with our fellow humans and with God should be because his person is the

---

17 Jonathan Edwards, "The Excellency of Christ," in *Works of President Edwards,* ed. Sereno E. Dwight , vol. 4 (New York, 182--30): 180.

18 Ibid., 183. This reiterates what Edwards noted elsewhere that "it appears to be unreasonable to suppose, as some do, that the Sonship of the second person in the Trinity consists only *in the relation He bears to the Father in His mediatorial character;* and that His generation or proceeding from the Father *as a Son*, consists only in His being appointed, constituted and authorized of the Father to the office of a mediator; and that there is no other priority of the Father to the Son but that which is voluntarily established in the covenant of redemption." Edwards, *Observations Concerning the Scripture Oeconomy of the Trinity and the Covenant of Redemption,* 56.

meeting point of so many diverse excellencies. By conjoining these numerous diverse excellencies Christ thereby communicates the divine more clearly, makes God more visible and brings the glory of God "more to a level with our conceptions, and suitableness to our nature and manner."[19]

The nearness of Christ makes of him a lion to our enemies and a lamb to us, and there should then be no hesitancy in approaching Christ, who unites the diverse excellencies of humanity and divinity. Because of the excellency of Christ "we shall come to an immensely higher, more intimate and full enjoyment of God, than otherwise could have been . . . for Christ being united to human nature, we have advantage for a more free and full enjoyment of him, than we could have if he had remained only in the divine nature."[20] Because of this intimacy with Christ the Son who unites humanity and divinity we in turn can have "more intimate union and intercourse with God the Father who is only in the divine nature." If Christ as the Second Person of the Trinity had also remained only in the divine nature then the nature of the divine-human encounter would have been quite different indeed.

The divine excellency consists not only in God's knowledge of and love for himself but also in the knowledge and love that God has of his creatures expressed through God's self-communication in the excellency of Christ. And through the excellency of Christ, which consists in his fullest consent to all beings and to being in general, we are called to partake in the excellency of God. The grand design of all this is that God, Christ, and his people through the Holy Spirit may be united in one and that the society of the Trinity may be realized on earth as it is in heaven. No wonder then that the perception of Christ as the visibility of God's excellence and beauty gives to the believer the greatest pleasure, because it is a pleasure and delight proportionate to the beauty that Christ represents. The excellency of Christ is defined not only with respect to the several parts but also to the whole system of being, on the basis of which it becomes apparent that the person and work of

---

19 Edwards, "The Excellency of Christ," 188.

20 Ibid., 198. See also Joseph Haroutunian, "Jonathan Edwards: Theologian of the Great Commandment," *Theology Today* 1 (October 1944): 361–77.

Christ are comprehensive to the last detail. The excellency of Christ is an invitation to view the bigger picture, to gain a wider vista on the great drama of redemption. And just as there is symmetry and harmony in nature, the perception of which gives pleasure to the perceiver, so too there are symmetries and harmonies of the spirit, the discovery of which gives even greater delight and pleasure to the believer. The harmonies of the spirit however are not the outcropping of natural laws working their course but the gift of grace working through the Spirit, whereby the excellency of Christ is made over into our consent to beings and to being in general. We begin modestly in this by the love or consent of one mind for another, which indeed is a beautiful thing, but is as nothing in contrast to the consent of the mind to being in general, which is now possible by our being of one mind with Christ through whom we have access to the very mind of God.

In his *Miscellanies* (#152), Edwards discerns that there is "an analogy or consent between the beauty of the skies, trees, fields, flowers, etc., and spiritual excellencies, though the agreement be more hid, and require a more discerning, feeling mind to perceive it, than the other."[21] Edwards was reasonably convinced that he in fact possessed "a more discerning, feeling mind," and he proceeds to show just how it is that nature may be made to yield up her mysteries. Because of its importance to any discussion of Edwards's Christology, this *Miscellany* on "The Excellency of Christ" deserves fuller quotation.

> Now we have shown that the Son of God created the world for this very end, to communicate Himself in an image of his own excellency. He communicates Himself, properly, only to spirits, and they only are capable of being proper images of his excellency, for they only are properly *beings* as we have shown. Yet he communicates a sort of shadow, or glimpse, of His excellencies to bodies, which, as we have shown, are but the shadow of beings and not real beings. He who, by His immediate influence, gives being every moment, and, by His Spirit, actuates the world, because He inclines to communicate Himself and His excellencies, doth

[21] Jonathan Edwards, *Miscellany* # 152, in eds. Clarence H. Faust and Thomas H. Johnson, *Jonathan Edwards: Representative Selections* (New York: Hill and Wang, 1962), 372.

doubtless communicate His excellency to bodies, as far as there is any consent or analogy. And the beauty of face and sweet airs in men are not always the effect of the corresponding excellencies of mind; yet the beauties of nature are really emanations or shadows of the excellencies of the Son of God.

So that, when we are delighted with flowery meadows, and gentle breezes of wind, we may consider that we see only the emanations of the sweet benevolence of Jesus Christ. When we behold the fragrant rose and lily, we see His love and purity. So the green trees, and fields, and singing of birds are the emanations of His infinite joy and benignity. The easiness and naturalness of trees and vines are shadows of His beauty and loveliness. The crystal rivers and murmuring streams are the footsteps of His favor, grace and beauty. When we behold the light and brightness of the sun, the golden edges of an evening cloud, or the beauteous bow, we behold the adumbrations of His glory and goodness; and, in the blue sky, of His mildness and gentleness. There are also many things wherein we may behold His awful majesty, in the sun in his strength, in comets, in thunder, in hovering thunder-clouds, in ragged rocks, and the brows of mountains. That beauteous light with which the world is filled on a clear day, is a lively shadow of His spotless holiness, and happiness and delight in communicating Himself; and doubtless this is a reason that Christ is compared so often to those things, and called by their names, as the sun of Righteousness, the morning star, the rose of Sharon, and lily of the valley, the apple tree amongst the trees of the wood, a bundle of myrrh, a roe, or a young hart. By this we may discover the beauty of many of those metaphors and similies, which to an unphilosophical person do seem so uncouth. In like manner, when we behold the beauty of man's body, in its perfection, we still see like emanations of Christ's divine perfections: although they do not always flow from the mental excellencies of the person that has them. But we see

> far the most proper image of the beauty of Christ when we see beauty in the human soul.[22]

This remarkable "miscellany" is reflected in another important treatise by Edwards entitled *Images or Shadows of Divine Things,* from which we learn that the things of the world are ordered and designed to shadow forth spiritual things, that natural things are types for which spiritual things are the antitypes. Here Edwards fleshes out in greater detail what was only sketched in the *Miscellany* on "The Excellence of Christ" by suggesting, for example, that "the silkworm is a remarkable type of Christ, which when it dies yields us that of which we make such glorious clothing," or carrying the metaphor further, just as the silkworm's "greatest work is weaving something for our beautiful clothing, and it dies in this work, it spends its life on it, finishes it in death (as Christ was obedient unto death, his righteousness was chiefly wrought out in dying), and then it rises again, as worm Christ was in his state of humiliation, but a more glorious creature when it rises."[23] Strictly speaking, God communicates himself in an image of his own excellency only to spiritual beings who in turn are capable of being themselves images of this excellency, but the shadow of divine excellency also may be glimpsed in the things of nature. The task then is one of reading from the things of this world evidences of the presence of things of the spiritual world. The world of nature is not opaque, but metaphors of excellency emanate through nature and may be detected "by a more discerning, feeling mind" that is capable of detecting in nature the shadows of the excellencies of Christ. Again, "as the silkworm, so the bee, seems to be designed as a type of Christ, who having spent his life in gathering with the greatest labour and industry, and laying up in store the most delicious food, having completed his work is killed, and by his death yield all his stores to the refreshment and delight of his murderers."[24] Once set in motion there was of course no end to this typological process, and from an early age Edwards took particular delight in reading the images and shadows of divine

---

22 Ibid., 373–74.

23 Jonathan Edwards, *Images or Shadows of Divine Things,* ed. Perry Miller (New Haven: Yale University Press, 1948), 101.

24 Ibid., 129.

things from the beauties of the Connecticut valley. For Edwards the physical world was a direct expression of the being and nature of God, and his early readings in Newton's *Principia* alerted him to the world of "matter and bodies." And even though his interest in "mind and spirits" was to take ascendency in his thought, the worlds of the natural and the supernatural, of matter and mind, of body and spirit were never completely divorced.

In Perry Miller's introduction to *Images and Shadows of Divine Things,* an essay that has become almost as famous as the Edwards treatise itself, he suggests that Edwards turned to typology as a means of interpreting the rhetoric of the Bible, so that the events of the Old Testament for example were "types" or precursors of the events whose "antitypes" were to be found in the New Testament. So too in nature, there are types that image antitypes, and when nature is read correctly together with sacred history the two deliver a unitary vision of the universe. According to Miller, what "accentuates the lonely grandeur of this isolated figure in the Connecticut Valley" was that he "comprehended in a flash that the old rhetoric would have to be jettisoned if the old physics was dead. There must now be established, he perceived, a closer alliance between the two realms of being, the object in nature or the event in history, and the thesis in the mind."[25] Edwards was able to cut through the haze and establish a direct living relation between the mind and its object and to see that the visible "metaphors and similies" of God's presence may be apprehended by the regenerate mind in not only in the events of sacred history but also in the objects of nature. One could therefore move from a natural type to a spiritual antitype or truth, and just as Christ is the ultimate antitype for the figures and events of the Old Testament, so too is Christ the ultimate antitype of natural types. Armed not only with the types and antitypes of sacred history in the Scripture but also now with the types and antitypes of nature, Edwards was able to find and to know Christ through both history and nature.[26]

---

25 Perry Miller, introduction to *Images or Shadows of Divine Things*, 8.

26 See Mason I. Lowance, "Images or Shadows of Divine Things in the Thought of Jonathan Edwards," in *Typology and Early American Literature,* ed. Sacvan Bercovitch (Amherst: University of Massachusetts Press, 1972), 209-44.

In 1793 a section of the *Miscellanies* which had been copied by Jonathan Edwards, Jr., was published in Scotland by President Edwards's friend and correspondent John Erskine, who entitled the volume "Miscellaneous Observations." This was then re-edited by Sereno Dwight and published in his edition of Edwards's *Works*, along with a fragment entitled "Observations Concerning the Divinity of Christ and the Doctrine of the Trinity." These "Observations" present Edwards very much as the traditional Calvinist defending the person of Christ from the vantage point of the Westminster Confession against what he perceived to be the too strong inroads of Arianism in New England. As a bulwark against Arianism he argues for example that for God to make a mere creature the instrument of salvation and its benefits would result in idolatry, and creature worship is hardly what either the Old or the New Testament has in mind. Therefore Christ must be more than a mere creature; he is in fact divine because he performs "the peculiar work of Deity" in both creation and redemption. The evidences of Christ's divinity abound in Scripture, and Edwards assembles a barrage of scriptural evidence that attests to the divine names, perfections, work and worship that are ascribed to Christ in the sacred text. As a conclusive note he finds it "a great evidence that Christ is one being with the supreme God, that the Spirit proceeds from and is sent and directed by Him."[27] In defending the divinity of Christ, Edwards argues that the Spirit of God is the Spirit of Christ, and to suppose that a mere creature has the Spirit as Christ has the Spirit is both unscriptural and unreasonable. In creating, preserving, governing and redeeming the world Christ is divine, and we may safely conclude that God would not have given us any person to be our redeemer unless he was of divine and absolutely supreme dignity and excellence, in short unless he was the supreme God. These "Observations" may not present Edwards at his creative best on the subject of the person of Christ, but they do represent the traditional side of Edwards as the defender of the Christology of the Westminster Confession.

Another more important but somewhat neglected extract from Edwards's writings is from his "Remarks on Important

---

27 Jonathan Edwards, "Miscellaneous Observations on Important theological Subjects," *Works of President Edwards*, ed. Sereno Dwight, vol. 7, 275.

Theological Controversies," edited again from the *Miscellanies* by John Erskine and published in Scotland in 1796. Like the "Observations" these "Remarks" were re-edited and published by Sereno Dwight in his edition of Edwards's *Works*. The section of particular interest here is entitled "Concerning the Necessity and Reasonableness of the Christian Doctrine of Satisfaction for Sin," which ties the other side of Edwards's Christology to his doctrine of the atonement just as its first side was tied to the doctrine of the Trinity. It is a straightforward assertion that "justice requires that sin be punished" and that further the punishment fit the crime. In this light, it is therefore requisite "that God should punish all sin with infinite punishment; because all sin, as it is against God, is infinitely heinous."[28] Because of its infinite magnitude no amount of mere sorrow or repentance is sufficient to satisfy the injury done by sin. But sin simply cannot go unpunished, therefore the infinite punishment that it deserves will be meted out in vindication of God's majesty and supremacy. The holiness of God consists of the opposition to sin even as the righteousness of God stands for the divine law that must be honored and upheld. It is a deception of the worst order to think that human sin has the power to abrogate the divine law, and moral agents know full well that the law will be fulfilled "in every punctilio."

In light therefore of the sovereignty of God and the majesty of the law "the satisfaction of Christ by his death is certainly a very rational thing."[29] God certainly would not accept as adequate any sacrifice beneath the value of what was to be remitted, in this case the remission of human sin. Enter then the person of Christ, who alone is adequate to the task, because "it was needful, that he that was a Mediator between the two parties, that are distant and alienated one from the other, to be the middle person to unite them together, should himself be united to both."[30] The atonement no less than the Trinity attests to the union of divinity and humanity in the person of Christ, and Edwards's Christology is a concerted effort to maintain the unity of the two natures in one person,

---

28 Jonathan Edwards, "Remarks on Important Theological Subjects," in *Works of President Edwards,* ed. Sereno Dwight, vol. 1, 588.

29 Ibid., 568.

30 Ibid., 576.

simultaneously pointing to the Trinity in one direction and to the atonement in the other.

But the task is ultimately one not of presenting right doctrines of the person of Christ but of presenting Christ and of making Christ our most apparent good. As James P. Carse has noted of Edwards, "His Christ is not one we are to think about, his is a Christ we are to see. Edwards does not want to teach us a doctrine about Christ, he wants to make Christ a fact that has great force in our lives. Therefore one has the impression that he is painting a verbal picture of Christ. The metaphors translate easily into visible components. We are ever reminded that Christ must be seen to be Christ."[31] The Northampton sage struggled throughout his life to read and to interpret the images and shadows of nature and the events of sacred history as evidences of the visibility of God, who in Christ has disclosed to us the excellency and beauty of both things human and things divine, of things natural and things historical; the same Christ whose own person is a perfect unity of humanity and divinity. As with virtually every other aspect of his thought so too in Christology, some of the Edwards legacy was lost and some of it was carried forward in his successors; it is to the fate of that legacy that we now turn.

## 1

What came to be known as "the New Divinity" owes its existence as much to Samuel Hopkins (1721–1803) as to any other single figure. Hopkins was a prolific writer, an active social reformer, notorious for his undistinguished preaching style and for many years the pastor of the Congregational Church in Newport, Rhode Island.[32] Hopkins's widely read

---

31 James P. Carse, *Jonathan Edwards and the Visibility of God* (New York: Charles Scribner's Sons, 1967), 100.

32 Biographical information on Samuel Hopkins may be found in *Sketches of the Life of Samuel Hopkins* by Stephen West (Hartford: Hudson and Goodwin, 1805); *Memoir* by Edwards A. Park, in Samuel Hopkins, *Works* (Boston: Doctrinal Book Society, 1852), vol. 1, 7-264. Hopkins's role in the development of the New Divinity movement is carefully traced by Joseph A. Conforti in *Samuel Hopkins and the New Divinity Movement: Calvinism, the Congregational Ministry and Reform between the Great Awakenings* (Grand Rapids: Wm. B. Eerdmans Publishing Co., 1981). See also George Nye Boardman, *A History of New England Theology* (New York: A. D. F. Randolph Co., 1899); Frank Hugh

*System of Doctrines* was an attempt to consolidate and set forth the New Divinity in a clear and comprehensive system of theology, which of course included a heading on the person of Christ.[33]

Hopkins approaches the subject of Christology with a mixture of confidence and consternation, confident that the proper knowledge of the person of Christ includes the whole of divinity and that this knowledge is clearly set forth in Scripture, yet distressed that Christology is the one subject about which Christians historically have differed perhaps more than any other. Admittedly the person of Christ is a topic surrounded with numerous mysteries that place it well beyond full comprehension and expression. But there is no mystery as to the need for a redeemer of Christ's personal stature—it is the immensity of human sin. Hopkins is extremely sensitive to the danger of constructing a system of theology and then finding himself with a redeemer unequal to the magnitude of the work of redemption at hand, for at the heart of any system of doctrine must be a redeemer whose person will measure up to the work of redemption. For Hopkins, the point of departure in Christology is anchored less in the doctrine of the Trinity and God's need for self-communication (as it was in Edwards) and more to anthropology and original sin and man's need for redemption.

Hopkins struggles to find the best way he can to express the "two natures in one person" Christology of Chalcedon and Westminster, sensing that this is the foundation upon which he needs to build. But the person of Christ is clearly a topic with which he is not completely comfortable, and despite its importance he is anxious to press on to other issues. Somehow

---

Foster, *A Genetic History of the New England Theology* (Chicago: University of Chicago Press, 1907); Williston Walker, *Ten New England Leaders* (New York: Silver, Burdett & Co.,1901).

33 Samuel Hopkins's *System of Doctrines Contained in Divine Revelation* (Boston: Isaiah Thomas, 1793) in two volumes was the first indigenous American systematic theology. Hopkins set to work on his *System* in 1782 and worked on it for ten years, holding to a rigid sixteen-hour workday that began at 4:00 a.m. The finished *System* provided Hopkins with an unexpected $900, which eased considerably his always embarrassing pecuniary circumstances. It sold a surprising 1,200 subscriptions, and of it Hopkins said that this work was "the greatest public service that I have done." The *System* became standard reading for theological students for well over a generation.

the true humanity of Christ must be acknowledged in his one nature, while at the same time the true divinity must be recognized in his other nature—all of this without making Christ two persons. The two natures of Christ, the human and the divine, are separate and must be kept distinct from each other, yet there are not two Christs. For example, the human nature of Christ had both a body and a soul while the divine nature had neither, but this does not allow for the conclusion that there are two persons in Christ. Hopkins finds that he can speak easily of the divine nature of Christ but not so easily of Christ as a human person; Christ is a divine person who has taken on human nature. The person of Christ is always the union of the divine and the human natures, and therefore it is impossible to speak of his human nature with a distinct human personality: "the human nature never was a distinct person by itself, and personality cannot be ascribed to it."[34] Despite his best efforts to balance the human and the divine, in the end Hopkins compromises the real humanity of Christ in favor of an overzealous protection of the divinity of Christ, although he does acknowledge that Christ's human nature is "doubtless unspeakably greater and more excellent than any other creature."[35]

The notion of the preexistence of Christ's soul is in turn dismissed by Hopkins as an Arian fabrication, simply because the human nature of Christ began to exist only at the incarnation. There was a preexistence of Christ's divine nature as the eternal Second Person of the Trinity, but the existence of Christ's human nature is strictly a work in time. The son that Mary bore in time had a real body and a real soul, and Hopkins rejects the notion of the preexistence of Christ's soul precisely because he sees it to be a threat to the genuine humanity of Christ. As a genuine human being and therefore as a moral agent, Christ faced the obligation and expectation of obedience to the divine law of the Moral Governor of the universe just as all moral agents do. If Christ therefore is not a genuine human being but only some kind of great creature who does not have to submit himself to the demands of the law, then God emerges as

---

34 Samuel Hopkins, *System of Doctrines,* vol. 1, 348.
35 Ibid., 349.

both unreasonable and immoral, and Christ is made into a deceiver.

But Hopkins finds also that the doctrine of the preexistence of Christ's soul is no less a threat to the divinity of Christ because it infringes on the Trinity and the *ad intra* relations of the three persons. The notion of the preexistence of Christ's soul threatens to unhinge the Second Person from the Godhead by transmuting Christ into one who possesses only some kind of a divine presence or assistance during the time of his incarnation, but who does not possess a genuine divine nature. As he sees it, one of the first steps in rejecting the doctrine of the Trinity is the promulgation of the doctrine of the preexistence of Christ's soul, and Hopkins is prepared to combat Arianism in whatever guise it appears. His real interest is in the divinity of Christ, and he wants to turn the discussion away from the notion of the preexistence of Christ's soul to the doctrine of the eternal sonship of Christ.

At this point Hopkins digs in his heels against all would-be "anti-Trinitarian" compromisers of the faith once delivered to the saints and sets himself the task of defining more precisely what is meant by the sonship of Christ. In opposition to the Arians, Socinians and Sabellians, who have misunderstood and distorted the meaning of Christ's true sonship, Hopkins wants to make it clear that the sonship of Christ necessarily includes his divinity and therefore that this sonship is eternal. While the humanity of Christ is denoted and subsumed especially under the title of Son of man, it is as the Son of God that Christ exists antecedently to the incarnation and independent of it, even to eternity. The nature of the sonship of Christ was becoming and would continue to be a thorny issue among New England Divines, and Hopkins is forced at this point to pause and make himself as perfectly clear on this troublesome matter as he can.

First of all, Christ did not become the Son by becoming man: "his Sonship does not consist in the union of the divine and human natures in one person."[36] Sonship rather belongs to Christ as God, as the Second Person of the Trinity, and

---

36 Ibid., 373. George Park Fisher has noted that "Hopkins was the last to hold to the Nicene doctrine of the primacy of the Father and the eternal sonship of Christ." *Discussions in History and Theology* (New York: Scribner's, 1880), 273.

therefore it is an eternal and not merely a temporal sonship. To be sure there is a temporal sonship, as indicated by the title "Son of Man," which the Arians are guilty of seizing on to the neglect of Christ as the eternal Son of God. Hopkins then proceeds to scour the Scriptures for support of the doctrine of the eternal generation of the Son. The view that Christ is Son of God as a consequence of the Second Person of the Trinity being united to human nature sets into motion a ripple effect that not only distorts the meaning of the phrase "Son of God" but also tends to lower our ideas of Christ's person and character, which leads to a neglect of his divinity and finally to a rejection of the Trinity itself. In short, taking away the eternal sonship of Christ leads to the loss of the divinity of Christ, and with that the distinctions of the persons in the Godhead collapse. It appears but in fact it is not really the case that the Arian view of Christ's exclusively temporal sonship eliminates the inconsistency of the Second Person of the Trinity being at once both eternal and yet dependent on the First Person of the Trinity. If the titles Son of God as referring to the eternal and Son of man as referring to the temporal are seen and understood in their proper meaning, the theology of smoke and mirrors created by the Arians will be exposed for what it is.

Admittedly, the question of the person of Christ involves great mystery that must be handled with extreme care, but at the same time it should be recognized that mystery is an essential ingredient to all human experience and to theology as well. Over against the charge that he is taking refuge in mystery as an escape from doing responsible theology, Hopkins embraces mystery, fearing that going too far into the metaphysics of the person of Christ is scripturally unsound and theologically unwarranted. Better to receive the eternal sonship of Christ as a mystery of the faith than to overstep the bounds set by Scripture and reason. The person of Christ is in fact a "revealed mystery," an oxymoron to his detractors but a source of inspiration and encouragement to Hopkins, for whom the phrase at once spelled out the magnitude of revelation and the limitations of reason. For Hopkins there is truth in mystery that we cannot comprehend, and if God has chosen the mystery of the eternal sonship of Christ as the manner of revelation best suited to the human mind then it behooves us to accept with meekness such means as have been divinely appointed and to acknowledge the limitations of reason to grasp and of language to express such mysteries. We should not fall victim to the Arian ploy of denouncing as absurd or inconsistent what in fact is beyond our capacity to know—in this case the exact manner of the union of two persons in one nature of Christ.

Hopkins is struggling at this point in his *System* to establish the person of Christ as a solid foundation for what he knows is coming later under the heading of the work of Christ, and he is determined that he will posit a person who in every way is able to work the redemption that is to come. As it turns out, Christ is in fact exactly the redeemer that sinners need because as the Son of man he suffers in the flesh, fulfilling the law as a human moral agent, and as the Son of God he is equipped by his divine nature to obey and thereby accomplish the greater work of redemption. When we contrast the greatness, dignity and excellence of Christ as the eternal Son of God with the ignominy, condescension and suffering of Christ as the temporal Son of man we see that Christ is indeed God's greatest exhibition of "disinterested benevolence." How else can the person of Christ be viewed, for the suffering of Christ is a grand display of disinterested benevolence by which the redeemed are exalted. Only in light of a right understanding of the person of Christ is the work of redemption fully seen and appreciated, or stated otherwise, the greatness of the Redeemer reveals both the misery of what sinners are and the grandeur of what they ought to be.

The divinity of Christ as attested in his eternal sonship equips him to suffer and to bear the penalty of human transgression against the law of God. The criminal violation of and rebellion against the perfect law of God is rightly deserving of eternal punishment, a punishment that no human being but only a redeemer with Christ's credentials could possibly bear. The demands of the law have been revealed and will prevail in the long run because the moral government of God is not mocked by the proximate violations of that law by human rebellion—otherwise the law is made mockery and chaos follows. But in the person of Christ as a moral agent and the work of Christ as redeemer the law of God is upheld in perfect consistency with the moral government of God. As God's greatest exercise of disinterested benevolence Christ does what no one else can do: removes the penalty of human disobedience to the eternal law of God through his own suffering. The penalty of the broken law will be paid in a manner consistent with the rectoral character of God, and this is accomplished by Christ, who suffers the curse of the law as the ideal and perfectly obedient citizen under God's moral government. Certainly God is not suddenly going to change the divine character by laying aside the demands of the law— that would be fatal both to the majesty of the law and to the moral government of God. Rather, in his person as a responsible moral agent and in his work as the redeemer, Christ demonstrates the majesty of the law by suffering its penalty, by vindicating divine justice and by delivering those who are most deserving of this penalty. Christ links the majesty of law with disinterested benevolence, and only as Christ is perceived as the greatest instance of disinterested benevolence, that is, only as we contrast the divine excellency of Christ as the Son of God against the depths of his suffering as the Son of man, will we be able to grasp both the fullness of his person and the magnitude of his work as the one who upheld the demands of the law of God. Both the depths of Christ's boundless suffering in fulfillment of the demands of the law as well as the dignity of the person who suffered are testimony to Christ as God's last and greatest display of disinterested benevolence. The infinite evil that Christ bore in his suffering and sacrifice brings in its wake an "overbalancing good," and this "happifying display" of disinterested benevolence is the occasion for the appearance of infinite moral goodness and happiness in the world. Indeed, it is not clear whether we have been made happier or holier or both by who Christ is and what Christ has accomplished, but the distinction between happiness and holiness is one that, following Hopkins, becomes increasingly blurred.[37]

The Christ who emerges from the pages of Samuel Hopkins is the obedient and suffering Christ whose role it is to vindicate the honor and rectitude of God, and thus the Christ of Samuel Hopkins is a figure caught up more in the machinations of the law than in the freedom of the gospel. The person of Christ is

---

37 Hopkins's emphasis on the benevolence of God created a tension with traditional Calvinism's emphasis on the sovereignty of God. The reconciliation of sovereignty with benevolence was a challenge that Hopkins met by compromise, at times with difficulty and with stiff opposition. On this tension in his thought see Joseph A. Conforti, *Samuel Hopkins and the New Divinity Movement*, 163f.

one who is equipped to confront and withstand the demands of justice. In the end Hopkins's whole discussion of the person of Christ is aimed at

> those who have such a low and dishonourable idea of the divine character, his law and moral government, as to believe sin to be infinitely less criminal than it really is, that it is not infinitely odious and criminal, and does not deserve infinity natural evil as the punishment of it: That it is not necessary that the threatening of the law should be in any sense executed, in order to the maintenance of public truth and righteousness: That man is not so depraved but that he may recover himself from sin to holiness when proper methods are taken with him, and motives set before him to induce him to repent, and renounce his rebellion, without any supernatural renovation by the Spirit of God; and that in this way he may obtain forgiveness, and recommend himself to the divine favour, so as to obtain eternal life: They who have such wrong notions of God, and his law, of sin and of themselves, do not, and cannot see the need of a divine person, of one that is really the true God united to the human nature, to be the Redeemer of men: Therefore they cannot believe that Jesus Christ is such an one.[38]

Perhaps Hopkins has yet to live down the reputation he earned during his first pastorate in Great Barrington, Massachusetts, from which he was dismissed by the congregation for the severity of his logic and the dullness of his sermons. The recollections of Hopkins by William Ellery Channing, one of his Newport, Rhode Island, parishioners, were that "his delivery in the pulpit was the worst I ever met with. Such tones never came from any human voice within my hearing. He was the very ideal of bad delivery. Then I must say that the matter was often as uninviting as the manner."[39] Despite his criticism of Hopkins's pulpit style and content Channing gratefully acknowledges the spirit of religious freedom and social progress that Hopkins represented, and he

---

38 Samuel Hopkins, *System of Doctrines*, vol. 1, 442.

39 William Ellery Channing, *Works* (Boston: American Unitarian Association, 1887), 423.

notes "the impression which he made was much greater than is now supposed. The churches of New England received a decided impression from his views."[40]

Channing knew well whereof he spoke, because Hopkins's work stands as a watershed in American religious thought, and the New Divinity that he represented found permanent expression in his *System of Doctrines*, which was to become standard reading for untold numbers of theological students in the century following his death. The metaphors and similies for Christ characteristic of Edwards are not picked up and carried forward by Hopkins, whose interest is rather in chiseling out right doctrine by means of more traditional language. In Hopkins's *System* one encounters a Christ who is the chief means by which the sovereignty of God is tempered by the benevolence of God, and as such a Christ in whom disinterested benevolence finds its highest expression. In short, the Christology of Samuel Hopkins reflects an important shift of emphasis from the sovereignty to the benevolence of God.

2

Joseph Bellamy (1719–90) was among the most loyal followers of Jonathan Edwards, and his widely circulated *True Religion Delineated* shows both the influence of and his independence from his friend and mentor from Northampton. Bellamy ranked second only to George Whitefield in reputation as a preacher in late eighteenth-century New England, and his fervent patriotism during the American Revolution served to extend even further his fame and influence. He was called to the Congregational Church in Bethlehem, Connecticut, in 1740 and remained in that position until his death in 1790. Though he lacked the creative talents of Edwards and the systematic bent of Hopkins, nevertheless through his numerous sermons, lectures, pamphlets and books Bellamy left a powerful legacy as a leading advocate of the New Divinity.

The point of departure for Bellamy's views on the person of Christ is his *Treatise on the Divinity of Christ,* which he

---

40 Ibid., 424. For a word of caution about making too much of the influence of Hopkins upon Channing see "The Rediscovery of Channing" by Conrad Wright in his *The Liberal Christians: Essays on American Unitarian History* (Boston: Beacon Press, 1970), 22–40.

opens with the disclaimer that just as there are many things in the natural and moral world that we know to be true but cannot understand, so too in the world of the Bible and divine revelation: "if some things, plainly revealed in the Bible, are as to the manner of them beyond our reach, it can be no objection against their truth."[41] This dictum applies perhaps especially to the text for his *Treatise*, which is taken from Phil. 2: 6–7, where Christ is presented as "the form of God." The argument here turns on Christ's existence before the incarnation, a doctrine that Bellamy establishes by a few deft references to the book of Genesis and to the Gospel of John. Bellamy finds for example that Christ in the form of God was genuinely the creator of the world, that Christ appeared to Moses as the angel of God in the burning bush and again at Mount Sinai in the giving of the law, and that it was Christ who appeared to Jacob at Bethel and to Isaiah in the temple. In each of these instances from sacred history Christ appeared in "the form of God" and spoke the language of supreme deity. Indeed, Bellamy even goes so far as to assert that Christ was the crown King of Israel who exercised the government of God over the people by himself dwelling in the tabernacle and the temple, which helps to explain how Christ was able to drive out the money changers from the temple in the days of his flesh, because he already had dwelt in the temple and exercised governmental authority in the time prior to his incarnation.

The preincarnation appearances of Christ are to be interpreted and understood as solid evidences of his supreme deity, and therefore to deny the divinity of Christ "is to say that the God of the Hebrews is an imposter, and to declare Abraham, Isaac and Jacob, Moses and all the Prophets, to be deluded idolators: for him they all believed to be supreme God, and him they worshipped as such."[42] Christ as "the form of God" is then foreshadowed on virtually every page of the Old

---

41 Joseph Bellamy, "Treatise on the Divinity of Christ," in *Works,* vol. 1 (New York: Stephen Dodge, 1811), 462. Biographical information on Bellamy may be found in Tyrone Edwards, "Memoir," in Bellamy's *Works,* vol. 1 (Boston, 1850); in William Sprague, *Annals of the American Pulpit,* vol. 1 (New York: R. Carter & Brothers, 1857), 404f; in Franklin B. Dexter, *Biographical Sketches of the Graduates of Yale College* (New York: H. Holt & Co., 1885), 525f.

42 Bellamy, *Works,* vol. 1, 474.

Testament, ensuring his divinity against the time when Christ would take on "the form of a servant" at his incarnation. According to Bellamy, Christ had many works to fulfill prior to his incarnation, and these works served as a prelude to the full unfolding of his divinity that comes in the great work of redemption. But on the evidence of the Old Testament alone it can be established that Christ partakes fully in both creation and redemption in the form of God and as such is divine, a fact that was recognized only slowly and in some instances never fully, even by his closest followers.

Christ also takes on "the form of a servant," in which form he was dependent on God, had no ability to perform miracles, groaned, wept, had no knowledge of the day of judgment and in every way bore the limitations of his humanity. The incarnate Christ partakes fully of humanity, just as he simultaneously partakes fully of divinity: "yet the natures remained distinct. And the human nature was not conscious to the ideas of the divine, only as they were imparted. . . . He knows not the secrets of divinity any further than they are communicated to him."[43] In the form of a servant Christ's power is derived, and only by an "infinite condescension" does he carry out the role of a mediator, through which God has exalted him and in which mediatorial form he shall remain until such time as he shall resign his dominion and God shall be all in all. In these two natures, in the form of God and the form of a servant, Christ is yet but one person, and it is nothing short of impious to deny or even to call into question the divinity of Christ on the ground that he laid aside, according to Bellamy's rough estimate, for "a long period of three or four thousand years," his equality with God to assume the form of a servant for thirty years.

Bellamy's patience runs thin, both with the Arians who want to subvert the plain evidence of Scripture in support of their wrong-headed views that end up denying the divinity of Christ, and with the Arminians whose views of human nature so blunt the effects of original sin that they end up denying the divinity of the person and the necessity of the work of Christ. Casting himself in the role of a self-appointed defender of the faith, Bellamy is determined not to allow the whole structure of Christian theology to collapse on his head while Arians,

---

43 Ibid., 479.

Arminians and Pelagians take over; or even worse to watch the demise of theology while increasing numbers of the faithful succumb to Deism, "which has been for some time growing to be the most fashionable scheme among the polite and genteel of the nation."[44] He is prepared rather to buttress the eroding foundations of faith by putting forth a Christ whose person is up to the immense task of restoring right relations between God and humankind. And this restoration can be accomplished only by a vindication of the honor of the divine law, so that whoever Christ is he must be equipped to carry out the task of perfect obedience to the law.

It is this Christ as the vindicator of the divine law who emerges from the pages of Joseph Bellamy, and he is concerned to present a Christ who in every way is prepared to execute flawlessly his task of upholding the majesty of the law. The person of Christ must in every way be adequate foundation for the work of Christ, and this means that he unites the two natures of humanity and divinity in one person. It is the honor and goodness of the law that is at stake, and this is not to be forfeited even if it should mean that the whole human race perished. Fortunately this extreme measure is not necessary because the divine government through the rule of law has been upheld, admittedly at an enormous cost in the work Christ, whose person as the union of humanity and divinity ensures the success of his work. The obligation of the law to love God perfectly and absolutely has been consistently violated by God's creatures, whose native bent of heart is to love themselves rather than God supremely. The principle of self-love has become the ordering law of life in violation of God's law, and herein is the source of all sin and false religion. Sinners are morally culpable for their consistent choice of self over God, which is in clear violation of the law of God, which demands rather the love of God over self. How to transform the native bent of the hearts of sinners from love of self to love of God is the great objective. This transformation is the end of all true religion, and the person and work of Christ alone are

---

44 Ibid., 488. As a Connecticut New Divinity clergyman, perhaps Bellamy sensed that he was not "among the polite and genteel of the nation," and he was not unaware of the intellectual, cultural and religious differences that divided the more revival-oriented Connecticut Valley from the rationalism of eastern Massachusetts and Boston.

the means to that end. Christ serves not only as the model of perfect obedience to the law of God but also as the visible sign of the cost of disobedience to the law.

The image of Christ as vindicator of the law is strengthened even further in Bellamy's "Essay on the Nature and Glory of the Gospel of Jesus Christ," where he notes forthrightly that "to do honour to the divine law was the only thing that rendered the mediatorial office and work of Christ needful in order to the salvation of sinners."[45] Because the law is that which ought to be most loved and obeyed, Bellamy cannot emphasize enough "the unreasonable, groundless, nay infinitely criminal" conduct in rebellion against the law. Adam was created in the moral image of God with the capacity to be perfectly answerable to the moral law of God. But that was before the Fall, in consequence of which we are now born into a world in which the moral image of God has been lost, a world in which humankind is moved by no higher principle than that of self-love. Enter then the person of Christ, who loves and obeys the law perfectly, not thereby to move the heart of God to abrogate the law or to be less severe in the punishment of sin—"a mediator for any such purpose had been an infinite reproach to the deity"[46]— but to satisfy all the demands of the law and to secure the ends of God's moral government. Christ's honoring of the beauty and glory of the law is in sum and substance the beauty and glory of the gospel. The Christ of Joseph Bellamy is a Christ defined by the law, one whose person restores Adam's original moral ability to obey the law perfectly and whose work vindicates the excellence of that law. Christ was a lover of the law, and for humans "to hate the divine law is to be an enemy of the cross of Christ," and furthermore smacks of antinomianism and infidelity.

Bellamy shied away from becoming entangled in the metaphysics of the union of two natures in one person and chose rather to define and understand Christ in other terms, specifically those of law and moral government. In the Christ of Joseph Bellamy the reflection of God is that of a sovereign fulfilling justice while simultaneously dispensing benevolence through Christ. Bellamy struggled to unite justice with mercy,

---

45 Joseph Bellamy, "Essay on the Nature and Glory of the Gospel," in *Works,* vol. 2, 381.

46 Ibid., 381.

sovereignty with benevolence through the moral government of God, a theme that took on increasing importance in the New Divinity. Christ is the vindicator of the law and the substitutionary object of divine wrath, but this presents only one side of his person and work. Christ is also the dispenser of the gospel and the expression of divine love and benevolence. Again, the sovereignty of God is tempered by the benevolence of God in the person and the work of Christ, in whom God becomes more the benevolent ruler of a moral government than the sovereign ruler of a predestined world.

In Joseph Bellamy also the emphasis shifts from the person of Christ as grounded in his eternal sonship as the Second Person of the Trinity to the character of Christ as grounded in his ability to vindicate the majesty of the law through suffering and obedience. The relation between Christology and atonement, between the person and the work of Christ is an enduring and, at times, a problematical one. Bellamy's theology is no exception to this, and a certain imbalance begins to set in between Christology and atonement, in which who Christ is becomes increasingly overshadowed and driven by what Christ does. If Christology begins to lose its moorings in the Trinity, then it begins increasingly to be subject to and driven by particular theories of the atonement. If the person of Christ is not grounded sufficiently in the divine essence by some immanent, eternal trinitarian necessity and is instead linked too exclusively to a particular view of the atonement, when that theory of the atonement comes under attack the person of Christ is likewise threatened. This theological drama of the ongoing relationship between the person and the work of Christ, along with the central plot of the relationship between justice and mercy, was to play itself out with an ever widening circle of participants in late eighteenth- and early nineteenth-century American Protestant thought.

## 3

From the pulpit of his Franklin, Massachusetts, church, which he served for forty-four years, and within the walls of his parsonage study to which a steady stream of nearly ninety ministerial candidates migrated over these years to study theology, Nathanael Emmons (1745–1840) exerted a considerable influence on the course of American Protestant thought during his lifetime and for a generation after. The life of Emmons revolved around his study and his pulpit, as four days a week were devoted to reading widely in exegetical and theological works, two days were given to the preparation and writing of his weekly sermon, and the Sabbath was the day to deliver the truth to the parishioners of Franklin as he had divined it in the course of the past week. Six volumes of his sermons were edited by Jacob Ide in 1842 and along with the obligatory "Memoir" make up Emmons's *Works.* Two of these volumes contain his "systematic theology," which stretches the point somewhat because they contain topically arranged sermons rather than a consciously written system of theology in the manner of Hopkins's *System of Doctrines.* It is then to this section of Emmons's *Works* that we turn first in an effort to reconstruct the views of this eminent divine under the theological heading of Christology.[47]

Emmons begins his discussion of the person of Christ by lamenting the long and sharp divisions in the church that have persisted from the earliest days (even Mary did not know for sure who Christ was!) and continue into the present when for sure Socinians, Unitarians and Arians do not know who Christ is. He yearns for the day when these unhappy divisions between and among Christians will be overcome and by means of a commonsense approach to the interpretation of Scripture agreement on the person of Christ will be reached at long last. A simple but careful examination of what Christ himself taught on these matters will go far toward uncovering the truth of his person, and will contribute significantly to overcoming the differences separating these several schools of thought.

47 For biographical information on Nathanael Emmons see his "Memoir of Nathanael Emmons, D. D., Written by Himself" in *Works*, vol. 1 (Boston: Crocker and Brewster, 1842), one of the most readable and moving of personal memoirs; Edwards Amasa Park, "Miscellaneous Reflections of a Visitor upon the Character of Dr. Emmons," in Emmons *Works*, vol. 1; an additional "Memoir" written by Jacob Ide, the editor of Emmons's *Works*, also in vol. 1; Edwards A. Park, *Memoir of Nathanael Emmons with Sketches of his Friends and Pupils* (Boston: Congregational Board of Publications, 1861), reviewed by George P. Fisher in *The New Englander* 19 (April 1861): 709ff. See also Sprague's *Annals of the American Pulpit*, vol. 1, 293f. Frank Hugh Foster, *A Genetic History of the New England Theology*, chap. 12, and Henry Boynton Smith, "The Theological System of Emmons," in *American Theological Review* 13 (January 1862): 8–53.

For example, Emmons argued that the Scriptures, if read through the lens of common sense, teach that Christ is certainly more than a man who is divinely inspired (as the Socinians teach), that Christ is not a derived and dependent being possessing divine attributes (as the Arians teach), and finally that Christ is not some kind of sui generis being who is neither man nor angel nor God (as the Unitarians teach).[48]

Accordingly, Christ called himself the Son of God, by which he clearly meant to assert his divinity, and despite the offense that this gave and continues to give to some, the commonsense meaning of the title Son of God is that Christ is divine. The title Son of God also implies the eternity of Christ as well as his authority to forgive sins and to perform miracles. All of this may be arrived at, not by elaborate philosophical or metaphysical speculation about the person of Christ, but by merely following the principles of common sense and sticking to the simple language of life and experience. Further, since Christ himself never denied his divinity (a correction he certainly would have made to the thinking of his disciples if he were not in fact divine), for anyone then to deny the divinity of Christ is nothing short of impeaching his moral character. Beyond this, to deny the divinity of Christ has serious consequences for the remainder of faith and doctrine, so that finally the issue cannot be evaded and a choice has to be made: either Christ is divine or he is not, and the commonsense simple language of Scripture affirms undeniably that Christ is divine.

Despite his penchant for applauding the power of reason and promoting Christianity as a rational faith, Emmons gives wide berth to the doctrine of the two natures in one person of Christ. He accepts in principle but does not elaborate in any detail the classical Christology of either Chalcedon or Westminster, choosing rather to approach the topic *via negativa* by saying what it is not and relegating the remainder to the realm of mystery. Concerning the doctrine of the two natures in one person, he notes only that it "does not mean that his human nature was made divine nature . . . nor on the other hand, does his human nature's being personally united with his divine nature mean that his divine nature was made human nature. For there was the same impossibility of degrading his divinity

48 Emmons, *Works*, vol. 4, 490.

into humanity, as of exalting his humanity into divinity."[49] The distinction without mixture of the two natures in Christ's single person was a standard Reformed teaching, but Emmons shows genuine reluctance to wander much beyond this into the wider stream of christological reflection. Better to accept the whole matter of Christ's person and the manner of the union of the human and the divine as a common sense truth of Scripture delivered in the form of a mystery and let it go at that. The conjoining if not confusion of commonsense and mystery irritated Emmons's detractors, but to the satisfaction of his own mind he found that there is truth in the mystery of Christ's person that is acceptable by commonsense. What is not acceptable is the charge of those who assert that there is only absurdity and not truth in the mystery of the union of humanity and divinity in Christ's person. Emmons is infuriated by the charge, delivered with increasing frequency by his opponents, that mystery contains only absurdity, and he responds with the counterclaim that real absurdity erupts with the denial of the divinity of Christ because then only the humanity of Christ is left. To ascribe such scriptural attributes as his eternity, his creation and governing of the world, his ability to judge the hearts of men and his power to raise the dead to Christ's humanity alone is of course impossible. The absurdities of accepting the teachings of the Arians, the Socinians and the Unitarians are far in excess of anything that could possibly ensue from accepting the simple commonsense scriptural teaching of the divinity of Christ. The divinity of Christ is therefore a scriptural truth so obvious and essential to the character and conduct of Christ and to the whole gospel that Emmons finds its rejection simply unthinkable.

But Emmons is also extremely sensitive that the presentation of the person of Christ must be balanced; the divinity must not be allowed to swallow up the humanity of Christ. He labors then to establish that Christ had not only a real human body but likewise a real human soul, which taken together constitute his essential humanity. Like all responsible human moral agents, Christ was dependent on God and placed under the law of God more or less in a state of probation. Christ is not exempt from the demands of the law, indeed he is subject to and in his

---

49 Ibid., 391.

lifetime obeys strictly and cheerfully the precepts of the law to the last detail. Since virtually everything hinges on the perfection of Christ's obedience to the law and faithfulness to the will of God, his fulfillment of the law and of God's will bring rewards to unworthy sinners that exceed all expectations. This fulfillment of the law by Christ in the flesh as a man is a demonstration that "there is no natural impossibility of men's becoming perfectly holy in this life . . . . Christ knew that no man is under a natural necessity of sinning, and therefore this requires. . . sinless perfection."[50]

The problem is not then with the natural faculty of reason; the problem is with the moral faculty of the will: sinners can but sinners do not obey the law. Like all persons, Christ was a free and responsible moral agent, albeit one who united perfect knowledge and perfect obedience. Yet it was not an infringement of his freedom that God preserved him from sinning, so it follows that "God is able to keep men from sinning consistently with their moral agency."[51] The Christ of Nathanael Emmons is less the one whose person unites the two natures of humanity and divinity and more the one who unites the natural and the moral image of God. And since the natural faculties of God's creatures are basically untouched by the Fall, it is the moral faculties that need restoration. The Christ who emerges from the pages of Emmons's *Works* is therefore the Christ of moral encouragement, the sinless example who serves as the beacon by which moral agents are to be guided in their moral exercises on the path to moral perfection.

The spurning of the moral law and the subsequent collapse of the moral image in humankind is testimony to the necessity for a work of redemption by a redeemer sufficient to the task. Again, Christ is both naturally and morally fit to carry out the assignment of taking upon himself what sinful humankind deserves as just punishment for disobeying the law. God is under no obligation to act on humankind's behalf, but he is obligated in light of the blatant violation of the divine law to see to it that the demands of divine justice and of divine goodness are simultaneously fulfilled. The person of Christ fits exactly the work assigned to him, a work made necessary it

50 Ibid., 603.
51 Ibid.

must be remembered, not on humankind's account, but on God's account—that the demands of the law must in every way be fulfilled. To be sure, God might have acted in some sovereign manner quite apart from an atonement in rescuing humankind, but the work of Christ brings together perfect justice and perfect goodness in such a way that both the sovereignty and the benevolence of God are revealed. The work of Christ in the remission of human sin for disobeying the divine law is therefore something that only God could scheme and only the person of Christ as the union of humanity and divinity could carry out. Adam, for example, even if he did perceive the need for an atonement because of his violation of the law, could not possibly have figured out how it was to be effectively accomplished and lacked the personal prerequisites to make it happen anyway. The bringing together of justice and mercy, of divine sovereignty and divine benevolence, is something that God alone can and did solve in both the person and the work of Christ.

Emmons was never shy about facing down any theological problem, and in this case he concludes that Christ in effect did nothing for sinners because strictly speaking he did not obey the law for them—that obligation remains with the sinner, as it always has and always will. "The atonement which Christ has made, has left sinners in the same state that they were in before. Its whole efficacy respects God's character."[52] It is respect for the majesty of the law and the upholding of the moral government of God that are the controlling motifs, not the benefits bestowed by the merits of Christ on undeserving sinners, all of which is secondary to the satisfaction of divine justice. The image of who Christ is and what Christ does is driven by the awesomeness of the law and the rectoral nature of God, and Christ emerges as the one through whose person and work alone the fulfillment of the justice of God is possible. The obedience and suffering that Christ endured in fulfilling the law by no means carry with them an obligation on God to forgive sinners. The obedience and suffering of Christ are first and foremost a public display of the awful cost of divine justice, to which only then is added by divine grace the pardon of sinners. A too simple ascription of "merit" to the work of Christ

52 Emmons, *Works,* vol. 5, 24.

is a mistake because again, strictly speaking, Christ did not merit anything for anybody. God in divine sovereignty still may or may not pardon even after the satisfaction of divine justice has been accomplished by Christ. That God does pardon is an act of grace beyond justice, but it is by no means a necessity inherent within the machinery of the atonement itself. The important thing is not to be drawn into thinking that the work of Christ was designed and executed to pay the debt of punishment that sinners owe to God. The work of Christ serves primarily to satisfy the justice of God, and only secondarily does it make the salvation of sinners possible by making it consistent for God to offer pardon. Stated in its most stark terms "the nature and design of Christ's atonement was merely to display the vindictive justice of God, and not to pay the debt of suffering which sinners had incurred by their transgressions of his holy law."[53] Overall Emmons is more interested in what Christ does than who Christ is, although he is aware that the two are closely related and that an inadequate Christology will not bear the weight of an adequate atonement.

This lends a certain remoteness to the Christ who walks the pages of Emmons's *Works*, a Christ whose person is made distant and rather cold by his work, which is more a matter of the intramural affairs of the Godhead and less a matter of the needs and experiences of human beings. The warmth, affection and "excellency" of the Christ of Jonathan Edwards is missing. Again the person of Christ is muted in favor of the work of Christ and a particular governmental view of the atonement to which Christ's person is tied. The consequences of this linkage bear watching as both the classical christological formulation of two natures in one person as well as the governmental theory of the atonement came increasingly under attack.

## 4

Both the office of the president and the pulpit in the chapel at Yale became platforms from which Timothy Dwight (1752-1817) exerted an enormous influence over many aspects of the ecclesiastical, educational and civil lives of the young republic. From the age of four when he had mastered the catechism, to

53 Emmons, *Works,* vol. 5, 37.

the age of eight when he was well advanced in his study of Latin, to the age of thirteen when he passed his entrance exam to Yale, it was clear that this precocious grandson of Jonathan Edwards was destined for great things. His graduation from Yale was followed immediately by a tutorship there, during which the young scholar's eyesight was weakened and his health broken by endless twenty-hour days of study. He left Yale to serve briefly as a chaplain in the Continental Army, following which the death of his father left him the inheritor of rather extensive landholdings and responsibility for his twelve brothers and sisters. A brief stint in politics was followed by the acceptance of a call from the congregation of the church at Greenfield Hill, Connecticut, where Dwight served as pastor before being called in 1795 to the presidency of Yale as the successor to Ezra Stiles.[54]

A four-year cycle of sermons delivered by Dwight to the undergraduates in the Yale chapel were collected and first published in 1818 as his *Theology Explained and Defended,* which became a standard source for theological students and preachers alike. As might be expected, the subject of Christology did not escape Dwight's attention; indeed, the doctrine of the person of Christ brings Dwight to a critical juncture in the overall structure of his systematic theology. Up to this point in his theological system Dwight had confined himself to an investigation of "the religion of nature" or the religion of law. The Christian system is rooted and grounded in the system of nature or law, the whole of which is presented in Scripture "in its native beauty, freed from every defect and every mixture."[55] Christianity has its foundation firmly

---

54 For biographical information on Dwight see Sereno E. Dwight, "Memoir of the Life of Timothy Dwight," in Timothy Dwight, *Theology Explained and Defended in a Series of Sermons,* vol. 1 (New York: Harper & Brothers, 1850); Jared Sparks, *The Library of American Biography,* vol. 4 (Boston: Little & Brown, 1855); Charles E. Cunningham, *Timothy Dwight: 1752–1817* (New York: The Macmillen Co., 1942); Kenneth E. Silverman, *Timothy Dwight* (New York: Twayne Publishing Co., 1969); Stephen E. Berk, *Calvinism vs. Democracy* (Hamden, Conn.: Archon Books, 1974); Annabelle Wenzke, *God and Evil in the Benevolent World of Timothy Dwight* (Lewiston, N.Y.: Edwin Mellen Press, 1991); Leon Howard, *The Connecticut Wits* (Chicago: University of Chicago Press, 1943), chaps. 3 and 10.

55 Timothy Dwight, *Theology Explained and Defended in a Series of Sermons* (Middletown, Conn.: 1818), vol. 2, 54. Leon Howard makes the somewhat contradictory observation of the sermons that comprise

planted in this religion of nature or law, but its genuine introduction to the world of course awaits revelation in the person of Christ. The religion of nature or law, no matter how important or beautiful it may be, is then but the prelude to Christianity, which has now become "the religion of fallen Beings, a religion furnishing effectual means of redemption from their apostasy, guilt and punishment; and of their restoration to the favor of God, to virtue, to future happiness. The means provided for this end; the truths to be believed, and the duties to be done, by such beings, in order to their escape from sin, condemnation and misery, and their attainment of justification, holiness and happiness constitute the sum and substance of the Christian religion."[56] The religion of nature or law is not a religion of redemption and offers no effectual means of either restoration to favor with God or of human holiness and happiness. The truths and duties of natural religion yield to the higher truths and duties of Christianity, which are revealed in the person and work of Christ.

The beginning of his discussion of the divinity of Christ marks then a critical juncture in the basic structure of Dwight's theology. It is the breaking point from the first major division detailing the ruined condition of humankind under the law and the religion of nature to the second major division of his theology describing the restoration of humankind in Christ. Christology opens onto the religion of grace, a subject that Dwight notes, in something of a major understatement, "will furnish an ample field for many discourses." And these "many discourses" must get off to a proper start by delineating a Christology that will at once drive the Arians and the Socinians from the field and be acceptable to the Orthodox. As a watchman on the walls of Zion, Dwight was ever alert to shifting theological currents and always ready to do battle for the truth of the doctrines and duties of the faith in accord with his own evangelical perspective. He detected with some alarm the growth in New England of views regarding the person of Christ that he found unacceptable if not

---

Dwight's *Theology* that "while they make no important contribution to the history of theology, they do provide an extraordinarily good illustration of the way in which a highly systematized body of doctrines, conscientiously held, might become adapted to different times and manners." *The Connecticut Wits*, 36.

56 Dwight, *Theology Explained and Defended*, vol. 2, 54.

reprehensible, and he sounded the alarm against them. Particularly objectionable were the views of the Arians and the Socinians, and he warned the Orthodox against the increasing danger and growing numbers of those who had fallen victim to these two misled and misleading parties. The Arian view that Christ was subordinate and inferior to the Father yet, because he existed before creation, he was in some ill-defined sense more than a mere man was a perspective that Dwight found particularly threatening. Likewise, Dwight found equally objectionable the more radical, though admittedly less prevalent, views of the Socinians, who asserted that in relation to God no special claims may be made for Christ and especially for his divinity but that as an example of the virtuous life Christ was the perfect man for all to follow.

Against these Arian and Socinian views Dwight simply barrages his reader with proof texts focusing on the biblical title "Son of God," an ascription that according to Dwight contains much more meaning and content than its detractors could ever imagine. Accordingly, with no hidden tricks or fancy principles of interpretation, the Scriptures yield "their plain, customary, obvious meaning," which can be understood by the common sense of common people. In this case the commonsense meaning of the title "Son of God" is that Christ is truly and properly God, and to arrive at an understanding of Christ that comes up short of acknowledging his genuine divinity, as the Arians and Socinians have done, is to compromise the very sum and substance of the gospel. It is against the backdrop of this perceived as well as real threat of Arianism that Dwight, with his customary sense of urgency, sets about the task of combing the Scriptures for evidences of the divinity of Christ.

For every passage of Scripture that the Arians put forth as evidence of the humanity of Christ, Dwight doubles the count and more with prooftexts for the divinity of Christ. For example, it is clear that in Scripture Christ is called God, the "true God," the "mighty God," and that he bears the attributes of God such as eternity, self-existence, omnipotence and omniscience, and that finally Christ performs the actions of God such as the creation, preservation and government of the world. Dwight has no serious argument with the Arians over the humanity of Christ, for everyone rather much agrees, with some admitted variations and differences, on Christ's human nature. There is no argument that Christ is represented in Scripture as a man who was born, suffered and died and who in the flesh was subject to the limitations of human nature. But by representing Christ as only a man the Arians have in effect neglected more than half of the Scriptures, which also represent Christ as divine and possessing all the names, the attributes, the actions, the relations and finally the worship of God. This latter is the obvious commonsense meaning of the Scriptures, which "were written for mankind at large. Of these, ninety nine hundredths, to say the least, are plain, uninformed men, incapable of understanding language in any other manner than the known, customary one. If then, the obvious meaning is not the true one; they are absolutely unable even to find the true one; and so far the Scriptures were written in vain."[57] But not to worry, the plain and uninformed are not fooled and will stay the evangelical course between Arian impiety and infidel idolatry by holding firm to the commonsense biblical fundamental of Christ's divinity.

Dwight subscribed to the Westminster formulation that the human and the divine natures exist together in the one person of Christ without confusion. For example, God did not suffer and die, but Christ as a man did both. But if pressed to explain and illustrate further the idea of two natures in one person Dwight "cheerfully acknowledges" that this is a doctrine "wholly mysterious and inexplicable." As with others before him, the Yale president finds that mystery is no problem, for the very texture of life and faith is interwoven with mystery and it cannot be laundered out of human experience. The matter of the scriptural *fact* of the unity of humanity and divinity in Christ's person, as set forth in the plain language of Scripture,

---

57 Ibid., 179. Leon Howard observes that Dwight had "completely rejected the Scottish philosophers in whom he had been interested during his tutorship. He had made the contrary systems of Locke and Paley the basis of his presidential instruction; he had redefined the term 'common sense' before he left Greenfield; and when he used the term in his *Theology* he usually indicated clearly that he was using it in its nontechnical, popular signification. Occasionally he slipped back into a use of the phrase that Thomas Reid would have accepted or into the statement of an idea that Dugald Stewart would have approved." *The Connecticut Wits*, 36. Sydney E. Ahlstrom notes of Dwight that "the impact of wide reading in the Scottish philosophers is clearly visible" in "The Scottish Philosophy and American Theology," *Church History* 24 (Sept. 1955): 263.

is not to be obscured by the manner in which the mystery of this union of humanity and divinity in one person finds expression. If we can but keep the matter of the scriptural fact of the person of Christ separate from the manner of the metaphysical expression of the person Christ, and be guided by the facts of the Bible rather than the mysteries of metaphysics, all will be well. Regarding the philosophical attempts to unlock the mystery of the two natures in one person, Dwight scolds those "who first make a philosophical system of religion and then endeavor to reconcile Scripture with it."[58]

However, the line between the facts of Scripture and the mysteries of metaphysics could not be drawn in the sand as clear and straight as Dwight imagined, and his own thought was more tinged by philosophy than he was willing to admit. The influences of the Enlightenment show through in his struggle to define the relation between reason and revelation or between philosophy and faith. For example, he acknowledges that "should it be objected, that mankind know something of God by their reason independent of revelation, and therefore possess a knowledge of God which is not derived from Christ: I answer that with some qualifications, that I admit the premises but deny the consequences."[59] Dwight wanted to acknowledge both the power and the limitations of reason and charged his opponents with promoting the former but failing to recognize the latter. The study of theology necessarily entails the use of reason in discerning the will of God, for theology is "the science of the will of God concerning the duty and destination of man."[60] The problem is that the will of God is disclosed only in "imperfect degrees," and against this reason is a weak reed that needs the supplement of revelation. Such revelation has in fact occurred in the authoritative and unchanging doctrines and duties that constitute "the scriptural system of theology." The divinity of Christ is one of these revealed doctrines, as is the doctrine of the two natures in the one person of Christ. Just as with the doctrine of the Trinity, so too with Christology: the nature of the matter is quite

58 Dwight, *Theology Explained and Defended,* vol. 2, 131.

59 Ibid., 116. On rationalism and the relation of Dwight's thought to the Enlightenment see Annabelle Wenzke, *God and Evil in the Benevolent World of Timothy Dwight*, chap. 3.

60 Dwight, *Theology Explained and Defended,* vol. 2, 134.

unintelligible and mysterious, but the fact of the matter is neither. We should be prepared then to accept both the fact as well as the mystery of the person of Christ, who is both human and divine.

None of this of course was very persuasive to Dwight's opponents, but at least to the satisfaction of his own mind he had quieted if not subdued his detractors by marshalling every fragment of scriptural evidence and hurling it at them in his demonstration of the divinity of Christ. Dwight argued with conviction that the divinity of Christ is the linchpin of Christianity, which, if it is pulled from the scriptural system of theology, would cause the whole to collapse into a heap of Arian or Unitarian rubble. To deny the divinity of Christ carries down with it other central doctrines of the Christian system, including human depravity, the atonement, regeneration and justification by faith. Dwight is convinced that if the divinity of Christ goes under everything else goes with it, because a consistent scheme of redemption and a reasonable system of theology are grounded in the mysterious but scriptural fact of the deity of Christ. It is therefore somewhat surprising that, given the ostensible importance that Dwight assigns to maintaining classical Christology, the overall amount of space he devotes to discussion the person of Christ is rather limited—especially in contrast to the almost unlimited space that he devotes to the doctrine of regeneration. In the end his interest in Christology is stimulated more by the refutation of views that he finds objectionable than by a felt need to develop his own Christology. While Dwight recognized the centrality and importance of the christological debate, it can hardly be said that he was a genuinely christological thinker and that the person of Christ was either adequately explained or defended in his theology.

One of Dwight's particular interests is in the role of Christ as mediator and the threefold traditional offices of Christ as prophet, priest and (only incidentally) as king. In the role of prophet Christ is an especially exemplary preacher who teaches plainly and directly with beauty and candor, thereby bestowing on the gospel his own authority and revealing its divine origins. Christ as the prophet-mediator unifies as no preacher/theologian before or after him ever has the two poles of life and instruction, of duties and doctrines. Christ is the great luminary who brings together his teaching and his life; he is the systematic theologian par excellence who unfolds "the doctrines and duties, by means of which apostate creatures are restored to obedience and favor."[61] By going beyond "the peculiarities of the Mosaic system," Christ "cleansed the intellect" and opened a new system of salvation that supersedes the old dispensation. As the prophet-mediator Christ is not the dispenser of advice and personal opinions on matters of salvation, but he speaks and acts as one whose authority is set forth in a perfect system of doctrines and duties.

But Christ is also the mediator-priest who carries out the assignment of the atonement, which according to Dwight "appears evidently to have been a part and the chief part, of the divine economy in the present world, in all ages from the beginning."[62] The question might arise in the minds of some, given the apparent perfection of the moral government of God, What in the world is left for Christ to do? The answer of course is plenty. Christ has a role in the scheme of moral government which is indispensable for its success, and he fulfills this role in his office as priest. As the mediator-priest Christ breaks down what was otherwise an insurmountable barrier between sinners and God, that is, Christ fulfills the demands of justice and upholds the rectitude of the law, something that could never be accomplished from the human side alone. The perfections of Christ's character stand forth most clearly in his office as priest, for it is evident that he is the model of good citizenship under the moral government of God. Christ's piety, candor, integrity, benevolence, fortitude and meekness are but samples of those character traits prerequisite to the fulfillment of the demands of the law.

The overall shift of emphasis then is away from the nature of Christ's person as the unity of the divine and the human to the nature of Christ's character as a model citizen of God's moral government. In the end, Dwight was not all that interested in sorting out the complication of classical Christology with its problems of the two natures in one person

61 Ibid., 242.

62 Ibid., 315. Dwight in fact was less interested in the theology of the incarnation, that is, in the question of how the eternal invades time, and more interested in the problem of relating the justice to the mercy of God, that is, the problem of the atonement.

and the relation between the human and the divine in Christ. But if Dwight was not interested in the metaphysics of the person of Christ, he was surely interested in the moral character of Christ. In this shift of interest from the person to the character of Christ, from metaphysics to morality, Dwight shared more with his Unitarian adversaries than he realized.

It is then not so much the person of Christ as the union of divine and human natures but the character of Christ that serves as the basis of the work of redemption. If there is any question about the adequacy of Christ's character to sustain this work, then by the time Dwight finishes with his lengthy description of the holiness of the character of Christ there should be no doubt in the reader's mind that as mediator-priest Christ is indeed endowed with the character traits necessary to fulfill the law and to achieve the ends of the atonement. For Dwight, the work of Christ in the atonement is based less on the person of Christ as grounded in the Trinity and more on the character of Christ as possessing those traits prerequisite to obeying and fulfilling the law. Christ honors the law by fulfilling its demands as a man and not as God, demonstrating that the law is in fact capable of being understood and obeyed by all moral agents: "There is no reason to believe that Christ possessed any other natural powers than those which are possessed by mankind generally."[63] Through the natural capacity of reason the sinner can know and understand the demands of the law even as Christ did; the problem is that, unlike Christ, sinners do not possess the disposition to obey the law because their moral capacity has been damaged by the Fall. But Christ does not suffer from this human deficiency because as the mediator-priest he is the one in whom the understanding and the will, the head and the heart were perfectly disposed to obeying the law of God.

The work of Christ consists then primarily in demonstrating the reasonableness of honoring the law and the practicality of obeying it, revealing to us that it is in our best interest to follow the example not of a metaphysical but of a moral Christ by obeying the law ourselves. Unlike Emmons, whose interest was primarily in the effect of Christ's obedience on God, Dwight's interest focuses more on the effects of Christ's obedience on

63 Ibid., 351.

humankind and the changes its brings in the lives of human beings. Christ's obedience of the law of God is an example to all believers: if Christ obeyed the law as a human being then believers too can and should obey the law. Of course the suffering and obedience of Christ as the priest-mediator leave an impression on God also, for through Christ's suffering and obedience both the divine law and the moral government of God are vindicated, and naturally this pleases God. But overall who Christ is becomes muted in Dwight in favor of what Christ does, of which in sum it may be said that "all his employments were directed to no other earthly end, than the promotion of human happiness."[64]

The great good that has accrued not so much through the metaphysical person as through the moral character of Christ is that the law has been fulfilled thereby vindicating the moral government of God and promoting the happiness of humankind. That Christ through his person and work was the promoter of the holiness and glory of God was an idea long recognized and approved by traditional Calvinists. That Christ's person and work equally promoted human happiness was an idea much less familiar to traditional Calvinists but one that was rapidly gaining acceptability. This transition from holiness to happiness, from the image of Christ as the one who makes sinners holy to the Christ who makes them happy, is part of what has been described elsewhere as the transition "from piety to moralism." The transformation of Christ from the promoter of holiness to the promoter of happiness suited better the demands of a new republic in which the pursuit of happiness was to overtake the pursuit of holiness. Dwight possessed a remarkable capacity to hold on with one hand to the Edwardsean tradition out of which he came while at the same time grasping firmly the spirit of the age with his other hand. Dwight's theology is a complex mixture of several strands of influence, including the New Divinity, the American Enlightenment plus the influence of Locke and Newton. The traditional portrait of Dwight as the implacable defender of evangelical Protestantism against the inroads of infidelity does not capture the complexity of this figure who deserves a more comprehensive treatment than is generally given.

---

64 Ibid., 373.

The Christ who emerges from the pages of Dwight's *Theology* is not a distant figure whose composition equips him to satisfy God's thirst for justice, but an amiable figure whose moral character equips him to satisfy the human thirst for happiness. Christ is the close friend and moral example who mediates between heaven and earth, between God and humankind, not so much on the basis of his prior status as the Second Person of the Trinity but on the basis of his character, which has been molded and shaped into a model of human happiness by his obedience to the law. The "excellency of Christ" as the one who gives consent to being in general in the thought of Dwight's grandfather gives way to the amiability of Christ as the one who promotes human happiness in the thought of the grandson, opening up new possibilities for Christology.

# Chapter II

# WILLIAM ELLERY CHANNING AND THE UNITARIANS: CHRIST AS DIVINE BENEVOLENCE AND HUMAN PERFECTION

The patience and skills of the historian of doctrine are taxed by the attempt to trace the quiet but real doctrinal development that occurred in New England following the First Great Awakening. The movement away from Calvinism in what has been identified by Conrad Wright as the development of "supernatural rationalism" produced no systematic theologies to which one may turn, and the pieces must be retrieved from a wide variety of sources and fitted together with difficulty.[1] The beginning stages of the story however generally center on the life and work of three major figures: Ebenezer Gay (1696–1787) of Hingham, Charles Chauncy (1705–87) of First Church,

---

1 Standard works to be consulted include Conrad Wright, *The Beginnings of Unitarianism in America* (Boston: Beacon Press, 1955), and *The Liberal Christians: Essays on American Unitarian History* (Boston: Beacon Press, 1970), especially the essay on "Rational Religion in Eighteenth Century America," 1–21. William Channing Gannett, "The Rise of Unitarianism in New England," in *Ezra Stiles Gannett: Unitarian Minister in Boston* (Boston, 1875), chap. 3; George W. Cooke, *Unitarianism in America: Its Origin and Development* (Boston: American Unitarian Association, 1902). Joseph Henry Allen and Richard Eddy, *A History of the Unitarians and Universalists*, in The American Church History Series (Boston: The Christian Literature, 1894). Wilbur Earl Morse, *A History of the Unitarians in Transylvania, England and America*, vol. 2 (Boston: Beacon Press, 1945), 378–487. Charles C. Forman, "Elected Now by Time: The Unitarian Controversy 1805–1835," in *A Stream of Light*, ed. Conrad Wright (Boston: Unitarian Universalist Association, 1975). Daniel Walker Howe, "At Morning Blest and Golden Browed: Unitarians, Transcendentalists and Reformers, 1835–1865," in *A Stream of Light*, ed. Conrad Wright (Boston: Unitarian Universalist Association, 1975). Wilbur Earl Morse, *Our Unitarian Heritage* (Boston, 1925). David Robinson, *The Unitarians and Universalists* (Westport, Conn.: Greenwood Press, 1985), 9–46. William Fenn, "The Unitarians," in *The Religious History of New England* (Cambridge: Harvard University Press, 1917). Sydney Ahlstrom and Jonathan S. Carey, eds., *An American Reformation: A Documentary History of Unitarianism in America* (Middletown: Wesleyan University Press, 1985), 3–41.

Boston, and Jonathan Mayhew (1720–66) of West Church, Boston.

Ebenezer Gay was a Harvard graduate who became an early and outspoken critic of the doctrine of the Trinity and other cardinal doctrines of Calvinism during his unprecedented sixty-nine year pastorate at Hingham. An ardent opponent of the formulation and use of creedal statements of any kind and a cleric firmly convinced that natural and revealed religion are not antagonistic to but instead complementary of each other, Gay stands as a primary representative of the growing rationalism of eastern Massachusetts.[2] Since there is no inherent contradiction between revelation and reason or between revealed and natural religion, it follows that Scripture and the doctrines of theology are dependably rational. Gay insisted that he had no desire to displace revealed religion with natural religion, for these two manifestations of religion do not exist independent of but rather complement each other. Reason then is a pillar of faith, and Gay made no apologies for the prominence that he assigned to the role of reason in his unfolding of the Christian religion.[3] The doctrine of the person of Christ was included among those teachings that would have to be submitted to rational scrutiny, and if parts of it failed the test of reason they would then simply have to be jettisoned. According to Gay the doctrine of the two natures in one person of classical Christology failed to meet the criteria of reason, and in this more enlightened age it was a teaching that would have to be abandoned.

Charles Chauncy is another central figure of eighteenth-century religion in America who represents the drift toward "supernatural rationalism." Chauncy was a devotee of logic and reason in theology, a practitioner of the critical-historical approach to the biblical text, and most widely remembered as a vocal critic of Jonathan Edwards and the excesses of the First

---

2 Ebenezer Gay, *Natural Religion as Distinguished from Revealed* (Boston: John Draper, 1759). Reprinted in *An American Reformation: A Documentary History of Unitarianism in America*, eds., Sydney Ahlstrom and Jonathan Carey, 45–60. See also Robert J. Wilson, *The Benevolent Deity: Ebenezer Gay and the Rise of Rational Religion in New England, 1696–1787* (Philadelphia: University of Pennsylvania Press, 1984), especially chaps. 4 and 7.

3 Gay, *Natural Religion as Distinguished from Revealed*, in Ahlstrom and Carey, *An American Reformation*, 48f.

Great Awakening. He was widely read in the works of English Unitarians, including Archbishop Tillotson, John Taylor and Samuel Clarke. But Chauncy was by no means ready to identify himself with these English Divines whose views of the person of Christ he did not fully share. While it is impossible to reconstruct a fully developed Christology from his writings, it is safe to say that Chauncy found in Christ one whose moral conduct was exemplary and worthy of emulation by those who would be led from sin to salvation. He "placed great emphasis on the mediatorial and exemplary roles of Christ. Christ served as mediator between humanity and divinity because he did not fall into sin, but suffered death in obedience to the divine will and therefore demonstrated that attainment of ultimate happiness was a real possibility for ordinary human beings."[4] Chauncy showed little if any interest in exploring the themes of classical Christology and the composition of the person of Christ. He was perfectly content to treat the notion of two natures in one person with benign neglect simply because this kind of inquiry into the person of Christ was a diversion from his primary interests in the mediatorial and exemplary roles of Christ.

Jonathan Mayhew was also a prominent eastern Massachusetts clergyman who quietly gave up the historical points of Calvinism in favor of a view of God that stressed benevolence, an understanding of Christ that stressed his human perfection, and a perception of the Spirit that stressed regeneration through education and growth over time. A graduate of Harvard (with a Doctor of Divinity from Aberdeen University) and a student of Ebenezer Gay, Mayhew was as outspoken as his teacher in his opposition to creeds and never tired of voicing his support of the right of private judgment over traditional creeds in matters of religion, including the Trinity and the person of Christ. He was an ecclesiastical maverick who willingly absorbed the criticism heaped on him because of his liberal views in religion, but he held firm and was unwilling to relinquish his undying confidence in the power of reason in religion. Mayhew had imbibed too deeply of the

---

4 Charles H. Lippy, *Seasonable Revolutionary: The Mind of Charles Chauncy* (Chicago: Nelson, Hall, 1980), 117–18. See also Edward M. Griffin, *Old Brick: Charles Chauncy of Boston, 1705–1787* (Minneapolis: University of Minnesota Press, 1980), especially chap. 8, 109ff.

spirit of the Enlightenment to turn back, and the reading of John Locke and Samuel Clarke left an indelible imprint on his mind.

Mayhew was an early critic of the doctrine of the Trinity and rejected the notion that the three persons of the Trinity are "coeternal and coequal," insisting instead on the strict unity of God. He simply notes that "with the metaphysical abstract nature, or essence of the Deity, I am not bold enough to meddle," and he was willing to leave such philosophical inquiry "to the temerity of the Athanasians."[5] But then Mayhew added a footnote that sent something more than a ripple through the ranks of the Congregational standing order: "Christians ought not, surely, to pay any such obedience or homage to the Son, as has a tendency to eclipse the Glory of God the Father; who is without Rival or Competitor. The Dominion and Sovereignty of the universe is necessarily one, and in ONE; the *only* living and true GOD, who delegates such measures of power and authority to other Beings, as seemeth good in his sight; but will not give his [peculiar] glory to another."[6] The authority that Christ has is only that which has been granted to him by God the Father, in what is primarily a mediatorial role—Christ as

---

5 Jonathan Mayhew, "On Hearing the Word," in *Sermons* (Boston: Richard Draper, 1755), 268; quoted in Charles W. Akers, *Called Unto Liberty: A Life of Jonathan Mayhew* (Cambridge: Harvard University Press, 1964), 117.

6 Mayhew, *Sermons*, 269n. From his Indian mission outpost in Stockbridge, Jonathan Edwards read Mayhew's footnote on the person of Christ with no little discomfort and solicited his colleague Thomas Foxcroft to make immediate reply. Edwards's "uneasiness" about Mayhew's Christology only increased when Thomas Emlyn's *Humble Inquiry* was reprinted in Boston the following year, perhaps at the instigation of Mayhew. This time Edwards wrote to none other than Professor Thomas Wigglesworth of Harvard stressing the need to make reply to Mayhew and Emlyn and urging the Harvard professor to take up this pressing challenge, telling him that "I think Zion calls for help . . . If nothing can be done, I dread the consequences." (From Joseph S. Clark, *Historical Sketch of the Congregational Church in Massachusetts* [Boston, 1858], 181–2). Wigglesworth declined Edwards's plea and deferred instead to a defense of the divinity of Christ recently published by Ebenezer Pemberton entitled "All Power in Heaven and in Earth Given unto Jesus Christ" (Boston, 1756) as an adequate bulwark against Mayhew and others. But Edwards must have read Pemberton's sermon and wept, for it was indeed a weak reed upon which to defend the divinity of Christ. The challenge was finally taken up by Edwards's son-in-law, President Aaron Burr of the College in New Jersey, in his *The Supreme Divinity of Our Lord Jesus Christ, Maintained* (Boston: J. Draper, 1757). But the opaque and turgid style of this pamphlet rendered little comfort to the cause of Orthodox views of the person of Christ.

"the image of the invisible God" is distinctly subordinate to the Father. Whenever possible Mayhew avoided sustained doctrinal disputes and viewed especially the controversy over the doctrine of the Trinity and its christological consequences as a major and unnecessary source of discord among Christians: "Some contend and foam, and curse their brethren, for the sake of the Athanasian trinity, till 'tis evident they do not love and fear the ONE living and true God as they ought to do."[7] The measures of religion are reason and practicality, and Mayhew argued that in light of these criteria the doctrines of the Trinity and of the two natures in one person of Christ simply do not measure up because both doctrines are unreasonable and impractical.

The demise of Calvinism was ushered along by other notable clerical leaders in eastern Massachusetts, including Thomas Barnard (1748–1814) and John Prince (1751–1836), both of whom from the pulpits of their Salem parishes quietly set the doctrines of the Trinity and the divinity of Christ adrift. They were joined in this process by William Bentley (1759–1819), a Harvard graduate, master of twenty-two languages, insatiable collector of books and trinkets brought to him from around the world by the seafaring captains of his congregation, an ardent supporter of Thomas Jefferson and a notoriously terrible preacher. Bentley read widely in the works of English Unitarians and, unlike virtually all of his liberal colleagues, he was especially attracted to and embraced the works of Joseph Priestley. With a very few notable exceptions such as Bentley, New England liberals did not want to be identified too closely with Priestley whose essentially Socinian Christology, which viewed Christ as a mere man, was reason enough to give this scientist-theologian a wide berth even in Boston. Those who turned their backs on classical Christology and wanted to see Christ as beneath and dependent on the Father nonetheless wanted to retain a Christ who was a supernatural being. For this reason the leaders of the more liberal wing of the standing order in New England for the most part found the teachings of the leaders of English Unitarianism unacceptable because they "were advocating views of Christ that made the very name

---

7 Mayhew, *Sermons* (Boston, 1755), 417–18n. See also Mayhew's sermon "On the Unity of God," in *Sixteen Sermons* (Boston, 1755).

Unitarian repugnant to most of the liberal Congregationalists of America."[8]

In his embrace of Joseph Priestley, William Bentley was joined by his Harvard classmate James Freeman (1759–1835), under whose leadership the congregation of King's Chapel (Episcopal) in Boston voted in June 1785 to delete from the liturgy any references to the doctrine of the Trinity. Freeman, like Bentley, was widely read in the English Unitarians and was devoted to promulgating in various ways his liberal views in religion, which included the presentation of a generous gift of Priestley's *Works* to the Harvard library.[9] Freeman refuted the Thirty-Nine Articles of the Church of England and proceeded to have himself ordained by his congregation in 1787. He carried on a sustained correspondence with the liberal English Anglican Theophilus Lindsey, who had urged the liturgical reforms at King's Chapel on Freeman, and also with William Hazlitt, who worked directly with him in the implementation of the reforms and in the first open espousal of Unitarianism in name and substance in America.

But Bentley and Freeman were the aggressive exceptions. For the most part the drift away from Calvinism and the erosion of classical Christology are marked by a certain vagueness and gradualism, and there are no clear lines of demarcation or distinctive events marking the transition from one camp to the other. Religious leaders are described as "probably Arian" or as being "classed with the liberals" or it is noted that "the

---

8 Wilbur, *A History of Unitarianism in Transylvania, England and America*, vol. 2, 380. Wilbur goes on to note that "the decay of Calvinism in most of the other old churches came from their independent study of the Bible as the fountain of their doctrine, and it passed slowly through the stages of Arminianism and Arianism; but the more rapid transition of the Salem churches seems to have been due to the fact that James Freeman directly interested them in the advanced writings of Priestley, who had already outgrown Arianism.""*A History of Unitarianism in Transylvania, England and America,* 349. Sydney Ahlstrom has observed that the doctrines promulgated by Priestley, Lindsey and Belsham "were by and large uncongenial to most American liberals. The system they evolved was dogmatic, crabbed and narrow; indeed it was liberal scholasticism." See the introduction to Ahlstrom and Carey, *An American Reformation*, 11.

9 Earl Morse Wilbur notes that "the Harvard College Library catalogue of 1773 lists hardly a single Unitarian author; but from the late eighties on, entries are frequent." Wilbur, *A History of Unitarianism in Transylvania, England and America,* 393n.

type of his Unitarianism is unknown." Clearly these are not exact descriptions of theological positions, and the transition from Calvinism to Arminianism, from Trinitarianism to Unitarianism, from Orthodoxy to liberalism, however one wants to describe it, does not admit to theological or chronological precision. There are few if any instant conversions of individuals, congregations or geographical regions from one to the other; there are instead more gradual shifts of emphases that result in the emergence of Unitarianism from the complex of Arminianism, supernatural rationalism and anti-Trinitarianism.[10]

For example, even William Bentley was not anxious for a break with the Congregational standing order, and as late as 1809 Joseph Buckmaster could write to Thomas Belsham that "except in the little town of Boston and its vicinity, there cannot be collected from any space of one hundred miles six clergymen who have any conception of rational theology, and who would not shrink from the suspicion of anti-Trinitarianism in any shape."[11] The "little town of Boston" served as headquarters for the minority party of rationalists and anti-Trinitarians for whom reason and common sense would blunt the sharper edges of Calvinism, reshape Christian doctrine into a more palatable form, and present a Christ who was more in accord with the intellectual temperment of the times. The liberal New England clergy of the late eighteenth and early nineteenth century found some inspiration and guidance in the rationalism and common sense of English Unitarians, but finally the American experience was theirs to shape on their own. They would filter the nature of God, the nature of human nature and the person of Christ through their own reason and experience and discover for themselves the benevolence of the deity, the perfectability of human nature and the person of Christ as the mirror of both divine benevolence and human perfection; and finally they would form themselves into a distinct denomination.

---

10 See Conrad Wright, *The Beginnings of Unitarianism in America* (Boston: Beacon Press, 1955), for an unfolding of the forces out of which American Unitarianism emerged.

11 Quoted in Joseph H. Allen, *History of the Unitarians and Universalists* (Boston: The Christian Literature, 1894), 187.

While considerable scholarly attention has been given to the role of anthropological issues and the doctrine of original sin in the process of the rise of Unitarianism, insufficient attention has been given to other theological issues that contributed to the separation of Unitarians from New England Congregationalism. Anthropological issues were important and widely diverse views of human nature emerged, but these views were part of a wider and more complex theological picture that also included increasingly divergent views on the doctrines of the Trinity, of the atonement, of regeneration and of course the person of Christ. We shall attempt to trace the the legacy of Ebenezer Gay, Charles Chauncy, Jonathan Mayhew and William Bentley by following the course of the subsequent christological debate and its role in the rise of Unitarianism.

1

The Reverend John Sherman, author of *One God in One Person Only and Jesus Christ a Being Distinct from God, Dependent Upon Him for His Existence, and His Various Powers; Maintained and Defended,* minced no words in this discourse rejecting the two natures in one person of Christ and in scorning the idea of the divinity of Christ. In sometimes distinctively caustic terms this upstate New York clergyman outlined his conviction that Christ is in every way a distinct, dependent and inferior person to the one God by whom he was sent as a servant, through whom he was delegated as mediator and to whom he prays as any human being prays.[12] Sherman in this connection also took exception to the doctrine of the Trinity, finding it to be a doctrine without foundation in the Scriptures, an affront to reason and therefore "a demonstrable absurdity." Together the doctrines of the Trinity and the divinity of Christ constitute little more than "the highest jargon" conceivable, and to Sherman's mind the time had long since passed to "clear away the rubbish of mystery and absurdity from the Christian

[12] John Sherman, *God in One Person Only and Jesus Christ a Being Distinct from God, Dependent Upon Him for His Existence, and His Various Powers; Maintained and Defended* (Worcester: Isaiah Thomas, 1805), 150f.

system." In an age of reason there was simply no justification for retaining that which was so patently unreasonable.

Sherman had found inspiration and encouragement in an earlier publication by Thomas Emlyn entitled *An Humble Inquiry into the Scripture Account of Jesus Christ, or a Short Argument Concerning His Deity and Glory According to the Gospel.* Emlyn essayed that Christ was clearly subordinate to God, distinct as the Son in every way from the Father, and therefore subject to and by no means equal with the Supreme Being. For example, Emlyn found that there is not a shred of scriptural evidence that Christ possesses the perfections of power and wisdom attributed to God. On the contrary, whatever power and wisdom Christ possesses is derived from God.[13] Further, Christ does not anywhere in Scripture claim such power and wisdom for himself, indicating that his own self-understanding was that of a derived and dependent being. To attribute to Christ a divine nature whereby he is the possessor of supreme goodness, power and knowledge not only is unscriptural, but also flies in the face of reason. Finally, it is not possible to have it both ways, for Christ was not a deceiver; he did not both know and not know; he did not both have and not have power; he was not now human and now divine. The simplicity and plainess of scriptural language attests to the fact that Christ is not God, that Christ understands the nature of his own person in that way and says as much himself.

That Christ is not divine does not however preclude his possessing all of the necessary prerequisites for the discharge of his office as redeemer. As a man, Christ was given all of the necessary mediatorial power to save humankind—why then add the unnecessary attribute of divinity to his nature? A commonsense reading of Scripture will readily reveal that the human nature of Christ alone is sufficient to his role as mediator and that divinity is an unnecessary add-on. Indeed, the single nature of Christ is to be much preferred to that of a mediator who consists of two natures in one person, which serves only to breed confusion in the hearts and minds of the

---

13 Thomas Emlyn, *An Humble Inquiry into the Scripture Account of Jesus Christ, or a Short Argument Concerning His Deity and Glory According to the Gospel* (Boston: Edes and Gill, at their office next to the Prison in Queen Street, 1756), p. 18. See also Wright, *The Beginnings of Unitarianism in America,* especially chap. 9.

faithful. Such confusion can be avoided very easily "by believing God and his Christ to be two beings, that so there may be room for one to mediate with the other; and that these two are not two equal supreme beings, but one subordinate to the other, that so we may preserve the unity of the Supreme God."[14] Emlyn was well aware that his views of the person of Christ would meet with strong criticism, but he confidently predicted that the Orthodox response would be "lame, confused and contradictory." The important thing is that the simple truths of the gospel regarding the person of Christ should be neither lost in the clouds of theological obscurity nor exposed to the derision of ungodly scoffers. One of the best available means to prevent either one or both of these from happening is simply to jettison the idea of the divinity of Christ, as the main source of theological obscurity and ungodly scoffing, and cling to the simple humanity of Christ. It was with this firm conviction regarding the person of Christ that Emlyn sent forth his *Humble Inquiry* as a defense of the faith and as an apologetic for the reasonableness and simplicity of Christianity.

The gathering momentum against the doctrine of the Trinity and its christological corollary of the divinity of Christ found clear and articulate expression in a series of letters in four parts written by Noah Worcester (1736–1837) and published in 1810 under the title *Bible News of the Father, Son and Holy Ghost.* Worcester, a sometime cobbler, farmer, preacher, essayist and editor, was eulogized by William Ellery Channing as a man who "was distinguished above all I have known by his comprehension and deep feeling of the Spirit of Christianity."[15] Worcester begins by assuring his readers that he did not arrive quickly or easily at the views expressed in his *Bible News,* but that he simply now had to confess that over the years he found it increasingly embarrassing and finally impossible to maintain belief in the Trinity and the divinity of Christ, and that he had at last given up on these

---

14 Ibid., 49.

15 William Ellery Channing, "The Philanthropist: A Tribute to the Memory of the Rev. Noah Worcester, D. D.," in *Works* (Boston, 1893), 599. See also Noah Worcester, *Bible News of Father, Son and Holy Spirit, in a Series of Letters in Four Parts* (Concord: George Hough, 1810), especially part 2, "On the Real Divinity and Glory of Christ."

theological fictions as indefensible. He documents how his own study of Scripture led him to search for the natural meaning and plain sense in lieu of the metaphorical or mystical meanings of language. On this basis of the plain, commonsense, simple usage of scriptural language it is clear enough to the common reader that Christ is the Son of God, and only mystical or metaphorical usage of language could ever arrive at the notion that Christ is the self-existent or eternal Son of God. In fact, Worcester finds that talk of a "self-existent" Son is nothing short of a palpable contradiction and of using words without meaning. The perfectly clear and natural meaning of the term *son* both inside and outside of the Bible is to denote a derived existence. Splitting the person of Christ into two distinct intelligent beings, into the self-existent Son of God and the derived Son of man, has no warrant in Scripture, and the whole notion of the two natures in one person of Christ is a distortion of sacred writ. Christ is appointed and anointed by God and sent as a derived and dependent being as the medium of God's presence in the world.

Encouraged by the rather wide circulation that his *Bible News* enjoyed, Worcester followed it up with a pamphlet entitled "An Impartial Review of Testimonies in Favor of the Divinity of the Son of God, as Given by the Most Eminent Christian Bishops and Martyrs of the First Three Centuries and by the Council of Nice, A.D. 325." Whereas his *Bible News* drew its support for the doctrine of Christ's person strictly from Scripture citations, here Worcester casts a wider net and turns to the church fathers to gather support for his Christology. He literally ransacks two well-known sources, Jacob Milner's *History of the Church* and John Mosheim's *An Ecclesiastical History*, for quotes supporting his position on the derivation and dependence of Christ. Both Milner, who was master of the grammar school at Kingston upon Hull, and Mosheim, who was chancellor of the University of Goettingen, were sources frequently cited by all sides of the christological debate, especially when it came to marshalling patristic support for one's position.[16] While the christological debates ostensibly

---

16 See Noah Worcester, "An Impartial Review of Testimonies in Favor of the Divinity of the Son of God, as given by the Most Eminent Christian Bishops and Martyrs of the First Three Centuries and by the Council of Nice, A.D. 325" (Concord: George Hough, 1810). Also Jacob Milner,

took their point of departure from and focused on scriptural references, few of the participants on either side missed the opportunity to amass support from the early church fathers both to attack the position of their opponents and to support their own point of view. In this case, Worcester's survey of the bishops and martyrs of the first three centuries of the church leaves him with little doubt that they perceived Christ as a derived and dependent being, and he is confident that on the basis of both scriptural and patristic evidence no other conclusion can be reached regarding the person of Christ.

Naturally Worcester's *Bible News* and his "Impartial Review" did not go unnoticed, and many among his readers were not impressed. One reviewer in particular pronounced boldly that the *Bible News* was "NOT CORRECT." Thomas Andros warned that despite Worcester's protestations, his views of the person of Christ boiled down to a jumbled form of Arianism. According to Andros, "By talking about a derived being as essentially different from a mere creature, an uncreated essence without uncreated attributes, about a divine nature without any essential properties that distinguish it from a created nature, Mr. W. raises a kind of magic mist, in which dazzling, though unreal objects are presented to view, calculated to beguile minds thirsting for wisdom, and yet not aware how often error chains her victims under this enchanted form."[17] Worcester, according to Andros, is guilty therefore of engaging in exactly what he had warned against, that is, he uses terms in ways that have no meaning and thereby creates little more than theological fog or a "magic mist." For example, Worcester has simply failed to tell how God could take a part of his own uncreated essence and form it into a distinct person without dissecting himself. He has failed further to say exactly what he means by personality; and even the Arians are much more clear and consistent in their view of the person of Christ than Worcester. He would do much better simply to adopt Arianism,

---

*History of the Church* (Cambridge, 1795), and John Lawrence Mosheim, *Ecclesiastical History* (London: S. Etheridge, 1810). While the assessment of the Bible in American religious life and thought has received recent attention, a similar assessment of the role of patristics is a desideratum.

17 Thomas Andros, *Bible News of the Father, Son and Holy Ghost, as Reported by Rev. Noah Worcester, A.M., NOT CORRECT, in a Letter to a Friend Inclined to Credit that News* (Boston: Samuel T. Armstrong, 1813), 19.

which would at least be a considerable improvement over his own muddled thinking about who Christ is. According to Andros, Worcester, the cobbler turned pamphleteer, would do well "to realize that in the grand scheme of godliness there are some things above our comprehension, and attempts to explain them have no tendency to promote the cause of truth, righteousness and salvation."[18] The faith once delivered to the saints would be better served if Worcester would return to the fold of Orthodoxy with its doctrines of the Trinity and the two natures in one person of Christ rather than inventing schemes that are far more unbelievable and incomprehensible than either of these.

Stung by the criticism of Andros and others, Worcester took up his pen once again in self-defense in a pamphlet entitled "A Respectful Address to the Trinitarian Clergy Relating to their Manner of Treating Opponents." Worcester's was not the first nor would it be the last such pamphlet addressing the proper manner of conducting theological debate, but he wanted to make it clear that he did not appreciate being smeared with the views of Joseph Priestley or stigmatized by Socinianism, sectarianism, infidelity or Arianism. Rather, he wished to be seen merely as a simple and honest man freely inquiring after truth by doing nothing more complicated than searching the Scriptures for their plain natural meaning. To be treated by his fellow clergy as a heretic and an apostate for his simple search after truth was a source of great personal pain, and he fought back with the rhetorical question: "Was my understanding given me for no higher purpose than to know what you believe?"[19] In theological debate, as in all things within the community of faith, Worcester pleads that a greater spirit of humility and forbearance is prerequisite, and he humbly proposes that his simple principles of biblical interpretation, according to which Christ is a derived and dependent being, are preferable to those principles of interpretation according to which Christ is divine. To be sure, right doctrine is important, but so too is the temper in which it is formulated and propagated, and on this latter point the conduct of the

---

18 Ibid., 40.

19 Noah Worcester, *A Respectful Address to the Trinitarian Clergy, Relating to their Manner of Treating Opponents* (Boston: Bradford and Read, 1812), 22.

Trinitarians leaves much to be desired. If only the majority party would take time to ask what the majority of people really believe concerning the person of Christ they would soon discover that "by far the greater part of your own hearers do really consider Jesus Christ as a being properly distinct from God."[20] Worcester is convinced that the greater part of simple commonsense Christians do not in fact see Christ as self-existent or the same being as the Father.

Among the favorable reviews that Worcester received was that of Andrews Norton of Harvard, who noted of the *Bible News* that "the work which we are now to examine, has, we think, claims to be considered the most valuable which has yet been produced among us."[21] Norton was especially impressed with Worcester's desire to abandon metaphysical speculation on the Trinity and the person of Christ in favor of starting anew with the Scripture alone as the basis of theological inquiry. Aside from a slight quibble over Worcester's failure to extend his understanding of the phrase "Son of God" beyond its more narrow literal meaning to encompass "the greater latitude and variety of signification," the Harvard professor could only applaud Worcester's effort on behalf of more liberal religious views as "perfectly inestimable."

Not only did Worcester's publications receive favorable notice from reviewers such as Andrews Norton, whose own christological views we shall summarize momentarily, they also gave encouragement to others such as the Rev. Aaron Kinne to publish their views on the person of Christ. In *An Essay on the Sonship of Jesus Christ, with remarks on Bible News by N. Worcester, A.M.*, Kinne took up and developed Worcester's strong criticism of the doctrine of the eternal generation of the Son as a teaching that was destitute of scriptural authority and involved a manifest contradiction. Kinne found no verifiable link between the eternal sonship and the divinity of Christ, and therefore the rejection of the former was not in any way a threat to the latter. While the defenders of the eternal sonship of Christ may think that it is a doctrine that serves as a bulwark against the rise and spread of Arianism, in truth it is a doctrine that only contributes to the same and would

---

20 Ibid., 40.

21 A review of Noah Worcester's *Bible News* in *The General Repository and Review* (April 1812), 352.

therefore better be jettisoned. Kinne agreed with Norton that Worcester had performed a great service by calling the eternal sonship of Christ into question and exposing it for what it is: a teaching "too obscure to be comprehended and too absurd to be admitted."[22] Sonship is an attribute separate from divinity and applies only to the humanity of Christ, and any notion of the sonship of Christ prior to his appearance in the flesh must be rejected in defense of the divinity of Christ because "divine filiation subverts the divinity of Christ, while human sonship supports it."[23] The issue of the nature of Christ's sonship was one that would not go away, and the doctrine of eternal generation of the Son became a flash point in the debates over the person of Christ and the relation between the human and the divine natures.

Noah Worcester also found some partial support in several publications of his brother Thomas, who began delivering himself on theological matters in 1810 with the publication of a sermon entitled "Our Savior's Divinity in Primitive Purity." Thomas Worcester followed his brother Noah's lead in the search for the simplicity of the Scriptures behind the obscurity of theological speculation, and found in the simple title "Son of God" the proper compromise between the Orthodox extreme of Christ's self-existence on the one hand and the Arian extreme of his mere humanity on the other. Christ is the mediator between heaven and earth and as such is both distinct from and dependent on God, yet he possesses a dignity far in excess of any man. It is proper and fitting to speak of Christ as the Son of God because he is just that; but Christ is not God, and to call him such goes beyond the natural meaning of the terms *father* and *son* as employed not only in everyday usage but also in the Bible. However, unlike his brother Noah, Thomas Worcester accepted Christ's divine sonship as a fundamental article of the Christian faith and warned that care should be taken that this sonship "should be expressed, not in words of man's wisdom

---

22 Aaron Kinne, *An Essay on the Sonship of Jesus Christ, with Remarks on the Bible News by N. Worcester, A.M.* (Boston: Samuel T. Armstrong, 1814), 26.

23 Ibid., 28.

but with the most sacred respect to the language of the Holy Spirit."[24]

In a sermon entitled "An Appeal to the Testimony of Christ with Respect to what Dishonors Him," Thomas Worcester's struggle to clarify and expand his views on the person of Christ continued. Searching once again for the plain truth of Scripture, he discovers that it is neither necessary nor proper to assign two natures to the one person of Christ. A close reading of Scripture will reveal that it dishonors Christ to say that he is the same as God for he does not say this of himself. Scripture, reason and common sense combine to make it perfectly clear that Christ "is another being from the one only true God, that he is properly the only begotten Son of God, who has received all his divine properties and all his fulness from him."[25] That Christ has received his divine properties from God does not however necessarily translate into a lower estimation of his person. Quite the contrary, it honors only what Christ has said of himself in his own scriptural testimony. If that is not being faithful to the witness of Scripture then Worcester is at a loss to know what is.

Thomas Worcester quotes approvingly several passages from his brother's *Bible News* vindicating the notion that the great corruptions of Christianity, notably the doctrines of the Trinity and the divinity of Christ, entered the life and thought of the church late in the fourth century, and are therefore irregularities to be laid at the feet of certain of the church fathers. After these many centuries of doctrinal corruption only now, in nineteenth-century New England, has the opportunity finally presented itself for the church once again to drink the pristine waters of scriptural Christianity and to meet the real Christ untainted by centuries of theological misrepresentation. How perfectly liberating then to live in an age free from the darkness and confusion generated by the teachings of the early church fathers and councils; how exhilarating to live in an age now in the process of overcoming the corruptions of history and

---

24 Thomas Worcester, *Our Savior's Divinity in Primitive Purity* (Concord: George Hough, 1810), 30.

25 Thomas Worcester, *An Appeal to the Testimony of Christ with Respect to what Dishonors Him* (Boston: S. T. Armstrong, 1810), 21. Worcester was not the first nor would he be the last to employ this line of argument that ascribing divinity to Christ was in fact a dishonor to him.

of recovering the wellsprings of the faith once delivered to the saints. Not since the apostolic age had any Christians stood so close to the pure and simple truths of Scripture, and as a result at long last the recovery of the real person of Christ was well under way. The rescue of Christ from the shackles of history and the chains of philosophy filled the Worcester brothers with hope and high expectations.

Finally, in *A New Chain of Plain Argument Deemed Conclusive Against Trinitarianism*, Thomas Worcester brought his new found theological self-confidence to full expression by blasting the whole of Trinitarianism and its Christology as "an error exceedingly detrimental to Christianity."[26] As the product of conciliar corruptions and human devisings, the unscriptural doctrines of the Trinity and of the divinity of Christ simply will not withstand the scrutiny of an enlightened age in which absurdities passed off as mysteries will be exposed for what they really are. Why the christological confusion and disorder of the fourth century with its ecclesiastical factionalism and doctrinal impurities should persist in the life and thought of the church in the present enlightened age is simply beyond Worcester. The fourth century witnessed the rise of Trinitarianism and the decline of piety, even as the present age is witnessing the decline of Trinitarianism and the rise of piety. The final link in the chain of his "plain argument" is that "it appears to me impossible for any rational creature to remain a Trinitarian after a patient, impartial, and thorough examination of the subject."[27]

The Worcester brothers were not alone in their rejection of the doctrine of the divinity of Christ, and they were joined by other critics from home and abroad, including the English Baptist clergyman Samuel Cooper Thacher. In a sermon on

---

[26] Thomas Worcester, *A New Chain of Plain Argument Deemed Conclusive Against Trinitarianism* (Boston: John Eliot, 1817), 6. See also Worcester's letter to Rev. Samuel Spring entitled "Call for Scripture Evidence that Christ is the Self-Existent Eternal God" (Boston: Printed for the author, 1811), critical of Spring's *Discourses on Christ's Self Existence* (Newburyport: Edmund M. Blunt, 1805), in which Worcester reiterates his conviction that the self-existence of Christ is a fabrication of human wisdom and a product of "the degenerate Council of Constantinople."

[27] Ibid., 42.

"The Unity of God," published and distributed in Massachusetts, Thacher created quite a stir with his outspoken criticism of the doctrines of the Trinity and the two natures in one person of Christ, both of which he found to be among "the accumulated errors and absurdities which the human mind in its most pitiable weakness engenders."[28] In place of these "accumulated errors and absurdities" Cooper determined to set the record straight concerning the person of Christ by means of a simple appeal to Scripture and reason. Accordingly, Christ represents the glory of God and has divine power, but Christ has this glory and power "without supposing that our Saviour is himself that very God in whose name he tells us he spoke."[29] To call Christ God is to distort language beyond meaning and in so doing to manufacture a wholly unintelligible phrase. However, Thacher assured his listeners that the denial of the divinity of Christ does not in the least jeopardize the salvation of humankind by placing it in the hands of an inferior being. As the divinely appointed "instrument of redemption," Christ is wholly sufficient to the task assigned him. This argument became an important and recurring theme in the christological debates from the liberal side, that any revision in the doctrine of the person of Christ denying his divinity and stressing his humanity by no means lessened or eliminated his ability to save humankind as its mediator. It is just that now the work of Christ as mediator is not tied to a divine nature in his person; divinity is not among the attributes prerequisite to Christ's saving work as redeemer.

## 2

The quintessential statement of liberal views on the interpretation of Scripture, the person of Christ and the doctrine of the atonement was set forth by William Ellery Channing (1780–1842) in his famous *Unitarian Christianity: A Sermon Delivered at the Ordination of the Rev. Jared Sparks to the Pastoral Care of the First Independent Church of Baltimore*

---

28 Samuel Cooper Thacher, *The Unity of God, a sermon delivered in America* (Worcester: Wells and Lilly, 1817), 18. See also Thacher's *Letter to the Moderator of the New Hampshire Association* (Boston, 1812).

29 Thacher, *The Unity of God*, 24.

on May 5, 1819.[30] Choosing as his text I Thess. 5: 21, "Prove all things; hold fast that which is good," Channing seized the occasion to launch a tour de force of American religious literature that went quickly through five editions and is said to have been more widely read than any other sermon in the history of the young republic. With precision and clarity he mapped out the territory that he wished to cover, including a shorter introductory section outlining Unitarian principles of Scripture interpretation and a much longer second section examining "some of the doctrines which the Scriptures, so interpreted, seem to us clearly to express."[31]

Among these doctrines clearly expressed in Scripture and now to be interpreted according to Unitarian principles is, in addition to the nature of God and the atonement, the person of Christ. Channing goes directly to the heart of the matter by linking the Orthodox doctrine of the two natures in one person of Christ to the doctrine of the Trinity. He finds each of these teachings equally repugnant to commonsense and the "general strain" of Scripture, and each is "an enormous tax on human credulity." No matter how one approaches the issue, one person is one person consisting of one mind and one soul, and there is no need in the case of Christ to change the rules and contort the language of Scripture into some insoluble puzzle on this point. But this is precisely what has happened to the person of Christ

---

30 William Ellery Channing, *Unitarian Christianity: A Sermon Delivered at the Ordination of the Rev. Jared Sparks to the Pastoral Care of the First Independent Church of Baltimore,* May 5, 1819 (Baltimore: Benjamin Edes, 1819), reprinted in numerous other sources including Channing's *Works* (Boston: American Unitarian Association, 1893), 367ff, and in Conrad Wright's *Three Prophets of Religious Liberalism* (Boston: Beacon Press, 1961), 47ff., with an especially helpful introduction by Wright. Biographical information on Channing may be found in a number of sources including WIlliam Henry Channing, *Memoir of Williams Ellery Channing with Extracts from his Correspondence and Manuscripts,* (Boston: American Unitarian Association, 1874); Elizabeth Palmer Peabody, *Reminiscences of Rev. William Ellery Channing, D.D.,* (Boston, 1880); John White Chadwick, *William Ellery Channing, Minister of Religion* (Boston: Houghton, Mifflin, 1903); David P. Edgell, *William Ellery Channing: An Intellectual Portrait* (Boston: Beacon Press, 1955); Arthur W. Brown, *Always Young for Liberty: A Biography of William Ellery Channing* (Syracuse: Syracuse University Press, 1956); and Conrad Wright, "The Rediscovery of Channing," in *The Liberal Christians: Essays on American Unitarian History,* ed. Conrad Wright (Boston: Beacon Press, 1965), 22-40.

31 Channing, "Unitarian Christianity" (Baltimore, 1819), 3.

at the hands of the Trinitarians, who have made him to "consist of two souls, two minds, the one divine, the other human; the one weak, the other almighty, the one ignorant, the other omniscient."[32] Channing finds himself at a loss to identify a single passage of Scripture to support the two natures in one person hypothesis and labels the whole thing "a gross absurdity." Especially irritating is the fact that this teaching is a violation of the use of language, notably the language Jesus uses to describe himself. The Jesus of history simply would not recognize himself in the formulations of Chalcedon, for Jesus never once used the word God to refer to himself. He is rather a distinct being from the one God, dependent on and sent by the one supreme deity. The only scriptural and rational conclusion that can be reached on this point is that "the inferiority of Christ pervades the New Testament."[33] As to those comparatively few passages of Scripture that seem to imply that Christ possesses divine properties, if correct principles of interpretation are applied then any notion of the divinity of Christ melts away. The person of Christ is no exception to the general rule that "language is to be explained according to the known properties of the subject to which it is applied," and the known property of Christ is "his distinct and inferior nature." When this use of language is consistently applied throughout the Scripture there is no way by which divinity becomes a property of Christ.[34]

Further, the gains imagined by the Trinitarians in ascribing divinity to Christ are really not all that impressive, as for example the claim that an infinite atonement is made possible only by the suffering of an infinite being. When pressed on the issue, it turns out that for Trinitarians only Christ's human nature suffered the pain of death; so what has been gained by the ascription of divinity to him? Trinitarians likewise argue

32 Ibid., 20.

33 Ibid., 23. Channing was careful from start to finish to ground his "Unitarian Christianity" in scripture to forestall the charge that Unitarianism exalted reason above revelation. Given the correct principles of interpretation, scripture and reason according to Channing do not conflict but in fact complement each other.

34 Ibid., 24. Channing alludes to but does not here or elsewhere in his works expand on an issue that became increasingly troublesome in the christological debates, and that was the problem of the nature of language.

that the love and mercy of Christ as a divine being are somehow more affecting on the hearts of sinners. Channing finds this argument unconvincing because exactly the opposite is the case: it is the love and mercy of a human Christ that is more affecting. Because the Trinitarian doctrine "reduces Christ's humiliation to a fiction, it almost wholly destroys the impression with which his cross ought to be viewed."[35] The Unitarian doctrine of the person of Christ on the other hand brings him closer to the believer and makes his love and mercy more affecting precisely because it presents the whole Christ and not just part of him.

The shift that Channing wants to achieve is away from the divinity of Christ's person and toward the divinity of Christ's mission, about which again "there seems to be no possibility of mistake. We believe that he was sent by the Father to effect a moral or spiritual deliverance of mankind."[36] The accomplishment of this moral deliverance is not focused exclusively on his death but is spread out across the entirety of his earthly ministry. Christ's mission includes his teachings, his promise of pardon to those who repent, his moral example, as well as his suffering and death, and finally his resurrection and intercession. Channing acknowledges that regarding the matter of the role of Christ's death in the forgiveness of humankind there is not complete agreement among Unitarians, not that complete agreement on any theological issue is a necessary or even desirable objective. But there is at least relative agreement among Unitarians that Christ's death does not serve to placate God's wrath and in turn awaken God's mercy. The notion of God's justice being satisfied by the suffering of an innocent victim who is substituted to suffer the penalty for the sins of humankind "seems to carry on its front the strong marks of absurdity."[37] Such a person is not the Christ who is presented to the believer in the New Testament, and it should not be the Christ who is presented in the pulpits of Boston, or anywhere else for that matter. Not one word in Scripture turns Christ into a substitutionary victim, and the

---

35 Ibid., 25.

36 Ibid., 32.

37 Ibid., 34. The calm, calculated controlled tone throughout Channing's sermon almost breaks down at this point in his discussion, but his irenic spirit wins out in the end.

whole fabric of such a doctrine is woven from "the fictions of theologians." Who Christ is and what Christ does are integrally linked together, and in each case the Orthodox have gotten it all wrong, and the spiral of a wrong-headed Christology feeding off a wrong-headed atonement and vice versa must be brought to a halt.

Transforming Christ into an innocent victim of divine justice mocks the paternal nature of God, whose mercy does not have to be wrung from him by the odious scheme of a vicarious sacrifice. The Trinitarian perception of who Christ is only "leads men to think, that Christ came to change God's mind, rather than their own."[38] The result of such a notion is to weaken the sense of our need for the improvement of character through which each person must pass on the path to "the perfect life." Both the Trinitarian doctrine of the person as well as of the work of Christ end up diverting attention away from the real mission of Christ, which is "to form us to a sublime and heavenly virtue." The problem with the Trinitarian doctrines of Christology and atonement is that they hide from us the necessity of seeing "the doctrines, precepts, promises, and the whole life, character, sufferings and triumphs of Jesus as the means of purifying the mind, of changing it into the likeness of his celestial excellence."[39] The issue is not one of metaphysics whereby the two natures of humanity and divinity are subsumed in the single person of Christ, nor is the issue one of litigation whereby the demands of divine justice are satisfied in the work of Christ. The issue is one of the character of Christ and the formation of character in believers, and by focusing too exclusively on the metaphysics of Christ's person and the litigation supposedly accomplished by Christ's death the Trinitarians have undercut divine mission of Christ. Unitarianism on the other hand is simply calling the faithful back from the metaphysics of Christ's person to the morality of Christ's character by displacing the Christ of the creeds with the Christ of the New Testament.

Channing's sermon on "Unitarian Christianity" is a high-water mark of his thought and of American Unitarianism, and his views on the character of Christ expressed there were not to

38 Ibid., 35.
39 Ibid., 36.

change much if any over the ensuing years. Channing had not the slightest interest in constructing a systematic theology and left no sustained treatise on Christology, which means that his more complete views on the person of Christ must be woven together from selections in his *Works,* including for example his "Objections to Unitarian Christianity Considered." Here Channing is quick to defend Unitarians against the sensitive charge that they deny entirely the divinity of Christ, when the truth of the matter is that Unitarians "believe firmly in the divinity of Christ's mission and office." Christ is seen by Unitarians as "the most glorious display, expression and representation of God to mankind," but this by no means translates into the belief that Christ is the supreme God. Christ and God are not the same but very distinct beings, and to make the two one "seems to us a contradiction to reason and Scripture so flagrant, that the simple statement of it is a sufficient refutation."[40]

The Trinitarians have compounded the error of giving us the wrong person of Christ through the doctrine of the two natures in one person by wrongly presenting the work of Christ as a substitutionary satisfaction of divine justice. The result is that both the person and the work of Christ become something that leads away from rather than toward the Christ of the New Testament. Who Christ is and what Christ does should lead us closer to rather than farther from an understanding of both the nature of the God of the Bible and of human nature. As it is, the Trinitarians have assessed the nature of God as being so completely vengeful and the human condition as being so utterly corrupt that only the apparatus of a vicarious atonement by Christ is sufficient to bring God and humankind together again. The whole scheme of positing a second deity to win over the mercy of the first deity is muddled theology at best and totally unscriptural at worst. Christ's mission is not to change the character of God from vengence to mercy, because mercy is the very unchanging character of God. Christ's mission is rather to change human character, and the sooner the Trinitarians get their house in order on this point the better. In the meantime there is hope because "in these times of growing

---

[40] William Ellery Channing, "Objections to Unitarian Christianity Considered," in *Works* (Boston, 1893), 402. This essay originally appeared in *The Christian Disciple* 1 (1819): 436–49.

light" a more cheerful, amicable and rational system has resurfaced in the form of Unitarianism, which is nothing more or less than "Christianity stripped of those corrupt additions which shock reason and our moral feelings."[41]

Channing shared the conviction that the faith once delivered to the saints was at last in the process of repristination and the dogmatic weight of the past was being lifted in the present by enlightened scriptural interpretation. The last best hope of Christianity is to dissociate itself from the baggage of irrational dogmas that have weighted it down for centuries and to free itself from those obstacles that have become unnecessary roadblocks to its propagation as a "rational religion." For Channing "Christianity is reason in its most perfect form, and I plead for its disengagement from the irrational additions with which it has been clogged for years."[42] Metaphysical speculation about the *nature* of Christ, about the mixture of humanity and divinity in one person, has for too long distracted the the more important and central issue of the *character* of Christ. We are moved to piety, not by metaphysical speculations about Christ's nature, but by reflecting on the traits of Christ's character: his simplicity, benevolence, virtue, humility and so forth.[43] This emphasis on the character over against the nature of Christ, the shift to morality from metaphysics, becomes the dominant theme of Channing's Christology.

Elsewhere Channing argues that Unitarian Christianity is "most favorable to piety," among other reasons because it presents to the believer only one and not three separate persons claiming attention and affection equally and thereby distracting the focus of worship. Unitarian Christianity presents to the believer one pure spiritual and paternal deity, God the Father, who alone is the object of worship and whose deity is not undermined by claims to the deity of Christ. The doctrine of God precedes Christology, and only with the undisputed deity and unity of God the Father firmly in place can attention be turned to the question of the person of Christ.

---

41 Ibid., 407.

42 Channing, "Christianity a Rational Religion," in *Works* (Boston, 1893), 245.

43 See for example Channing's "The Evidences of Revealed Religion," in *Works*, 220ff.

Further, Unitarian Christianity is favorable to piety because it directs the believer to the proper understanding of the work of Christ, which like the character of Christ exemplifies piety to the believer and draws forth piety from the believer. By making pardon rather than piety the centerpiece of Christ's work, the Trinitarians have missed the whole meaning not only of who Christ is but also of what Christ does. It is not, as many have been deceived into believing, "a greater boon to escape, through Christ's sufferings, the fires of hell, than to receive through his influence, the Spirit of heaven, the spirit of devotion."[44] As a consequence, "the deep wants of the human spirit" are better served by Unitarianism, whose Christ warms our hearts by bringing a paternal God closer, rather than by Trinitarianism, whose Christ chills our spirits by transforming God into a vengeful moral governor seeking divine justice. Contrary to the frequent charge that Unitarianism is a cold religion lacking in spirituality and devoid of religious experience, Channing argues that Unitarianism nurtures devotional piety precisely because of its emphasis on the paternity of God and the humanity of Christ. The moral government of God does not by any means have to be abandoned under the Unitarian scheme; indeed it remains very much intact. But it is now headed by a paternal rather than a wrathful deity, within which Christ is the exhibit of moral character rather than the innocent victim of divine justice. Unlike Trinitarianism, whose doctrines of the Trinity, the divinity of Christ and the atonement are an affront to the intellect and the feelings alike, Unitarianism is most suitably fitted to address both reason and piety with its paternal God, its exemplary Christ and its nurturing Spirit.

After all, Channing argues, the great purpose of Christianity is to reveal the character of God, and God's great purpose in revealing himself is that he may "exalt and perfect human nature." God does this by setting the human mind free and by "cleansing it from evil, breathing into it the love of virtue, calling forth its noblest faculties and affections, enduing it with moral power, restoring it to order, health and liberty."[45] The perfection of human character has been made visible in

---

44 Channing, "Unitarian Christianity Most Favorable to Piety," in *Works*, 394.
45 Channing, "The Great Purpose of Christianity," in *Works*, 246.

Christ, who "is another name for intellectual and moral excellence." It is the intellectual and moral character of Christ and not some metaphysical union of the human and the divine in his person that reveals to us the character of God. Christ communicates the mind of God, elevating and enobling our minds, even as Christ communicates the character of God dwelling in the believer and forming character into his own. Salvation consists then not in something that Christ accomplishes for the believer via an external work transacted between himself and God; salvation is rather the restoration of the mind to freedom and of the heart to the path of moral perfection through the inward influence of the spirit of Christ working in concert with human agency. Both through who he is and what he does Christ "raises the mind to celestial truth and virtue," renovating the intellectual and moral virtues of the individual and uniting the mind and heart of the believer with the mind and heart of God.

In this way we grow more into a "likeness to God" by the unfolding of the divine nature within us. Is this to claim too much for human nature? Not really, according to Channing, for "in Christianity, particularly, I meet perpetual testimonies to the divinity of human nature. . . . Lofty views of the nature of man are bound up and interwoven with the whole Christian system."[46] Divinity it would appear is an attribute of humankind in general and not of Christ in particular: it is a "likeness to God" into which persons grow by the influence of the Spirit. Christ stands as the perfect embodiment of the likeness to God by virtue of his intellectual and moral excellence and not by virtue of the union of the two natures of humanity and divinity in his person. The need therefore is to cut through the centuries of christological underbrush and to arrive at a common ground of plain truth about the person of Christ on which all

---

[46] Channing, "Likeness to God," a Discourse Delivered at the Ordination of Rev. F. A. Farley, Providence, Rhode Island, in *Works,* 292f. In later years Channing identified the title of this sermon as the central and unifying theme of his life and work. (See preface to his *Works*.) Herbert W. Schneider has noted that "throughout the Enlightenment this emphasis upon human nature was a familiar theme . . . Locke's aim was to find the origin of human understanding in order to reveal its natural limitations; Channing's aim was to find the perfection of human nature in order to realize its possibilities." See "The Intellectual Background of William Ellery Channing," in *Church History* 7 (March 1938):18.

Christians can at last agree. That common ground of agreement is of course the moral goodness of Christ—the benevolence, righteousness and holiness of his character and not the metaphysics of his nature. Believers can identify with and aspire to attain a moral character like the Christ of the New Testament; they cannot identify nor can they aspire to attain a metaphysical nature like the Christ of the historical creeds. Human beings can love the Christ of morality because such "love to Christ" is rooted and grounded in the very frame of human intelligence and morality; they cannot love the Christ of metaphysics because their intellectual and moral nature is not so framed.

The problem then is that theology generally has tended to obscure the living Christ rather than provide insight into his mind and heart. "And here I would observe, not in the spirit of reproach, but from a desire to do good, that I know not a more effectual method of hiding Jesus from us, of keeping us strangers to him, than the inculcation of the doctrine which makes him the same being with his Father—makes him God himself."[47] The doctrine of the two natures in one person totally eclipses the person of Christ, over against the Jesus of the Gospels who comes to us as "the unsullied image of God and a perfect model, a being who bears the marks of reality, whom I can understand, whom I can receive into my heart as the best of friends."[48] Theology as presently practiced will never give us Christ as "the best of friends" because of its chronic attachment to ideas that are unscriptural and irrational. Theology is obligated however to give us a Christ we can know, a Christ we can love and whose character we can emulate because of his moral and intellectual excellence. "Christ's nature and offices I, of course, would not disparage; but let them not be exalted above his moral worth."[49] It is finally not the dignity of Christ's office, his imagined eternal generation, or his mysterious nature to which the New Testament directs us, but all things point rather to that which alone counts—his intellectual and moral excellence.

---

47 Channing, "Love to Christ," in *Works*, 319.
48 Ibid., 319.
49 Ibid., 320.

Among the several mistakes that Trinitarian theology has made in the past is its tendency to focus too exclusively on the sufferings of Christ and to allow the atonement to determine who Christ is. Trinitiarians have let the work determine the person of Christ, thereby presenting a less than totally satisfactory image of Christ either to the church or to the world. Trinitarians have for too long allowed the tail to wag the dog, and the time has come for Christology to reassert itself and to redress the balance between the person and the work of Christ. It cannot be denied that Christ really suffered pain and ignominy, but to make suffering the chief instrumentality of his person and mission creates a wrong impression of the person of Christ and inhibits a wider and more palatable view of both his person and his work. Surely as compassionate human beings we are touched and moved by the sight of the cross, but "to approach the cross for the purpose of weeping over a bleeding, dying friend, is to lose the chief influence of the crucifixion . . . [which is] to acquire firmness of spirit and to fortify our minds for hardship and suffering in the cause of duty and of human happiness."[50] The character of Christ shines through in the atonement in ways that Trinitarians have missed completely, summoning us not to weeping and wailing but to strength and firmness of spirit in the face of hardship and suffering. For Channing, Jesus is the friend who does not bear the sins and griefs of the believer but who opens to the believer the mind of a paternal God whose image the believer bears in his or her own unlimited mind.

Trinitarian theology has made the further mistake of creating the impression that Christ is somehow more compassionate toward humankind than is God. This theological sleight of hand has been accomplished by stripping God of the qualities of paternal goodness and mercy, by sinking human beings into the torments of hell and by creating a divine savior who alone can intervene and rescue them. But this theology of smoke and mirrors designed ostensibly to magnify the tenderness of Christ ends up being a dishonor to God, to Christ and to human nature. The Christ who is the product of a theology that distorts the character of God and of human nature is a Christ who is of little or no moral worth. It is time

---

50 Ibid., 325.

for theology to stop driving a wedge between God and Christ and between God and human beings. It is time to recover the Christ of the New Testament, who as the image of God comes to address the mind, "for his chief sympathy was with the mind, with its sins and moral diseases, and especially with its capacity of improvement and everlasting greatness and joy."[51] Classical Christology, with all of its speculation on the nature of Christ and its preoccupation with fixing the place of Christ in the order of creation, simply does not fulfill the the intellectual needs of the mind "with its capacity of improvement and everlasting greatness and joy" or the moral needs of the heart with its capacity to develop "a likeness to God."

The Christ of William Ellery Channing is a friend who is not at all beyond the reach of human sympathy and imitation and who in the end is "an illustration of the capacities we all possess." Human beings need the intellectual and moral excellence that Christ provides, for these excellencies expand the mind and the soul, each of which has the capacity for the growth and development toward intellectual and moral perfection to which Christ summons the believer. The life and thought of William Ellery Channing was driven by the conviction that "I no longer see aught to prevent our becoming whatever was good and great in Jesus on earth."[52]

---

51 Ibid., 326.

52 Channing, "The Imitableness of Christ's Character," in *Works,* 312–13.

3

The venerable Andrews Norton (1786–1853) of Harvard entered the christological debate with the publication in 1819 of his widely circulated *Statement of Reasons for not Believing the Doctrines of Trinitarians Concerning the Nature of God and the Person of Christ.* Norton's *Statement* went through numerous editions and became for many but by no means for all Unitarians, a handbook of the liberal movement. Endowed with a temperment that was always ready for a theological debate, Norton mustered his rather considerable exegetical skills and launched a thoroughgoing denunciation of Trinitarian Christology by way of an attack on the doctrine of the Trinity. He simply could not contain his disdain for this doctrine, and after a survey of five different and distinct formulations of the doctrine of the Trinity he concludes that "if men will talk absurdity, and insist that they are teaching truths of infinite importance, it is unreasonable for them to expect to be understood as meaning something wholly different from what their words express."[53] Thus, concerning the Trinity no matter how it was formulated he could find nothing but absurdity in the words used to express it and therefore nothing but absurdity in the doctrine itself.

His rejection of the Trinity was but a prelude however to Norton's refutation of the equally unscriptural and irrational doctrine of the two natures in one person of Christ. Norton found the notion that Christ is both God and man not only contradictory but also incapable of being proved, tending to absurdity and therefore like the doctrine of the Trinity impossible to believe. Certainly the "double nature of Christ" is no part of scriptural revelation, for revelation cannot teach absurdities. If ever there was a doctrine beyond belief then the two natures in one person of Christ is it. Rummage the Scripture

---

53 Andrews Norton, *A Statement of Reasons for not Believing the Doctrines of Trinitarians Concerning the Nature of God and the Person of Christ* (Boston: American Unitarian Association, 1877), 41. Norton's *Statement* first appeared in the *Christian Disciple,* new series, 5 (Sept.–Oct. 1819): 370–431, reprinted numerous times and expanded through many editions including the tenth edition from which the quotes here are taken. Biographical information on Norton may be found in "Biographical Notion of Mr. Norton" in his *Statement of Reasons,* in Sprague's *Annals of the American Pulpit*, vol. 8, 432ff; and in Andrew P. Peabody, *Harvard Reminiscences* (Boston, 1888).

as you may, not one single passage can be cited in support of the proposition that Christ is God.[54] Norton then proceeds to unfold the results of his own scriptural rummaging by unleashing a volley of texts frequently cited by Trinitarians in support of the divinity of Christ, and one by one he demonstrates to the satisfaction of his own mind that the Trinitarians have misinterpreted and distorted the meaning of the text in question. In each instance, when these texts are properly interpreted, they yield up exactly the opposite meaning—that Christ is inferior to and not equal with God. The clear meaning of each text when properly interpreted is that Christ is appointed by, distinct from, dependent on and inferior to God, and by what other principles of interpretation one could arrive at any other conclusion is simply beyond Norton's comprehension. The evidence is clear that Christ is a man who agonizes, mourns, is troubled, suffers and dies, and these are not things that God does. It is immediately apparent that, if Christ in fact is God, such important and obvious information would not have been lost on his disciples and others who knew him in the flesh. Surely the realization of the divinity of Christ by those who knew him personally would have played an extremely significant and central role in the New Testament portrait of Christ. But as it is, there is not even a hint that the disciples sensed that Christ was God.

Further, the Jews in the time of Jesus certainly would have raised much more of a stir by seizing on the claim that Christ is God and attacking it more vigorously. But there is no evidence of such an attack in the New Testament or in other literature of the time reflecting Jewish objections to the claim that Christ is God. Because the divinity of Christ was not promulgated by either Christ or his earliest followers such an attack by the Jews of Jesus's time was simply unnecessary. The doctrine of the divinity of Christ is therefore not even a minor article of faith in the New Testament or the early church, much less anything approaching the claim that has been made for it as essential to the very foundation of Christianity itself. The patent falsity of the doctrine of Christ's divinity serves only to indicate what

---

54 Norton, *Statement of Reasons*, 58. Ostensibly Norton wrote his *Statement* to refute Moses Stuart's *Letters to Channing*, but for the most part he ignores Stuart altogether and proceeds to write what he calls "a general view of the subject in controversy."

a singularly remarkable phenomenon this idea is in the history of Christian doctrine, that so many have adhered to it as a teaching containing any merit whatsoever. One senses that the Harvard professor did not know quite whether to laugh or to cry over this.

The self-assurance that characterizes Norton's survey and refutation of favorite Trinitarian scriptural texts on the Trinity and the divinity of Christ is lacking in his survey of the writings of the early church fathers on the same subjects, doubtlessly because he was considerably more comfortable with exegesis and biblical criticism than with patristics and church history. But the results in both Scripture and in the writings of early church fathers remain the same: the deity of Christ "exists, I conceive, merely as a form of words, not significant of any conceptions, however dim or incongruous."[55] The christological views of Justin Martyr, Irenaeus, Clement of Alexandria, Tertullian and Origen are examined and in turn judged by Norton to be unintelligible, incomplete, vague or self-contradictory. Overall, he is not impressed with the early church fathers, but in all fairness the faults in Christology are not entirely theirs. The transmission of tradition is risky business at best, and the chances of corruptions creeping into the tradition are always present. In the case of Christianity, "in the passage of our religion from the Jews to whom it had been taught, to the Gentiles through whom it has been transmitted to us, the current of tradition was interrupted. . . . The Christianity of the Gospels is not that of the earliest Christian fathers."[56] The early church fathers may have been pious and honest men, but unwittingly they were victims of the philosophy of their time, hostages of the Platonism through which the gospel became filtered and by which they sought to express the truths of Christianity. Now, after centuries of captivity, the Christian faith may at long last break free from the bondage of the philosophy of Plato and the theology of the church fathers to recover the pure, rational religion of the Gospels. With that, Christ too can break the clutches of Plato and the church fathers to walk forth from the Gospels as a pure, free, rational human being.

---

55 Ibid., 107.
56 Ibid., 119.

But recovering the primitive purity of the New Testament and the true religion of the Gospels by going behind the councils and the philosophy of the early church fathers is no easy task. Historical Christianity slid off base sometime in the second century and subsequently has become encrusted with layers of doctrinal corruption that only now have begun to be peeled back so that the true faith may once again appear. Surveying the wreckage of doctrinal corruptions and false religion, which has wrapped itself in the cloak of Orthodoxy, Norton simply cannot contain his rage at what it has done to the human mind: "In the history of other departments of science, we find abundant errors and extravagances; but Orthodox theology seems to have been the peculiar region of words without meaning; of doctrines confessedly false in their proper sense, and explained in no other; of the most portentous absurdities put forward as truths of the highest import; and of contradictory prop"[57] At long last the shackles of Orthodoxy have been broken and the faithful may once again drink the pure waters of gospel truth and meet the Christ not of Plato but of the New Testament. The Christ who emerges from the tedious and labored pages of Norton's *Statement* is a Christ devoid of divine attributes who is human in every way and therefore approachable by rational and pious believers.

---

[57] Ibid., 125. See also Norton's "A Defense of Liberal Christianity, "*The General Repository and Review* (Jan. 1812), 12–23, and his response to Ralph Waldo Emerson's famous "Divinity School Address," in *A Discourse on the Latest Form of Infidelity, delivered at the request of the Cambridge Theological School, 19 July 1839* (Cambridge: John Owen, 1839).

## 4

In 1821, the *Unitarian Miscellany and Christian Monitor* began publication in Baltimore under the editorship of Jared Sparks. Though modest in size and circulation, the *Miscellany* aimed at becoming a principle organ for the dissemination of Unitarian views, and in its first issue set forth an "Abstract of Unitarian Belief." The "Abstract" is an articulate and concise presentation of fundamental Unitarian doctrines, including of course the person of Christ. Accordingly, Christ is described as a messenger, as a distinct and subordinate being who is not God and whose wisdom and power are strictly derived from God. To believe that in his person Christ is God is to misread Scripture and to violate reason; yet it is clearly the case that Christ does make "a divine revelation to the world. We believe in the divinity of his mission, not of his person."[58] The miracles, teachings and character of Christ all reveal the power, wisdom and virtue of God, who in Christ has accomplished a divine mission without the necessity of a divine person. And just as God is one, so too is Christ one. To wrench the one person of Christ into two natures necessarily ends up making of him two distinct beings or persons, and that of course is absurd. Since the Scriptures do not deal in absurdities, we may safely assume that the two natures in one person Christology is an impossibility that rational and pious Christians will therefore reject out of hand.

The short-lived *Unitarian Miscellany and Christian Monitor* published several essays of high quality that were later reprinted and distributed by the American Unitarian Association as part of its extensive tract series. These tracts were spread "as seeds upon the wind," serving as one of the primary instruments by which the reasonableness of Christianity in its Unitarian garb would be carried to a much wider audience beyond "the neighborhood of Boston." The leading lights of liberal Christianity were enlisted to contribute their views on a wide range of theological and devotional topics, and the measure of American Unitarianism on a number of issues, including the person of Christ, may be taken by a survey of the tracts printed in this valuable and

---

58 *Unitarian Miscellany and Christian Monitor,* vol. 1, no. 1 (Jan. 1815): 15.

interesting series.[59] For example, among these Unitarian tracts is an essay by Alan Lamson on "The Doctrine of Two Natures in Jesus Christ," reprinted from the *Unitarian Miscellany.* According to Lamson's findings, the great majority of early Christians "viewed Jesus as a finite and dependent being," that is, until the early church fathers became corrupted by Platonism. The influence of this "worst philosophy of the worst times" subsequently flowed through the church and became calcified in the Council of Chalcedon, which left its enduring imprint on the church through its mistatement of the person of Christ. But not even the vote of a church council can permanently transform absurdity into truth, and the Platonizing notion of two natures in one person is only now at long last being unmasked by Scripture and reason. It has become clear to the enlightened that any attempt to unite the divine and the human in one person is quite beyond doing, for this "brings together an assemblage of qualities which are incompatible with each other."[60]

Further, the doctrine of two natures in one person destroys the personal unity of Christ and divides him into two distinct persons or intelligent agents, each with its own individuality and consciousness. Even more serious, traditional Christology casts aspersions on the character of Christ because it "impedes his veracity and attributes to him deceit, equivocation and

---

59 In a twenty-five year span from 1825 to 1850, the American Unitarian Association published 272 individual tracts, which were subsequently collected and bound in three handsome volumes. Of these, approximately 113 tracts were devoted to practical issues while 93 were devoted to doctrinal issues, including the important topic of the person of Christ. The tracts were viewed by the AUA as a permanent contribution to American letters generally and to American religious literature specifically. The Committee on Tracts noted that "no religious connection of the same extent has, in its periodical literature or its occasional pamphlets, shown more vigor of thought or industry of pen, while the larger works that have been given to the public proclaim the scholarship and integrity of our writers." (From the Twenty-Fifth Report of the American Unitarian Association, with the Proceedings of the Annual Meeting, May 26, 1850, 46). This was not just an idle boast, and while the Unitarian tracts did not have their hoped for effect of sweeping a waiting nation into the arms of religious liberalism, nonetheless the legacy of this tract series is one of importance to the wider stream of American religious life and thought and deserves more attention than it has received.

60 Alvan Lamson, *The Doctrine of Two Natures in Jesus Christ* (American Unitarian Tract Series, I:20, n.d.), 8.

falsehood."[61] Finally, the doctrine of the two natures in one person weakens if it does not destroy the example of Christ's own piety because we are left confused, to take but one example, as to whether one of his natures (the human) prayed to the other nature (the divine). Since there is no scriptural guidance given for sorting out which words and deeds of Christ are to be ascribed to which of the two natures, Lamson concludes that the doctrine in question only throws a veil over Scripture. Classical Christology displaces the ordinary language of the Bible and its established laws of interpretation with confusion and obscurity, whereby the Scriptures "may mean anything or everything, according to the prejudices and fancy of the reader."[62] That the faithful should have to suffer such absurdities as this in the name of right belief and piety is more than Lamson can bear, especially when all of this difficulty and confusion could be quickly and easily dissipated if the person of Christ were seen in the whole of his nature to be inferior and subordinate to God.

In an 1827 sermon entitled "The Foundation of Our Confidence in the Saviour," Lamson sounded a recurring Unitarian theme by declaring that Christianity is "built not on the dignity of Christ's nature, but upon the divinity of his mission."[63] In effect, the Orthodox have wasted their energy by focusing on and defending the wrong divinity, for the salvation of humankind is predicated not on the divinity of Christ's person but rather on the divinity of Christ's mission, and therein consists "the foundation of our confidence." In another of Lamson's several tracts written for the American Unitarian Association he marshalls scriptural evidence for the view that Christ is distinct from, subordinate to and sent by God to fulfill a divine mission among humankind, and so far at least as Unitarians are concerned "the question of his nature they do not consider as important."[64] He had no difficulty with the divinity of Christ's mission and office, but any suggestion that Christ's person was divine in nature was rejected out of hand.

---

61 Ibid., 18.

62 Ibid., 23.

63 Lamson, *The Foundation of Our Confidence in the Saviour* (Dedham, Mass: H. & W. H. Mann, 1827), 7.

64 Lamson, *What is Unitarianism?* (American Unitarian Association, Tract Series 1: 202, 1833), 12.

Others from the ranks of liberal religion joined Lamson in the effort to clarify the nature of the person of Christ, including for example the Rev. William B. O. Peabody. In a tract entitled *Come and See*, Peabody attempted to present a fair, rigorous and candid synopsis of what Unitarians believe, including "what we teach of Christ." Unitarians do not teach, as some too readily assume, that Christ was a mere man. In truth, "our doctrine is simply this, that Jesus Christ was inferior to the Father, and to the Father alone; of all beings, with one exception, he is by far the most exalted."[65] Does this mean that the world thereby has been deprived of a savior adequate to the task of salvation? This is by no means the case, and Unitarians cannot be accused under any circumstance of placing the salvation of the world in the hands of a mere man. In fact, Christ is armed with the power derived from God prerequisite to accomplishing all that is required of him in the great drama of salvation. The denial of the divinity of Christ does not in any way either undercut his adequacy as a redeemer or detract from the proper reverence for Christ that Unitarians always and everywhere have consistently shown. Peabody is exasperated by the charge that the Unitarian failure to pay high honor to the person of Christ results in spiritual coldness and indifference. Indeed quite the opposite is the case, for it is precisely the Unitarian understanding of the person of Christ that leads to the highest honor for him. A theological attack on Unitarian views of the person of Christ was one thing; but linking this to personal attacks on Unitarian piety was something else, and Peabody was quick to come to the defense of both the theology and the piety of his fellow liberal religionists.

A contribution to the AUA tract series entitled *The Moral Power of Christ's Character* was written by yet another New England Peabody, and it attempts to distinguish more sharply between two essentially differing views of Christ's person. Ephraiam Peabody drew a clear distinction between "one class deeming the metaphysical view of Christ the most essential; the other the moral view. That is, one has deemed it of primary importance that men should have just notions of the *nature* of Christ; the other, that men should have just

---

65 William B. O. Peabody, *Come and See* (American Unitarian Association, Tract Series 1: 71, 1844), 14.

conceptions of his *character*."[66] Peabody elaborated on this useful distinction between a Christology focusing on the nature versus a Christology focusing on the character of Christ and charged that the church and its creeds have shown a regrettable preoccupation with the metaphysical to the neglect of the moral view of Christ's person. Inquisitions have been set up and armies have marched in defense of metaphysics of Christ's nature while the morality of Christ's character has lain in shameful neglect. If the nature of Christ's person was really all that important, the New Testament would have settled the issue long ago. But the fundamental question is "What has belief in Christ's nature, whether it be understood to be divine, or super-angelic, or angelic, or human, to do with a virtuous and holy life?"[67] Peabody ingeniously turns the tables on the Orthodox, charging them with allowing the intellect to overshadow the affections, the metaphysical to outweigh the moral in their preoccupation with the nature of Christ's person. By allowing the metaphysics of the historical creeds rather than the morality of the Bible to dictate the content of faith and especially the shape of christological debates, the Orthodox are guilty of diverting attention away from the moral character to the metaphysical person of Christ, thereby distorting who Christ is and in turn what Christianity is.

The character of Christ is likewise the key to the character of God, and who God is should be shaped in the human mind and heart not by metaphysical speculation but by the image that is revealed in the character of Christ. Over against the nature of Christ, about which the New Testament is silent, stands in bold relief the almost tangible presence of the character of Christ. Therefore, constituted as they are, the only way that human beings can arrive at any just notions of the character of God is by seeing the divine character revealed through human character. That is precisely what has happened in the character of Christ, through whom "God as it were stooped from his heavens, and humbled himself to our feeble comprehensions, and revealed his infinite glories in the softer light of the visible life of Jesus."[68] The character of

---

66 Ephraiam Peabody, *The Moral Power of Christ's Character* (American Unitarian Association, Tract Series 1: 151, 1840), 3, 4.
67 Ibid., 5.
68 Ibid., 10.

Christ reveals the character of God in ways that metaphysical speculation about the nature of Christ never could, but also the character of Christianity as as religion "not for the philosophers alone, but also for the poor and ignorant." The great virtue of Unitarianism therefore is that through it Christianity will be restored to the common people from whom it has been taken by the speculations of Trinitarianism. The coming triumph of religious liberalism will then be attributable in no small part to the Christ who it presents to the masses, for the Christ of Unitarianism is far more recognizable to them than is the Christ of the philosophers.

If the moral character rather than the metaphysical nature of Christ becomes the criterion of Christology then "the dark places of Scripture" and "the doubtful doctrines of Christianity" are given new illumination and seen in a new light. Salvation comes not through the intellect philosophically reflecting on the metaphysical nature of Christ, but through the affections identifying with the moral character of Christ in whom we have a perfect standard of excellence. Christ is the one who "stands before the world, not merely the image of God, but the standard of perfected humanity."[69] Christ does not stand before the world as the one whose person unifies the two natures of humanity and divinity and therefore as some kind of metaphysical puzzle. Christ stands as the model of moral excellence whose character is proleptically at work in the world, slowly but surely elevating humankind to higher levels of moral good.

The list of contributors to the American Unitarian Association's first series of tracts reads like a virtual who's who of liberal religion in America, including Ezra Stiles Gannett, one of Unitarianism's most astute apologists. One of Gannett's tracts entitled *The Faith of the Unitarian Christian* was devoted to defending against the charge that among other things the christological views of Unitarians represent little more than unbelief and infidelity. According to Gannett, these charges against Unitarians are painted with a wide brush, when in fact a closer and more fair examination of their views on the person of Christ will reveal that unlike infidels and unbelievers, Unitarians do not deny Christ's supernatural

---

69 Ibid., 19.

mission and his moral excellence. Gannett was determined that Unitarians "will not be seduced from our faith by the ingenious theories or mystical discourse of some who affect to honor Jesus while they throw suspicion over his whole history. We cannot divorce the history from the Divine influence which it conveys."[70] The doctrine of two natures in one person of Christ is just such an instance of dishonoring Jesus and obscuring the historical basis of the Christian faith by wrapping its founder in "ingenious theories or mystical discourse." The link between doctrinal Christianity and spiritual Christianity is a vital one, and if the history of doctrine is filled with corruption we can expect that spirituality will be filled with the same. Spiritual Christianity is grounded in historical Christianity, which is why it is all the more urgent in the present to get beyond the christological corruptions of historical Christianity to the real historical basis of the faith in the New Testament. Only then will the historical and the spiritual be brought back into alignment with each other, and the spiritual will be able once again to drink from the unpolluted streams of the historical. Right doctrine must be allowed to work its salutary effects on Christian piety, something that has not happened within Trinitarianism for centuries.

## 5

Not every sermon, discourse or essay of liberal religious thinkers made its way into the American Unitarian Association tract series, including for example a sermon delivered by the Rev. Abiel Abbot Livermore on the occasion of the dedication of the Unitarian meeting house in Windsor, Vermont, in December 1846. Discoursing on "The Faith Once Delivered to the Saints," Livermore informed his listeners that this faith does not contain anything at all about the divinity of Christ or his equality with God. The teaching of the twofold nature of Christ should be exposed for what it is: "a pure theological fiction" that has been concocted to explain away

70 Ezra Stiles Gannett, *The Faith of the Unitarian Christian* (American Unitarian Association, Tract Series 1:220, 1845), 21. Gannett had read carefully and was following closely Andrews Norton's *Latest Form of Infidelity* at this point.

the difficulties of another theological fiction, the doctrine of the Trinity. Christ should be seen as what he is revealed to be in the New Testament, that is, as neither God nor man "but an exalted being midway between the two, or as the record says, a Mediator."[71] Moreover, its was time according to Livermore for theology in general and the doctrine of the person of Christ in particular to catch up to "the spirit of the age, which is in league, we believe, with a more earnest practical faith, with a more resolute religious spirit, a more sober, real, living, everyday piety and morality, cleansed from the mists and speculations and traditions of dark and distant ages, and in harmony with the progress of society, the advances of science, the triumph of the arts, the spread of popular institutions, the diffusion of useful knowledge, the universal education of the people, and the glorious movements of modern reform against the hoary vices of the past."[72] Livermore was merely sounding themes that were echoed repeatedly by his liberal colleagues, including the conviction that Christ simply could not be expected to walk into an enlightened age of rational religion encumbered by the weight of past christological formulations. Livermore does not flesh out the Christ who has been "cleansed from the mists and speculations and traditions of dark and distant ages" and who therefore would meet the criteria of "modern reform against the hoary vices of the past," but certainly it is not the Christ of Chalcedon or of Orthodoxy in general.

Others, including Daniel Whitaker, took the liberating message of liberal religion far beyond the boundaries of New England, in this case to Charleston, South Carolina, where the Rev. Mr. Whitaker discoursed at some length and in considerable detail on "The Unity and Supremacy of God the Father." Whitaker attacked the doctrine of the divinity of Christ as an improbable and inconsistent teaching that was not found in the Scripture and that ends up doing far more harm than good. The doctrine of the divinity of Christ undermines the strict unity of God and therefore serves as an opening for

71 Abiel Abbot Livermore, *The Faith Once Delivered to the Saints* (Boston: Wm. Crosby & H. P. Nichols, 1847), 11. Livermore followed the westward course of Unitarianism to Meadville, Pennsylvania, where he taught New Testament at the Meadville Theological School.
72 Ibid., 22.

and encouragement to Deists, skeptics, infidels and others to launch their attacks on the Christian faith. Whitaker pounded the Charleston pulpit as an expression of his dismay and impatience with those who read the same Bible that he did and discovered there another supreme God alongside God the Father. He is frustrated that Christ as this other supreme God has been extracted from texts in which there "is no ambiguity, no circumlocution, no metaphor, no far-fetched allegory, no mysterious combination of scholastic terms to bewilder the unsophisticated mind."[73] These are texts that assert in straightforward commonsense terms that Christ is not a supreme God but distinct from and inferior to the one supreme God. How much simpler can it get than to accept the common sense of Scripture according to which Christ is subordinate to and not equal with God? The attempt of classical Christology to transform the finite into the infinite is simply impossible because two such dissimilar natures as the human and the divine cannot be united in one person. Shrouding the plain and simple truths of the gospel in ambiguity, circumlocution, metaphor, allegory and scholastic terms and then trying to promulgate this concoction as the essentials of Christianity is an enormous tax on not only the unsophisticated but also the enlightened mind, and Whitaker will have none of it. Promoting mysteries in the name of Christianity is a great disservice, for it only serves to diminish rather than enhance the truths of religion. But most important, it is impossible "that divine revelation should contain any mysteries. As soon as a proposition is revealed, it ceases to be a mystery."[74] There are therefore certainly no mysteries surrounding the person of Christ because it has been so clearly revealed exactly who he is, and the Orthodox for too long have hidden behind the theological masks of mystery.

Whitaker shared with many of his fellow liberal religionists the conviction that the finger of blame is to be pointed at the fourth century and the corrupting influences of Platonism, through which the councils and catechisms of the church were led astray, and regretfully these corruptions have persisted into the present. Fortunately, however, the tide of

---

73 Daniel Whitaker, *The Supremacy of God the Father* (Charleston, 1826), 12.
74 Ibid., 28.

history is turning and the primitive and pure faith of the New Testament is once again finding expression in the life and thought of the church. This turn has occurred only as the subversive doctrine of the Trinity and its christological corollary doctrine of the two natures in one person of Christ have given way. Slowly emerging from the ruins of a discredited metaphysics is the Christ of the New Testament who is the mediator of God and the friend of humankind. Turning his back on the divinity of Christ, Whitaker reached out to embrace this friendly and approachable Christ who was not God. He was convinced that the divinity of Christ contradicts the testimony of the prophets and the apostles and is therefore unscriptural; that the divinity of Christ defies the tenants of reason and common sense and is therefore irrational; that the divinity of Christ disregards the testimony of Christ himself and is therefore immoral; that the divinity of Christ flies in the face of history and is therefore ahistorical; that the divinity of Christ does not foster piety and is therefore impractical.

From the same Unitarian pulpit in Charleston, South Carolina, the Rev. Samuel Gilman held forth in a sermon that took its text from the introduction to the Gospel according to St. John, in which Gilman informed his listeners that the use of the term "Logos" by St. John refers not to a separate intelligent agent but to God alone. The simple fact is that "if St. John intended to begin his gospel by informing his readers that Jesus Christ was truly God, he would probably have told us so in plain and clear terms, and not involved his meaning in a cloud of figurative obscurity."[75] A commonsense reading of John's prologue will reveal that Christ is not the Logos of God and does not possess a divine nature, but that nevertheless he does possess "a character of inimitable perfection" and "a destiny and a dignity of infinite and unrivaled excellence." The human nature of Christ has been filled by the divine with "its unspeakable effluences," and in this view of Christ it is clear that he is not a mere man. It is therefore most unfair and unfortunate that Unitarians have been charged with a doctrine of Christ that they do not believe, and that their teachings have been mistreated by the Orthodox as something monstrous

75 Samuel Gilman, *A Sermon on the Introduction to St. John* (Boston: C. C. Sebring, 1826), 8.

and horrid. If you want to see something monstrous and horrid, look at some German theology, of which Gilman can only say that "none more than Unitarians lament and discredit the extravagant speculations into which some of the German theologians have been borne."[76] It is the Unitarians who are the true defenders of the person of Christ against the Orthodox on the one side and German theology on the other.

Three well-organized and lucid sermons by the Rev. Jacob Norton that appeared in 1819 as *A Humble Attempt to Ascertain the Scripture Doctrine of the Father, Son and Holy Spirit* deserve mention at this point. Regarding the relation between the first two persons of the Trinity Norton states in no uncertain terms that "the Father of our Lord Jesus Christ is alone the true God, and Jesus Christ is not the true God but inferior to him."[77] He then proceeds systematically to demonstrate this conviction by arguing that Christ is a man "approved of God," but this is by no means the same as saying that Christ is that same God. Christ is to be clearly distinguished from the supreme God because to posit two supreme Gods is obviously patent nonsense. Further, while the title "Son of God" may designate a miraculous conception, point to the high office of Messiah, and serve to remind us of Christ's resurrection and exaltation, all of this taken together does not add up to the divinity of Christ. It is simply gratuitous to assign both humanity and divinity to the person of Christ because in fact Christ was sent to fulfill the will of the one supreme God from whom he has derived all his power and authority. In a summative statement of his views on the person of Christ, Norton sought to touch every possible base in defense of his fundamental conviction that Christ is inferior to God and

> that he received commands from the Father—that the doctrine which he taught were not originally his own but delivered to him from the Father—that he was a Priest, a High Priest, in which character he transacted important and interesting concerns between his Father and sinful

---

76 Ibid., 37.

77 Jacob Norton, *A Humble Attempt to Ascertain the Scripture Doctrine of the Father, Son and Holy Ghost* (Boston: Palmeter & Balch, printers, 1819), 32. Jacob Norton is representative of the liberal wing of the Baptists.

> men—that he prayed to his Father—that he was subject to violent and grievous temptations from Satan—that he is the image of the Supreme God—that he is the beginning the creation of God, the first born of every creature—that he had not the disposal of the highest places of his kingdom—that he is not supremely good—that his knowledge was not unlimited—that his Father is greater than himself—that he has a God, or head or superior—that he died, and was raised from the dead by his Father—that he is subject to God, as his servant, his chosen, by faithfully obeying his Father, and giving up (hereafter) the kingdom of God, even the Father, from whom he had received it.[78]

After all of this, who for one minute could believe that Christ is God or as the Second Person of the Trinity that he is in any way equal to the First Person.

In his 1849 "Address before the Graduating Class of the Divinity School in Cambridge," Frederic Henry Hedge (1805–90) assured the graduates that the Trinitarian doctrine of the person of Christ was only a passing phase in the history of the church, albeit a rather lengthy phase. At long last however, this necessary phase of the church's history is drawing to a close as the creeds and confessions of this earlier era are yielding to the more enlightened needs of the present age. These needs are now being and will continue to be more than adequately met by the practical bent and tolerant spirit of Unitarianism. The creeds and confessions of an earlier age served only to invite theological speculation and doctrinal rigidity, thereby creating an atmosphere of divisiveness and intolerance toward opposing points of view. But the weight of the past is being lifted and the creeds of a former phase of the church's history are being displaced by a more liberal and nondogmatic spirit that is but a prelude to that day when "there will be neither Trinitarian nor Unitarian, nor orthodox nor liberal, but more adequate statements, let us hope, and more adequate illustrations, let us be sure, than any of these now furnish, of Christian truth."[79]

---

78 Ibid., 50.

79 Frederic Henry Hedge, *An Address before the Graduating Class of the Divinity School in Cambridge* (Cambridge, 1849), 28.

Hedge's optimism about the emergence of more adequate statements and illustrations of Christian truth included of course the doctrine of the person of Christ. His hope was that the Christology of the first century would become once again the Christology of the present century because "the Christians of the first century were strict monotheists, or Unitarians. They speculated very little, if at all, about the person of Christ."[80] With the passage of time however the Jesus of history became idealized into the Christ of the church and its creeds by a regretful but almost unavoidable tendency toward speculation. As the historical Jesus receded into the past and grew dim to memory the tendency was to transform the bare historical fact of Jesus into the idealized person of Christ, to transform the simplicity of the Gospels into the complexity of the creeds. But these doctrinal developments of the fourth century that found expression in the doctrine of the two natures in one person of Christ are not necessarily to be lamented. Better instead to see them as an important phase in the history of the church during which the early church fathers were indeed grappling with a serious theological issue: "the union of God with man is no quibble; it is a truth of profound significance."

The important thing to see is that the bad doctrinal formulations on which the early church fathers settled need not remain a lodestone around the neck of the church in the present. The solution of the early church fathers to the problem of the union of God with man leaves off too quickly, and the task is to carry their struggle forward into the present by recognizing, as they did not, that the rest of humankind shares at least some measure of Christ's union with God. "Of what avail to mankind at large," asks Hedge, "that a single individual, of the countless millions who in all the ages of human history have walked the earth, was substantially united to God, if all the rest are substantially separated from him?" Hedge concludes that "if Christ was really man, he differed from other men only in degree. What he by nature possessed without measure, all men in a manner must also

---

80 Frederic Henry Hedge, *Ways of the Spirit and other Essays* (Boston, 1877), 348f. On Hedge see also George H. Williams, *Rethinking the Unitarian Relationship with Protestantism: An Examination of the Thought of Frederic Henry Hedge* (Boston: Beacon Press, 1949).

possess."[81] The point is to detect and to trace the evolution of this measure of divinity in all persons and to chronicle the spirit of Christ coursing its way through the heart of Christendom and into the world, discovering along the way "unmistakable signs of deeper earnestness and truer devotion, of a more thorough penetration and occupation of this age by the spirit of Christ, than any past time has known."[82]

## 6

In 1837, George E. Ellis wrote *A Half Century of the Unitarian Controversy* in which he devoted a chapter to "Unitarianism and Orthodoxy on God and Christ." Ellis begins his discussion with the obligatory Unitarian denunciation of the doctrine of the Trinity as "an enormous waste of human thought upon a metaphysical abstraction," as an incomprehensible and inexplicable mass of rubbish heaped up at the threshold of Christianity and as an "amazing perplexity" that serves only as a stumbling block to the faithful.[83] In an ongoing torture of Scripture, Trinitarians have made matters worse by linking the divinity of Christ to the doctrine of the Trinity, with the result that they simply have given to the world the wrong Christ. Little wonder then that in the course of the continuing inquiry the question "What think ye of Christ?" has been met with a bewildering number of responses that serve only to divide rather than to unite the parties involved. The unhappy result is not only the division within the church between Trinitarians and Unitarians, but also, according to Ellis, the even more tragic loss of the real Christ, who has been eclipsed by extraneous, artificial and perplexing dogmas. The real Christ lies buried beneath absurdities that are wholly "unevangelical and anti-evangelical in all [their] character and element." The task at hand is one of healing these divisions by the recovery of the genuinely evangelical Christ who is not frayed and fragmented by endless theological controversy.

---

81 Ibid., 351.
82 Ibid., 93.
83 George E. Ellis, *A Half Century of the Unitarian Controversy* (Boston: Crosby & Nichols, 1857), 120.

Ellis is convinced that it is Unitarianism that has made the most significant contribution to the recovery of the real Christ of the New Testament, the Christ who leads us to God alone as the supreme object of our worship. It is simply not true that by asserting the derivation and dependence of Christ that Unitarians have thereby somehow dishonored him. It is true that Unitarians teach that to attribute divinity to Christ is both incongruous and incoherent, but this does not mean that Unitarians therefore think of Christ as a mere man. The person of Christ in Unitarian thought is distinguished from both deity on the one side and humanity on the other, although Ellis does not provide his readers with any details on the nature of these distinctions. He admits to a certain christological disarray within the Unitarian camp, but then universal agreement among Unitarians on anything, much less the person of Christ, is neither desirable nor possible.

Within this variety of Unitarian viewpoints are those who see Christ as a man miraculously endowed and holding rank above all others as a human being. There are within the Unitarian ranks those who are Arians and hold to Christ's preexistence and his dwelling before all the worlds, while at the same time there are those who reject the preexistence of Christ as an untenable teaching. There are likewise Unitarians who are not interested in the least in Christ's nature but whose interest focuses rather on his office as the mediator between heaven and earth. There are even Unitarians who subscribe to the doctrine of the eternal generation of the Son, although Ellis himself has to admit that while those who hold this position do not intend to utter an absurdity or to signify that they are "saying something while they are saying nothing," in fact he himself can "get no idea at all from their words." Finally there are those Unitarians who view Jesus as a mere man and under no circumstance will be persuaded otherwise regarding his person.[84] The point is that no matter in what form Unitarians express themselves on the person of Christ, their desire is to honor him and above all to think rightly about him on this most important theological topic.

Unitarians are as concerned as Trinitarians not to dishonor the person of Christ, and they therefore refuse to ascribe

---

84 Ibid., 158.

divinity to Christ's person. To call Christ divine is to lose "some of the highest and most precious uses for which God was manifested in the person of Christ . . . [as] a being nearer our conceptions and more available to some of our highest needs of guidance, knowledge and confidence."[85] By ascribing divinity to Christ as the Orthodox have done, he becomes remote and lost to human view, which is both tragic and unnecessary. But from the tomb of the barren metaphysics of traditional Christology a living Christ can and will be resurrected by a faithful remnant of scriptural, rational and experiential Christians. Ellis is confident that overall the Unitarian controversy has served the good by shifting the focus of the christological debate from the metaphysical to the devotional, from the philosophical to the practical. A spiritual or devotional Christ is much to be preferred to a metaphysical Christ, and this as he sees it is the great gain that has come out of the sometime rancorous debates over the person of Christ between Unitarians and Trinitarians.

7

The above survey is of necessity selective and incomplete, but it may serve to provide a representative sampling from sermons, tracts and books of the diversity within Unitarianism on the issue of the person of Christ. As they faced off against the Orthodox there was certainly no unanimity of opinion regarding the person of Christ among the Unitarians, a fact that many of their number cherished deeply. As the christological controversy between Trinitarians and Unitarians dragged on many things kept repeating themselves, including the same favorite scriptural texts that were staunchly defended by each side; the same charges of philosophical corruptions and historical distortions resurfaced time and again; the same misunderstandings and charges of misrepresentation regarding the nature of language cropped up and were hurled back and forth; the same sharp exchanges over reason and revelation and what qualifies as a mystery and what does not were rehashed; the same hurt feelings over exclusion and the impugning of character in print were

85 Ibid., 148.

expressed by both sides; the same arguments over whether Christ was an object of worship; as well as the same differences over the appropriateness of creeds and confessions all were expressed repeatedly. As the lines of difference hardened each side was increasingly convinced that the other had crucified the real Christ and did not know where they had laid him. Christ's haunting question "Who do you say that I am?" became increasingly explosive as the touchstone for who was most scriptural, who was most rational, who was most faithful, who was most Christian. No little amount of self-righteous fury found expression on both sides of the controversy over the person of Christ.

# Chapter III

# MOSES STUART AND LEONARD WOODS: CHRIST AS THE LOGOS AND AS THE SON

William Ellery Channing's Baltimore sermon elicited a number of critical responses, including a series of letters written by Moses Stuart (1780–1852), associate professor of sacred literature at the Theological Seminary at Andover.[1] When he assumed his teaching position at Andover, Stuart had virtually no acquaintance with either Hebrew or Greek. Despite both his poor eyesight, which imposed severe restrictions on the number of hours that he could spend in his study each day, and the enormous teaching workload that he undertook at the seminary, Stuart not only mastered both biblical languages but also in 1828 set the type for and published a *Grammar of the Hebrew Language.* In the midst of this flurry of activity he was also able to acquaint himself with a vast quantity of German scholarship, and at the time of his response to Channing's Baltimore sermon Stuart was on his way to becoming the most formidable biblical scholar in America. He launched his attack on Channing as an effort "impartially to weigh the arguments and examine the

---

1 For biographical information on Stuart see Sprague, *Annals of the American Pulpit,* vol. 2, 475f; "Moses Stuart" in Edwards A. Park, *Memorial Collection of Sermons,* comp. Agnes Park (Boston: The Pilgrim Press, 1902), 178–217; John H. Giltner, *Moses Stuart, 1780–1852* (Atlanta: Scholar's Press, 1988); Leonard Woods, *History of Andover Theological Seminary* (Boston: J. R. Osgood, 1885).

reasonings which it presents, with a wish to know and believe the truth."[2]

Not surprisingly, Stuart begins by taking exception to Channing's principles of biblical interpretation, suggesting that if reason and common sense are applied to Scriptures it is clear that the name of God is given to Christ in such a manner that there can be no question but that Christ is the supreme God. Drawing on the first three verses of the prologue to John's gospel, Stuart unfolds for Channing the meaning of the term Logos as that which is "bestowed upon Christ, in reference to his becoming the Instructor or Teacher of mankind; the medium of communication between God and them."[3] As such, the Logos is not just another of the many attributes of God, but it "appears to be a person." For according to John's prologue the Logos was not only "with God," the Logos "was God," a distinction that on closer examination will be discovered applies to no other divine attribute. And since Christ was the Logos, we cannot escape the conclusion that Christ was God. Stuart continues by patiently explaining to Channing that in the interpretation of Scripture, or for that matter in the interpretation of any text, "every word takes on a sense adapted to its connexion." If this principle of interpretation is followed faithfully and applied to the opening verses of John's gospel we soon see that the term "God" is used in two slightly different senses, one in saying that the Logos was with God and the other that the Logos was God. In other words, John is saying of the Logos "that he was truly divine, but still divine in such a manner, that there did exist a distinction between him and the Father."[4] But this distinction between "with God" and "was God" is not to be carried to extremes and inflated, as some are guilty of doing, by implying that Christ as the Logos means on the one hand his self-existence and independence, or on the other hand his derivation and dependence.

Channing might very well be interested in knowing exactly how the Logos is connected with God. To this inquiry Stuart candidly responds: "I answer freely that I cannot tell. The

---

2 Moses Stuart, *Letters to the Rev. William E. Channing, Containing Remarks on his Sermon Recently Preached and Published at Baltimore* (Andover: Flagg and Gould, 1819), 3.

3 Ibid., 59.

4 Ibid., 63.

Evangelist has asserted the *fact*, but has not added one word to explain the *modus*.[5] Much like the "fact" of the personal distinctions within the Godhead that constitute the Trinity but that do not yield to further explanation as to modus, so too here the "fact" of the connection between God and the Logos is a scriptural given that does not yield to further explanation. Arguments from such "facts" were not convincing to Channing and his followers, but to Stuart it was an unavoidable conclusion that the Logos is God in the true and supreme sense of the word based on the fact of Scripture. After rather lengthy exegetical excurses into Heb. 1:10–12 and Col. 1:15–17, he concludes that Christ as the Logos is the eternal, immutable and divine creator of the universe, and that creation under no circumstance could be delegated to an inferior and dependent being. Christ is therefore the supreme God, and contrary to Channing's assertion that there are only two or three texts in which Christ is called God, there are in fact numerous texts which can be added to the above that attest that as the Logos Christ is the supreme God. Not that the number of such texts is important, for even one text would be sufficient to prove the divinity of the Logos; Channing needs therefore to return to his New Testament with a more careful eye to what it is really saying and with greater sensitivity to the sense that every word takes on according to its context.

With these preliminaries out of the way, Stuart is now ready to unleash against Channing the full force of his considerable exegetical skills, linguistic talents, historical knowledge and familiarity with German scholarship. He accuses the Federal Street pastor of being mistaken in thinking that there is a paucity of texts proving the divinity of Christ when just the opposite is the case. The problem is quite simply that Channing has no solid basis on which to build his Christology, for the phenomenon of the one person of Christ combining the two natures of humanity and divinity "is a wonder, which no ground but that of Trinitarianism can ever explain. I mean the ground, that the divine and human natures co-existed in Christ, and that in the same sentence, he could with propriety speak of himself as human and divine. The sacred writers appear not to take the least pains to separate the two natures, in anything

5 Ibid., 64.

which they say of either. They everywhere speak of Christ (so it appears to me), as either human or divine, or both."[6] It is therefore simply not necessary to sort out the human and the divine usage every time Christ's name appears in Scripture; the original writers did not feel the necessity of doing this, why should we?

Stuart then proceeds to barrage Channing with a lengthy series of biblical texts that, according to principles of Trinitarian interpretation, attest to the equality of Christ with God. Special attention is given to Phil. 2:5–8, for which Stuart provides a fresh translation and a lengthy interpretation designed to support Christ's equality with God. In the midst of his detailed exegesis of this passage the Andover professor pauses to issue the disclaimer that "human language, (made up of terms, formed to express the ideas of finite and mutable beings about finite and mutable objects), is of course incompetent, fully to designate the mode of union between the divine and human natures. I must regard the language here, and in all other passages, on the awful subject, as only an approximation toward describing what exists in the Divinity or is done by him."[7] While Stuart is driven in his discussion of the two natures in one person of Christ to acknowledge the problem of language, and its inadequacies, he was not prepared to offer a new theory of language, much less to formulate a new Christology on the basis of it. But the problem of language as it related to Christology would not go away, and it remained for Horace Bushnell to take up that at which Stuart only hints at this point, that is, the reformulation of Christology in light of a new theory of language.

Meanwhile, the best that Moses Stuart can do is to document his awareness of the shortcomings of language and to express his dismay over the history of doctrine, which has failed to examine adequately the very language, with which it has

---

[6] Ibid., 85.

[7] Ibid., 97. Daniel Day Williams has noted that Stuart's controversy with Channing "shows him struggling to defend orthodoxy by the use of a theory of language definitely anticipating Horace Bushnell," and that he thought in terms of "a language of approximation toward complete description . . . [which] it may nevertheless express enough to excite our highest interest and to command our best obedience." Daniel Day Williams, *The Andover Liberals* (New York: King's Crown Press, 1941), 19.

formulated itself. He ends up falling back on the facts of Scripture by noting that "the history of past ages exhibits an appalling picture of disputes about the person of Christ; all springing from the denial of *facts* revealed in the New Testament, or from the unhallowed curiosity of men, who desired to know what God has not revealed."[8] Channing doubtless placed Stuart himself among those with an "unhallowed curiosity who desired to know what God has not revealed," but Stuart of course did not see himself in quite that light. He remained convinced that, Channing's principles of biblical interpretation notwithstanding, there are numerous New Testament texts in which particular divine attributes or works are ascribed to Christ, and he reels off a series of examples: omniscience in Matt. 11:27, divine power in Heb. 1:3, eternity in John 1:1, divine honor and worship in Rom. 10:9. Stuart simply delighted in scouring the New Testament for every conceivable witness to the divinity of Christ, who on the basis of overwhelming scriptural evidence is one with the infinite, almighty and all-sufficient God.

Stuart is forced to concede in his investigation into the person of Christ that the language of the creeds and confessions of the church has in some instances done harm to the Trinitarian cause. "That some of our *phraseology* has been derived from men, who *sometimes* speculated too boldly, and substituted names for ideas; I am ready to concede. I feel the embarrassments, that on account of this, are occasionally thrown in the way of inculcating truth, at the present time."[9] Exactly who these theologians are who have caused these embarrassments to the Trinitarian cause by speculating too boldly about the person of Christ Stuart does not say. But his lament reveals not only the burden of a more distant as well as an immediate doctrinal past, but also his sense of the urgency of clarifying the doctrine of the person of Christ within the present American theological context. Channing must have taken a certain amount of satisfaction from Stuart's complaint that among his fellow Trinitarians there were some who had "speculated too boldly, and substituted names for ideas," for that in essence was Channing's complaint about the

---

8 Stuart, *Letters to Channing,* 99.
9 Ibid., 119.

Christology of the Trinitarians also. But Stuart is quick to defend himself by reaffirming that his theology as well as that of the majority of his colleagues is shaped predominantly by the study of the Bible, with only very infrequent references to creeds or to historical theology.

In a conciliatory gesture to Channing and his followers, Stuart notes that the principles of biblical interpretation as guided by "the general laws of language" and in light of which he himself has studied the sacred text are largely the same as those outlined by Channing in his sermon. The Andover professor therefore has no real fundamental quarrel with the Federal Street pastor on the issue of the principles of biblical interpretation. He even goes so far as to inform his readers that "at least three quarters of my time have been spent among writers of the Unitarian class, from whom I have received, with gratitude, much instruction relative to philology, the exegesis, and the literary history of the Scripture."[10] He wonders aloud if the same can be said of Channing relative to his reading of Trinitarian authors. But in the end, Trinitarian or Unitarian, it really does not matter because the decision of Scripture is the final authority weighing "immeasurably above all human opinions." The divinity of Christ is not a decision of theology or the creeds but a fundamental fact of Scripture. The task of sorting out "human opinions" from "the facts of Scripture" would not be so easy as Stuart assumed. A little Christian charity at this point would then go a long way, and he warns Channing that it will not do for him to ascribe all virtue to the Unitarians and all vice to the Trinitarians. The issues are doctrinal and not personal, and in the future he hopes that Channing and his colleagues will cease casting aspersions on the Trinitarians by "representing us as gloomy, superstitious, malignant and unsocial; by appropriating to Unitarians all that is kind and noble and generous and exalted, and leaving us the opposite of these virtues."[11] Such aspersions may be good for controversy, but they are not good in the search for the truth, which is after all what both men are seeking. However,

---

10 Ibid., 120. Members of the Andover Seminary Board of Overseers must have read this line with considerable discomfort, and although Stuart was able to escape their censure, the Board did have to warn him against "the unrestrained cultivation of German studies."

11 Ibid., 125.

the argument for the "moral tendency" of either Unitarian or Trinitarian views was another one of those lines of argument that would not go away and that caused no small amount of tension and downright rancor between the two parties.

Stuart felt especially compelled to address himself to those texts that Channing had selected in his Baltimore sermon to prove the dependency and inferiority of Christ. He concludes his analysis with the confession that he is genuinely confused by and cannot quite figure out who Channing's Christ really is. In fact, given the choice between the Christ of Channing's sermon and outright Socinianism he prefers the latter, because the Socinians at least honestly adhere only to the strict humanity of Christ. As it is, Channing's Christology has transmuted Christ into some kind of unidentifiable compound, prompting Stuart to raise the query, "To what order or class of beings, then, does this new *compound*, and strangely mixed person belong? He is not divine; he is not human, for a human soul is surely essential to human nature; nor is he angelic, for angels have no corporeal forms."[12] The Unitarians may chide Trinitarians all they want for taking refuge behind mysteries in their discussions of the Trinity and the person of Christ, but to Stuart's mind who the person of Christ is in the thought of Channing is a mystery beyond all mysteries. In short, of Channing's Christology it can only be concluded that "if there be mystery in any theory which has ever been proposed respecting the person of Christ, it is surely here."[13] In light of

---

12 Ibid., 133. Channing was little interested in theological labels or in forming a theological party around himself. The use of the term Socinian in connection with his name would have made him bristle, but he was not unreceptive to being called an Arian. In any event, Stuart's assessment of Channing's Christology is at this point considerably more charitable than that of George Park Fisher, who noted that "according to Channing, Christ was a pre-existent rational creature, an angel or spirit of some sort, who had entered into a human body. He was not even a man except so far as his corporeal part is concerned, but was a creature from some upper sphere." Fisher concludes "that the particular conception which Channing set up in the room of the church doctrine of the Incarnation is one of the crudest notions which the history of speculation on this subject has ever presented. The transitional character of Channing's type of theology is strikingly indicated in this indefinite, unphilosophical sort of Arianism, to which it would seem that he adhered to the end." George Park Fisher, *Discussions in History and Theology* (New York: Scribner's, 1880), 272–73.

13 Stuart, *Letters to Channing,* 133.

the foregoing the Andover professor is rendered speechless by Channing's charge that it is Stuart's views on the person of Christ that are "a tax on credulity." It is rather Channing who has expressed himself so confusedly on the proper humanity of Christ that Stuart only hopes that he has misunderstood him, and will therefore await further clarification from Channing's pen on the matter. And in a moment of theological understatement bordering on humor, Stuart concludes that he cannot imagine under any circumstance that Channing would either deny the proper humanity of Christ or embrace Arianism in any of its several forms.

At this point in his *Letters* Stuart inserts a bit of instruction to Channing regarding one of his favorite exegetical themes on the troublesome phrase "Son of God." Admittedly this title is used in Scripture to designate a prior distinction in the Godhead, but this is only an "occasional and secondary" usage by the sacred penmen: "It does not appropriately designate Christ as divine, but as the incarnate Mediator."[14] This statement that the primary scriptural usage of the phrase Son of God is to designate Christ as acting in a subordinate capacity and is used only very occasionally to designate an eternal distinction in the Godhead brought down on Stuart's head the wrath of the Old Calvinists at Princeton Seminary. Stuart suddenly found himself having to devote time and attention to explaining himself more clearly and in greater detail on the nature of the sonship of Christ in a series of letters to Samuel Miller at Princeton. The Old Calvinist was simply not going to let Stuart get away with such shoddy thinking about what was to him such a central teaching of the New Testament and Christian doctrine as the eternal sonship of Christ, and so a rather sharp exchange between Stuart and Miller ensued.

Stuart could not bring his *Letters to Channing* to a close without taking a parting shot at what he perceived to be the Federal Street pastor's careless handling of Scripture texts having especially to do with the divinity of Christ. Regarding these texts, he charges Channing with willfully seeking "to modify, restrain and turn them from their obvious sense." He warns Channing "that the course of reasoning in which you

---

14 Ibid., 149. The issue of the nature of the sonship of Christ created a considerable volume of literature and dragged on for well over a dozen years.

have embarked, and the principles by which you explain away the divinity of the Saviour, must lead most men who approve them, eventually to the conclusion, that the Bible is not of divine origin, and does not oblige us to belief or obedience."[15] The charge is a serious one: whether in fact Channing did apply the principles of biblical interpretation that he outlined in the first part of his sermon to the specific doctrines he examined in the second part, or whether he simply abandoned Scripture and revelation altogether in favor of reason alone.

Channing of course would deny adamantly even the hint that he abandoned Scripture and revelation for reason alone, making Stuart's parting salvo the most unkind cut of all. The suggestion is that while Channing himself may not be guilty of undermining the authority of the Bible by his principles of interpretation, there is a "tendency" in that direction in the manner by which he has applied these principles to texts involving the divinity of Christ. As an illustration of what he means by this Stuart proceeds to parade for Channing's benefit his knowledge of the latest expressions of German scholarship, and what in turn he discerns as the direction of Continental theology. Stuart argued that there was currently running through German theology a "theory of accommodation" similar in effect to Channing's unfortunate phrase "to modify, restrain and turn from their obvious sense" words as used in the Bible. German scholars such as Eichorn have in effect turned the Old Testament into "poetical and philosophical speculations and patriotic wishes." Similarly, what Ferdinand Christian Bauer and others have done to the New Testament can only make one "smile or shudder." The pity is that in the midst of all this German theological scholarship "the question about the divinity of Christ has been entirely forgotten." What does all of this have to do with Channing and American Unitarianism? Perhaps not much at the present, but the "tendency" of Channing's sermon and the results of the application of his principles of biblical interpretation, especially to the person of Christ, are decidedly in the direction of German theology. Stuart viewed the denial of the divinity of Christ as but the prelude to the rejection of the authority and inspiration of

---

15 Ibid., 160.

Scripture, at which point all has been lost for the Christian faith.

Stuart was recognized as the American scholar most widely read in German theological and biblical literature, and therefore his opinion carried weight when he concluded that he found the Germans "fundamentally subversive of Christianity," and yet he conceded that "I am under great obligation to them for the instruction they have given me."[16] After a rather lengthy justification designed to ward off the fears and suspicions of the trustees and associates of Andover Seminary for his having read these heretical Germans in the first place, Stuart acknowledges that he has come away from his reading of them with a renewed sense of and enhanced appreciation for "evangelical orthodoxy" and that there is no need to fear that he has been tainted by his contact with Continental thought. His conclusion regarding the Germans is that generally "exegesis has come, by discussion among them, to a solid and permanent science. That the Scriptural writers taught substantially, what we believe to be orthodoxy, is now conceded by their most able expositors."[17] Channing must have wondered how the same people who had been pronounced "fundamentally subversive" could be proclaimed "substantially orthodox" within the range of a single paragraph. Nonetheless, the same tendency that has been stemmed within German theology must now also be stemmed in America, because the denial of the divinity of Christ leads in turn to Arianism, then to humanitarianism and finally to natural religion. Stuart saw developing within the American context "a great contest" in which the issue will be whether Christianity is to be retained or rejected. In this respect Stuart did not find Channing's sermon exactly salutary for the future course of Christianity in America, but he closes his letters by vowing that his pen is now retired from the argument and "that this

---

16 Ibid., 169–70. See also Jerry Wayne Brown, *The Rise of Biblical Criticism in America, 1800–1870: The New England Scholars* (Middletown, Conn.: Wesleyan University Press, 1969).

17 Stuart, *Letters to Channing*, 174. An example of Stuart's putting German theology into the service of evangelical orthodoxy may be seen in his translation of J. A. Dorner's "The Doctrine Respecting the Person of Christ," *Bibliotheca Sacra* 2 (Oct., 1850): 696–732, where Stuart offers a wholesale endorsement of Dorner's views.

investigation already is, with my most hearty concurrence, in the hands of a respected and beloved friend and brother."[18]

As we have noted, in the course of his *Letters to Channing* Stuart rather offhandedly observed that he simply could not make any sense of the phrase "the eternal generation of the Son" and that he found this doctrine of the eternal sonship of Christ to be "a palpable contradiction." Samuel Miller of Princeton read this passing observation by Stuart with considerable distress, and he was simply not content to let the statement pass unexamined and unchallenged. Stuart therefore found himself having to take up his pen once more not against Channing but in answer to the letters of an Old Calvinist at Princeton on the eternal sonship of Christ. In his correspondence with Miller, Stuart was forced both to sharpen his own views on the person of Christ and to reassure all interested and concerned parties that Orthodoxy was alive and well at Andover and not, according to the Princeton charges, yielding vast ground to Unitarianism. This defense was carried out in a series of *Letters on the Eternal Generation of the Son* which were addressed to the Princeton professor of ecclesiastical history. He begins by apologizing to Miller if he has offended the latter by a too casual treatment of the doctrine in question; it is just that he had to confess honestly that "during my whole theological life I had never once heard the doctrine seriously avowed and defended."[19] Stuart has no quarrel with the argument that the Logos is eternal, but "that the Logos was eternally the Son of God, I doubt." The appearance of the doctrine of eternal sonship in the history of the church may be laid at the doorstep of the Council of Nicaea and its over reaction to the rise of Arianism and the corrupting influences of Platonic philosophy. Sounding every bit like any of a number of Unitarians who lambasted the early church fathers for falling prey to Platonism and selling out the faith to a foreign philosophy, Stuart argues that the fathers of the church are guilty of misapplying the doctrine of emanation to

---

[18] Stuart, *Letters to Channing,* 150. Just as Channing was to withdraw from the controversy over the Trinity and leave it in the hands of Andrews Norton, so too here Stuart's "respected and beloved friend and brother" was Leonard Woods of Andover, who took over for him.

[19] Moses Stuart, *Letters on the Eternal Generation of the Son, Addressed to the Rev. Samuel Miller* (Andover: Flagg and Gould, 1820), 4.

the Logos, thus giving rise to the notion of the eternal sonship of Christ.

Charity however should be extended to the early fathers, and Stuart argues that it should be remember that they were not all that far removed in time from the influences of heathenism, for which a "derived deity" eternally generated by the Godhead was a common notion that posed no serious intellectual problems. But the person of Christ should be preserved from getting entangled in the nets of Platonism and heathenism, and "we who are taught from infancy to believe in the simplicity, spirituality, self-existence, independence and immutability of the divine nature, can be brought only by violence to reason as the Fathers did."[20] If they did in fact teach the doctrine of the eternal generation of the Son, the early church fathers were simply out of touch with Scripture and out of bounds with reason. Beside which, Stuart is simply not going to accept uncritically this or any teaching from patristic sources, much less cite the authority of the fathers over that of Scripture. But Stuart is not fully satisfied that the early church fathers did teach the eternal sonship of Christ, and after his own rather lengthy survey of patristic literature he is satisfied that they instead "believed that the Son of God was begotten at a period not long before the creation of the world; or in other words, that he became a separate hypostasis, at or near the time, when the work of creation was to be performed."[21] Miller would then be well advised to go back to his patristic sources and look more carefully at them on the topic under discussion. Needless to say, this little lesson in patristics by the biblical scholar from Andover did not sit well with the church historian from Princeton, who did not appreciate being lectured on ecclesiastical history by a biblical exegete.

It is the scriptural investigation of the eternal sonship of Christ and not its patristic roots which interests Stuart most and with which clearly he is more comfortable, convinced as he is that the final authority on this as on any doctrine rests with scriptural and not with patristic texts. The problem is that the sacred writers, unlike the patristic writers, have left

20 Ibid., 74.
21 Ibid., 17.

unexplained what the doctrine of the eternal generation of the Son seeks to explain. The task of biblical exegesis is to discover and to interpret what it is that makes the Logos the Son and what the relation is between the Logos and the sonship of Christ. And here Stuart uncovers a basic cleavage between exegesis and patristics, because the patristic doctrine of the eternal generation of the Son seeks to push back into Christ's essence the sonship, which belongs only to his personality. The sacred writers make sonship an attribute of Christ, but Scripture does not in fact extend sonship to the essence of Christ. Christ is essentially the Logos of God, but personally he is the Son of God. Christ is both the Logos and the Son, but these two must be kept separate: Logos as applying to the essence of Christ, sonship as applying to the person of Christ.

Stuart admits to the difficulty of the fine distinctions being drawn here between essence and attribute and of the challenge involved in unpacking the truth contained in mystery and that which in the end is even incomprehensible. But there is no reason to fear mystery or even to back away from it, for mystery contains a truth of its own that invites investigation. If, however, when one attempts to bring mysteries to expression through doctrines, such as in this case the eternal sonship of Christ, then one can be held accountable for the comprehensibility and intelligibility of the language used in that attempt at doctrinal expression. While mystery is a suitable attribute of things such as, in this instance, describing the relationship between the Logos and the Son, mystery is not an acceptable attribute of the language that we use to express the products of our understanding. It is precisely the task of the scholar to root mystery out of the words used in the expression of doctrine and to expose contradictions and incongruities passing as mysteries. Once the theologian decides to go public with a doctrine there is no hiding behind mystery, and the theologian cannot carry mystery over into the language used to express doctrine. The doctrine of the eternal generation of the Son fails this litmus test, and Stuart remains adamant that while the Logos is eternal and preexistent the Son is not.

With this in mind, it should be possible to speak of the fact of Christ as both the Logos and as the Son of God in language that has been laundered of mystery, even though the manner of the Logos and of Christ's sonship remains engulfed in mystery.

Separating the fact from the manner of Christ as Logos and Christ as Son was, to the satisfaction of Stuart's mind, a significant theological gain, and on this basis the eternal sonship of Christ falls to the ground because it is nowhere asserted as a "fact" of Scripture. The truth of the matter is that the doctrine of the eternal generation of the Son ends up doing just the opposite of what its proponents contend, that is, it undercuts rather than supports the divinity of Christ. It is a doctrine that impugns all of the attributes essential to the divinity of the Logos, including self-existence, immutability, independence and eternity. Rendering the Logos into a derived and subordinate being, as the doctrine of eternal generation does, vanishes the idea of supreme divinity and then "the Logos ranks with those who are *called* God, only from some resemblance either of station, or office, or of moral or intellectual qualities, to the self-existent Deity."[22] How then does the self-existent and eternal Logos become the subordinate and temporal Son? Certainly not by an eternal generation that in effect destroys the divinity of Christ by undermining the self-existence and eternity of the Logos.

How then is the phrase Son of God to be understood as applied to Christ in the Scriptures? One possibility is quickly disposed of: Christ is not the Son of God "simply on the ground of his *moral* resemblance to the Father."[23] So much for the Christology of the Unitarians. Christ is rather called the Son of God for two primary reasons: first, as respects his human nature, which is derived from the moment of his conception on. It is to this derived human nature that sonship applies, while the Logos applies to the eternal and divine nature; eternity and self-existence apply to the Logos, while temporality and derivation apply to the Son; Logos applies antecedent to the incarnation, sonship only after the incarnation. Second, by virtue of "the elevated dignity that was conferred on him as the Messiah," Christ is called the Son of God. After a rather lengthy exegetical survey of the relation between Messiah and sonship in which conclusive evidence is presented that the title Son of God pertains to the Messiah as incarnate and not to the Logos before the incarnation, Stuart is ready to offer his own

22 Ibid., 93.
23 Ibid., 109.

final analysis of the situation: "If I am correct then, the Logos, before his incarnation, was not, strictly speaking, Son of God, but only to become so by union with the person of Jesus . . . . That the Son (as Son) is subordinate and derived, I most freely grant as a doctrine of Scripture; but that the Logos is so, I have found no satisfactory evidence."[24] This distinction between time and eternity that Stuart drew in terms of the Son and the Logos was not designed to bring comfort to his more conservative supporters at Andover, while the Old Calvinist at Princeton only huffed that he knew all along that New England was being swallowed up by Unitarianism.

As a corollary to his position on the sonship of Christ, Stuart notes that to his mind it is not any more necessary that God existed eternally as the Father than that Christ existed eternally as the Son but not as the Logos. The titles Father, Son and Holy Spirit "designate the distinctions of the Godhead as manifested to us in the economy of redemption . . . . and are not intended to mark the eternal relations of the Godhead, as they are in themselves, and in respect to each other."[25] For the expression of similar views a few years later Horace Bushnell would bring down on himself the charge of heresy in the form of Sabellianism, but Stuart is able to escape this charge by his distinction between the Logos and the Son. Stuart is equally anxious to escape the charge that his Christology contains even so much as a hint of Arianism, and he turns the tables on his Old Calvinist adversary by arguing that to embrace the doctrine of the eternal generation of the Son is itself the first step in the direction of "an approximation of Arianism"—at which point Miller's blood must have frozen in his veins.

Stuart then advances his own position as a considerable improvement over Nicaea precisely because it preserves and protects the true and essential divinity of Christ by ascribing self-existence, independence, immutability and eternity to the Logos. It is then by no means the case, as Miller had charged, that denial of the doctrine of eternal generation carries down with it the divinity of Christ. Apostasy and heresy are not running rampant in New England; just the opposite is actually the case, for the divinity of Christ actually stands taller than

---

24 Ibid., 115.
25 Ibid., 151.

ever in light of Stuart's clarification of the relationship between the Logos as the divine and superior nature and the Son as the human and inferior nature in the one person of Christ. In any case, the doctrine of the eternal sonship of Christ should not be a source of alienation and division among Christians, especially since it may well be that the differences that divide them at this point are merely over words and the manner of expressing the truth about the person of Christ. If, however, on the basis of Scripture he can be shown any error in his position or any dishonor to the person of Christ in what he has written, Stuart will repent in dust and ashes and be eternally thankful for the correction of his ways. But with a self-confidence that may well have infuriated the rather mild-mannered Miller, Stuart is quite certain that nothing like this is about to happen, and once more he laid down his pen.

In two of his biblical commentaries, both published in 1833, Stuart had occasion to return to the topic of Christology and specifically to the issue of the sonship of Christ. Early in his *Commentary on the Epistle to the Romans* he offers an excursus on Rom. 1: 3, 4 and the phrase Son of God. It is a title that "designates the high and mysterious relation which subsisted between him and God the Father . . . [and] is often applied to Christ as a name of nature, as well as of office; yet I am fully satisfied, that it is not applied to him considered simply as divine, or simply as Logos."[26] He remains convinced, as in his *Letters to Channing*, that little or nothing is gained by trying to add an eternal generation to Christ's sonship because the term *generation* by necessity implies derivation, which in turn means dependence. But how can a derived and dependent being be truly God? And once the self-existence and independence of Christ are given up there is simply no line of adequate defense against the Arians with their notion of a derived and dependent divine being, an idea that Stuart finds "quite impossible." All the more reason then to distinguish clearly, as Stuart is convinced he has done, between Christ the Son and Christ the Logos if the true divinity of Christ is to prevail as a genuine doctrine of the Scriptures.

The Andover exegete found himself writing another rather lengthy christological excursus in his *Commentary on the*

---

26 Moses Stuart, *Commentary on the Epistle to the Romans* (Andover: Flag and Gould, 1833), 237.

*Epistle to the Hebrews,* this time focusing on Heb. 1: 2 and the question of the nature of the relation between Christ and creation. The question at stake is if the Logos is the author of creation, then does Christ create as an absolute and independent act or under the superintendence of God? The problem as always is to sort out what the Scripture teaches from the debris of metaphysical speculation, and the danger as always is one of trespassing the boundries of Scripture rather than remaining content with what they have taught. Just as the attempt to probe the interior nature of the Godhead and chart its trinitarian distinctions is out of bounds, so too here we would do well to recognize that we cannot probe the intricate details of God creating the world through the Logos. The scriptural fact of distinctions in the Godhead (the manner of which we cannot know because they have not been revealed in Scripture) and the scriptural fact of a subordination implied in God's creation of the world by the Logos (the manner of which we cannot know because it too has not been revealed in Scripture) should not cause us to despair or reduce us to total theological silence. Rather we must trust that any subordination "implicated" in the trinitarian *ad intra* distinctions of the Godhead or any subordination "implicated" in the creation of the world by the Logos do not in any way infringe on the divinity of Christ. Again, it is the doctrine of the Logos and not the doctrine of Christ's eternal sonship that protects against any infringement on the divinity of Christ in eternity or time, helping us to understand better what it means that God spoke formerly by the prophets, "but in these last days he has spoken to us by a Son, whom he appointed the heir of all things, through whom also he created the world " (Heb. 1:2).

Stuart returns to the theme of the nature of language, instructing his readers that "words are the signs of ideas," or even better yet that they are "merely *arbitrary* signs of ideas, so when employed in their original sense, they can never signify more than the things for which they stand."[27] But that is only half of the story regarding the nature of language, for words may be and are employed figuratively, as is the case with our reflection on the nature of God "for the description of

---

27 Moses Stuart, *Commentary on the Epistle to the Hebrews* (Andover, Mass.: Flagg and Gould, 1833), 543.

whom none of the words of our language were originally formed."[28] In our discussion of the nature of God or for that matter of any theological subject, we use words "nearly always" in a sense more or less qualified and differing from their original and literal sense. There is therefore not an exact correspondence between the same words applied to the divine nature as to human nature. But there is enough of a correspondence established over time and common usage that our words used figuratively are not rendered into meaningless gibberish. The invitation is not one to loosen up on the usage of language, but rather to see clearly that words have two distinct forms, the one original and the other figurative. The very misuse of language of which he had accused Channing in his *Letters* to the latter has here become rather attractive to Stuart, who struggled toward but never reached a new theory of language for theological discourse.

With this preliminary note about language firmly in mind, Heb. 1:2 becomes a more approachable text because, informed by the inability of language ever fully to express or describe the divine, we are sobered into realizing that we must therefore be guided by the qualified or figurative usage of language. So for example, usage of the term *person* in connection with the Logos; if applied in its original sense it will lead inevitably to the loss of both the unity of the Godhead and the divinity of the Logos. The use of the term *person* is an especially aggrieved case of what Stuart is talking about because the term does not appear in Scripture and "one might wish the word had never been introduced into ecclesiastical usage." Further, the Unitarians have seized upon this fact and temporarily turned it to their advantage, but once the distinction between the original and the figurative usage of language is established and made clear the Trinitarians will turn the argument around again and regain the high ground. The term *person* is certainly not unique and is only one example of the difficulty encountered with the use of language in theological discourse. In this particular case it has to do with a term applied to the distinctions within the Godhead, but the same objections to the term *person* as used here could be leveled against any term so employed. The point is that theological confusion will persist

28 Ibid., 543.

unless and until "we have seen that all language which is used in order to describe God, must be taken of course and by necessity, in a *qualified* sense."[29] Employing words literally when they were meant to be used figuratively leads to no end of theological mischief, as may be seen also in the case of the language used to express the manner in which the Logos is involved in creation. In both cases, either the distinction of the persons in the Godhead or the involvement of the Logos in creation, the fact of the matter is not in question for Stuart. The manner of the fact and the language used to express it are however open for question and debate, and that is what biblical theology is all about.

In a rather lengthy two-part article entitled "Exegetical and Theological Examination of John 1:1–18" that appeared in *Bibliotheca Sacra* in 1850, Stuart repeats but does not carry further his earlier observations about the nature of language and specifically the biblical usage of the term Logos. His concern is to show that the author of John did not employ the term Logos to designate the personification of God, but because the Logos was "with God" it is therefore the very hypostasis or particular embodiment of certain qualities such as the life and light of God. And for John and his listeners the employment of the term Logos in this sense would have been readily understood as the *usus loquendi* of that period and that accordingly "there can be no reasonable ground to doubt, that all this is figurative, or (in other words) that it is a symbolical representation of God's executive power or energy."[30] Just as words are the means by which we make known and execute our will, so by analogy the word or Logos is the means by which the internal desire or will of God is accomplished. The Logos is the principal medium of revelation or communication, and Christ as the Logos is the hypostasis or embodiment in the world of God's light, life and truth. While the biblical writers did in some cases form "new designations" or in other cases gave words "a more prolonged or shorter form," for the most part "they assigned to the old words a sense in some respects new, leaving it to the context and the nature of the case to point out the meaning of them. Nothing is plainer, than that, so far as the

29 Ibid., 547.

30 Moses Stuart, "Exegetical and Theological Examination of John 1:1–18," *Bibliotheca Sacra* 7 (Jan., 1850): 18.

invisible world is concerned, all the words, which designate objects there, have a meaning in some respects quite new attached to them."[31] It is a test of the mettle of every biblical scholar by means of "grammatico-historical" criticism to uncover not only the *usus loquendi* of a term but also the new sense of words used by a sacred writer in light of his own writings. At least to the satisfaction of his own mind Stuart had done this in the case of the term Logos, and he is convinced beyond doubt that the Gospel of John teaches the real and essential divinity or godhead of the Logos.

Stuart was keenly aware that the painstaking task of biblical criticism even at its best is not an exact science. Imparting human analogies one on one to things divine simply will not work, and therefore the best that exegesis and theology can hope for is an approximation of language that will enable the exegete and the theologian to pursue their respective tasks. Searching the syntax of sacred writ for the analogy between the literal meaning of words as applied to things of this world and the qualified or modified meaning of words as applied to things of God and the next world will tax the best of biblical scholars. Certainly the distinctions and relations of God, Son and Logos are difficult subjects, and while it is plain that the Logos appeared in human form, "how this incarnation was accomplished; whether it was by the mere indwelling of the higher nature with the man Jesus; or whether it was by some principle of union between the divine and human, utterly beyond our power of discovery or even comprehension; are questions that we cannot definitely answer, and need not attempt to answer, since the whole matter is beyond the present circle of human knowledge."[32] But if those involved in the discussion would only learn to sort out the difference between words and things and not pursue the illusion that an abundance of words grasp the thing itself then exegetical and theological discourse would generally go much smoother. The problem is compounded because so often the discussion drifts out of the bounds of Scripture and into the realm of metaphysics where all is lost. No less than Channing, Stuart also struggled to deliver the person of Christ from the

31 Ibid., 34.

32 Moses Stuart, "Exegetical and Theological Examination of John 1:1–18," *Bibliotheca Sacra* 7 (April, 1850): 310.

grip of the metaphysics of classical Christology and to recover the Christ of the New Testament from the philosophical baggage of the past. Both men turned to sacred writ for guidance in their search for the real Christ, and each came away from the Bible in the company of quite a different figure.

1

In 1808 an uneasy coalition of "consistent Calvinists" and New Divinity advocates who were dissatisfied with the theological developments at both Harvard and Yale banded together to found Andover Seminary. The professorship of theology in the newly founded seminary went to Leonard Woods (1774–1854), whose four-decade career at Andover left an enormous impact on New England Congregationalism through his writings and especially through the many students who faithfully copied out his lectures in systematic theology. Never one to pick a theological fight, yet at the same time never one to back away from a theological controversy once it was in motion, Woods is best remembered for his exchange with Henry Ware of Harvard in the famous Wood 'n Ware controversy.[33] Wood's views on the person of Christ are best set forth in his lectures on systematic theology that he delivered over the years at Andover and are collected as part of his multivolume *Works*. Woods had a keen sense of exactly who his opponents were, what they stood for and how he was going to go about equipping his students with sufficient theological defenses against any threats to consistent Calvinism. He therefore drew a rather careful bead on Arianism, Socinianism and Unitarianism and launched his volley in the direction of Cambridge.

Woods begins his christological section with the humanity of Christ and takes greater than usual pains to show that Christ really and truly was a man. He plods through a lengthy examination of the issue, replete with copious scriptural support, itemizing those features of Christ's character that demonstrate his humanity. Included among these features are the fact that he is called a man numerous times in Scripture,

---

[33] For biographical information on Leonard Woods see Sprague, *Annals of the American Pulpit*, vol. 2; Williston Walker, *Ten New England Leaders* (Boston, 1901).

that he had the form and features of a man, that he was subject to the trials and temptations of a man, that he sustained human relations with others, and that he possessed the mind of a man. The truth of Christ's full humanity is writ large in Scripture for plain and honest readers to discern and further secured against all error by the testimony of the Spirit. The true humanity of Christ is an uncontested truth to be preserved against the errors of the Arians, who, while they make much of the humanity of Christ, have in fact mismanaged the issues by misinterpreting Scripture and presenting the world with a Christ who is not really and truly human after all. The Arians hold "that the man Christ Jesus was constituted by the union of the pre-existent Spirit of Christ with a human body merely, without a proper human soul; or that the Logos became man by becoming the soul of a human body."[34] The Arian hypothesis regarding the person of Christ flies in the face of Scripture and common sense, both of which make it plain that all human beings, Christ included, possess a human body and a human soul united in one. Substituting a divine spirit for the human soul in Christ, as the Arians do, brings ruin upon his genuine humanity.

Likewise, simply implanting a divine mind or Logos in Christ in lieu of a human mind destroys the true humanity of Christ by displacing the normal mental growth through which any human mind, including the mind of Christ, goes in its development from infancy to adulthood. Or even more absurd, the implanting of "a pre-existent spirit" in Christ, so important to the Arian scheme of Christ's person, undercuts the genuine humanity of Christ by "supposing that the pre-existent spirit of Christ lost its fulness of divine knowledge and strength, by becoming incarnate—that it underwent such a mighty change that those intelligent and active powers, which were competent to create a universe, were all reduced to the compass of an infant's mind."[35] The humanity of Christ does not consist merely in his having a human body; Christ does not become man by becoming the soul of a human body. Representing Christ otherwise than as having not only a human body but a human soul and a human mind as well is to compromise his true humanity. According to Woods, the irony of the situation is

---

34 Leonard Woods, *Works,* vol. 1 (Boston: J. P. Jewett, 1851), 284–85.
35 Ibid., 287.

that the Arians, who trumpet most the humanity of Christ, have ended up losing the humanity of Christ.

The Arians are also guilty of wrongly accusing the Orthodox of adhering to a Christology that ends up with not one but two distinct persons. But who is to say that proper humanity cannot be united to proper divinity? Certainly the contrary assertions of a few Arians are not going to dissuade the faithful, especially when "it is important to remember that the human nature of Christ never existed *by itself*, that is, in a state of separation from his divine nature. And as Christ's human nature never had a separate *existence*, it never had a separate *personality*. It was created, and from the first existed, in a state of union with divinity. Accordingly, to speak of *two distinct persons* being united in Christ, or to represent Christ's human nature, or the man Christ Jesus, as having had a personal existence and agency separate from the divine Logos, is totally inadmissible."[36] Woods goes to rather extraordinary lengths to protect the human nature of Christ against the Arian charge that in the Orthodox scheme of things the human is overwhelmed by the divine nature. He insists at the same time that the human nature never had a separate existence apart from the divine nature and that the union of the human and the divine means just that in both time and eternity. Sensing the danger that it posed, Woods took to the offensive against Arianism, and he felt compelled to dismantle it piece by theological piece before the very eyes of his students. He shifts the burden of proof to those who assume that the union of the divine and the human natures in one person is not possible and proceeds at least to the satisfaction of his own mind to demonstrate the veracity of the scriptural and rational Christology of Orthodoxy and Andover over against the fatal flaws of Arianism and Harvard. It is simply not the case that the human nature is obliterated or transformed into something else through its union with the divine nature in the person of Christ, but that the human nature of Christ is and remains human in union with the divine.

The Arians (read Unitarians) regretfully have constructed unnecessary roadblocks to accepting the unity of the divine and human natures in Christ's person. They object, for instance, that

---

36 Ibid., 291.

it is impossible for the Godhead to suffer and that therefore Christ was capable of suffering only as a derived and dependent being. This is merely a theological red herring, argues Woods, and while it is true enough that as the Logos or the Second Person of the Trinity Christ is incapable of suffering, as God incarnate in human flesh he is capable of suffering and really does suffer. But "if it is consistent to say, that Christ walked, ate, slept and lived in poverty, *as a man*; it is equally consistent to say, that *he acknowledged his dependence on God, and prayed, and suffered and died* as a man."[37] The sufferings of Christ pertain to his human nature, but to a human nature that is inseparable from his divine nature and that does not exist by itself. Strictly speaking then, it is neither the divine nor the human nature of Christ that suffers and dies but Christ the complex person of two natures consisting in the union of humanity and divinity. Yet Woods, in keeping with his consistent Calvinism, will not accept the teaching that whatever is predicated of Christ must be true of both the human and divine natures that constitute his person.

Andover's professor of systematic theology struggled to preserve the unity of Christ's person against the Arian charge that the Orthodox have in effect ended up turning Christ into two persons. His way of fending off this charge, to which he was very sensitive, was to argue that the Orthodox "predicate of Christ all *human* attributes and works, and all *divine* attributes and works. The former we predicate of him *as man*, the latter *as God*. In this way we predicate of one complex person a greater variety of properties, than our opponents think *can belong* to one person."[38] Woods was convinced not only that he had covered the Orthodox flank but also that on this basis it could be determined whether an action of Christ was predicated on his humanity or on his divinity. In the case of Christ's suffering it was easy enough to determine that it is the human nature and its attributes that are involved and that the divine nature of Christ did not suffer. Just as human nature is constituted of body and mind to which acts peculiar to each are attributed, and yet they are spoken of as belonging to one and the same person, so Christ is constituted of humanity and

---

37 Ibid., 299.
38 Ibid., 301.

divinity in such a way that acts are spoken of as belonging to his human or to his divine nature, and yet he is not two but one person. The person of Christ is not constituted of his human nature or of his divine nature alone, but the person of Christ is a complex of both these natures taken together.

Beyond the argument from analogy for the two natures in one person of Christ and weighing in more heavily is the argument from Scripture, where evidence abounds to seal the case for classical Christology. With the assurance of a victor in battle Woods piles up the proof texts in support of his position and in opposition Arianism. In the end it is the Arians who are guilty of unnecessarily complicating, for example, the issue of who it was that really suffered and died on the cross. On the other hand, the two natures in one person Christology of the Orthodox is both a scriptural and commonsense doctrine that clearly and easily settles all such questions by honoring the complex person of Christ. Woods's opponents of course were not all that convinced that the "complex" Christ he drew out of the New Testament was the same Christ that they met there.

Woods was concerned to send forth his young Orthodox warriors well prepared to meet the challenge of Arianism and its mistaken views of the person of Christ, convinced that it is best to know the position of your opponent better even than your opponent does. On this basis he sought to acquaint his students with fundamental Arian views and to equip them with ways by which to confound and disarm the advocates of Arianism. For example, in opposition to what the Arians teach about the preexistence of Christ there is widespread agreement that the names and titles ascribed to Christ in Scripture demonstrate that he preexisted in a state vastly superior to the remainder of humankind, and that therefore "manhood was not his original character." Once again the doctrine of the preexistence of Christ is simply a matter of the combination of common sense and the revelation of Scripture, and Woods proceeds to compile and explicate his favorite texts on the subject, including John 8:58, John 1:1–3, and Heb. 1:10. While admittedly the emphasis of each of these texts is slightly different, their cumulative effect is "that Christ was in possession of whatever belonged to his state of dignity, *before* he was in his state of humiliation."[39] There is no argument that Christ was in the form of God before he took on the likeness of man and that therefore his dignity and glory are not derived from his obedience and death, as the Socinians in particular are inclined to teach. If it is the case that Christ's dignity and glory are predicated exclusively on his work of redemption, then the preexistence of Christ's nature as the eternal Logos is invalidated. The task then is one of not confusing the glory of Christ's nature as the eternal Logos with the glory of Christ's work as the temporal Son of man. It is better to recognize that there is both a dignity in Christ that is his by virtue of his nature as the eternal Logos or the Son of God and that there is a dignity that belongs to Christ by virtue of his office as the Word made flesh, as the Son of man whose humiliation is rewarded by the Father. Keeping in mind this distinction will aid considerably in distinguishing and interpreting those texts that apply primarily to the dignity and glory of Christ's nature from those texts that apply primarily to the dignity and glory of his office. In other words, we shall be spared letting the work of Christ overshadow the person of Christ and of allowing the atonement to dictate the terms of Christology. The doctrine of two natures in one person is then the best hedge against an imbalance between Christology and atonement, between the person and the work of Christ. But whatever ground of agreement there may be between Orthodox and Arians on the humanity of Christ the time has now come decisively to separate the two parties, and that separation becomes most apparent over differences regarding the divinity of Christ.

Woods launches his investigation into the divinity of Christ by an examination of the name of God as ascribed to him in Scripture. The challenge here is to distinguish the metaphorical from the literal or proper usage of the title of God as given to Christ in the Scripture. For example, there are admissible metaphorical usages of the name God in Scripture, as when the title is applied to men (e.g., to Moses in Exod. 7:1); but when it is applied to Christ the name or title God means properly and literally just that—Christ is the true God. By employing "the comparative view," that is, by letting

---

39 Ibid., 326.

Scripture be its own interpreter rather than forcing foreign principles of interpretation on it, one is driven to the inevitable conclusion that the names and titles that are peculiar to the supreme being are literally and properly applied likewise to Christ. To make his point, Woods walks his reader through a rather lengthy exegetical exercises on John 1:1, Ps. 82:6, Exod. 22:28, Rom. 9:5, Heb. 1:8 and John 10:33 as "unequivocal evidence" that Christ is the true God.

But the divinity of Christ does not hinge only on titles ascribed to him; it may also be proved from his divine attributes and works. Attributes such as eternity (Isa. 9:6 and John 1:1), omnipotence (Phil. 3:21, Heb. 3:1), omniscience (John 2:24, 25), omnipresence (Matt. 28:20) and so forth are so obvious in proving the divinity of Christ as to need little if any discussion, except to meet the objections of those who for whatever reason deny them. There are unfortunately those who have been seduced into either overlooking or misinterpreting the above and other passages, which clearly ascribe divine attributes to Christ. These oversights and misinterpretations may be attributable at least in part to the fact that the character and office of redeemer, in which Christ is most frequently represented in Scripture, naturally present him as possessing the marks of dependence and subordination characteristic of his incarnate state. But this by no means overshadows or furnishes proof against the divinity of Christ, and to conclude that it does is at best a narrow and one-sided reading of the Scriptures.

Likewise the works of Christ in creation and in his miracles are further proof of his divinity. It is clear from such texts as John 1:3, Col. 1:16,17 and Heb. 1:10 that Christ is properly the creator of the world and as such is therefore divine. The only way that Christ as creator can be denied is either first by insisting that the term creator cannot be understood in its proper sense simply because it is applied to Christ, which is to beg the question; or second by claiming that the term creator as applied to Christ cannot be so understood because the sense is qualified and restrained by something in these or other texts.[40] On the basis of this second objection and in light of the fact that the Bible is its own interpreter, those texts that assert that God is

40 Ibid., 351. Woods is struggling with the problem of language, but in a way less creative even than his colleague Moses Stuart.

the sole creator must be paralleled with those texts that explicitly declare that all things were created by Christ. When this is done, what other conclusion is there but that Christ is God, that "though Christ is in some respects distinct from the Father; yet in his original character, he possesses the same divine perfections, and is one with the Father."[41]

Part of the problem is that Socinians, Arians and Unitarians alike have lost sight of the original nature of Christ and have concentrated too exclusively on his assumed or mediatorial character. As a result they have failed to understand that any subordination or dependence of Christ in his mediatorial role does not infringe on the divinity of his original character, which remains intact throughout his humiliation in the work of redemption. The original character of Christ in the form of God has been eclipsed by the mediatorial character of Christ in the form of a servant. The result has been a benign neglect or even loss of the divinity of Christ, and the Orthodox have only themselves to blame for allowing this to happen. It is true that the Father and the Son are distinct and that there is a division of labor and an ordering of persons between them whereby the Son is subordinate to the Father in the work of redemption; yet the Father and the Son remain throughout one and the same as to their divine nature and perfections. This is a perfectly scriptural and necessary although finally "unfathomable" arrangement for the work of redemption, which unfortunately Unitarians have distorted into a permanent and consistent subordination and dependence of the Son that is both unscriptural and irreverent. Any subordination or dependence attributed to Christ in Scripture by no means translates directly into an infringement on his divinity, which always remains an unimpaired part of his original character.

Further evidence for the divinity of Christ is to be found in the miracles of the New Testament, which he performed in his own name with a peculiar divine power or authority according to his own will and for his own glory. What further possible proof is necessary for the divinity of Christ than the miracles that he worked as the promised Messiah? And despite the protests of the Unitarians that Christ always spoke of receiving power from God and disclaimed having any power of

---

41 Ibid., 353. Woods was far less willing than Stuart to show any charity toward Unitarian principles of biblical interpretation.

his own to work miracles, a closer look at the New Testament will reveal once again that texts that assert that Christ received power from God apply only to his assumed character as a man and not to his original character as the eternal divine Logos. All of the confusion that the Unitarians bring down on the person of Christ could be quickly dispelled if they would recognize not only the truth but also the practicality of the doctrine of the two natures in one person of Christ.

The same rules apply to the worship of Christ, a topic on which Woods labors at some length and with great earnestness to demonstrate that Christ is the proper object not of subordinate but of supreme worship by angels, saints and apostles alike. Unitarianism had launched heavy assaults on Orthodoxy over the issues of miracles and the question of the proper worship of Christ. Woods set out to turn back these attacks and to defend the citadel of Calvinism on these points by training up and sending forth watchmen worthy to defend the walls of Zion. Essential to this defense is a proper sense of the veneration tendered Christ throughout the New Testament, where texts abound as evidence that he is the object not of limited or subordinate but of supreme worship. The plain, commonsense, nonmetaphorical meaning of text after text is that Christ is the worthy object of supreme worship, and over against "the cautious, cold respect for Christ which Unitarians show, and which they inculcate upon others—what is it compared with the glowing affection, and the adoring praise, which warmed the hearts and elevated the devotions of the apostles? Who could ever suppose that Unitarianism caught its spirit from the sacred pages, or that it had ever attended to the song of the heavenly hosts?"[42]

Woods closes out his discussion of Christology with what in effect is a lengthy footnote on the troublesome issue of the sonship of Christ, a topic on which the influence of his colleague Moses Stuart is evident. Woods borrows Stuart's distinction between the original or literal sense of the term son, according to which "the father pre-exists, and has an agency in giving existence to the son, so that the son is derived from the father," and the term son in its metaphorical sense, according

[42] Ibid., 388–89. Obviously Woods did not find Unitarianism "most favorable to piety," but charged his opponents with the same kind of spiritual coldness of which they had accused him.

to which "the word son, may be applied to any one who bears a resemblance to a proper son in regard to the prominent circumstances attending the natural relation, though he has no resemblance to him as to the origin of that relation."[43] On the ground of this somewhat shaky distinction Woods proceeds to demonstrate that the literal usage of the term son is here precluded both by the nature of the character of God (that a son should be begotten of God or that God should have a son by proper generation is utterly inconsistent with the divine nature) and the character of Christ (who has existed from eternity and therefore to predicate a literal generation of that which is eternal is an absurdity). The problem with the title Son of God centers around the literal and the metaphorical usage of language and the tendency of "cleaving to the literal sense of Scripture expressions, which are more or less metaphorical." Woods admits that the Orthodox have not helped their own cause at this point with the confusing phrase that Christ is "very God of very God," which itself needs some careful explanation. But when literal explanation is mixed with metaphoric meaning, trouble arises so that "the literal sense of the phrases 'God of God', 'very God of very God,' has seemed to me to involve the self-contradictory idea, that an underived being is derived—that a self-existent Being owes his existence to another. And this makes it further necessary to explain the language which has been meant as an explanation of the words of Scripture. But, to my apprehension, all the explanations which have been used, fail of making the matter any more clear, and do themselves need explanation."[44] But Woods himself is unwilling or unable to undertake the necessary rethinking of the nature of language that would allow for the more clear explanations for which he yearns.

And so downward the theological spiral goes, and where language is used literally to explain language that elsewhere is used metaphorically it will necessarily end in confusion and obscurity. The irony of the case under consideration is that a phrase designed to combat Arianism, i.e., "very God of very God," has in fact ended up expressing and promoting Arianism. In their understanding of the nature of the sonship of Christ the

43 Ibid., 393–94.
44 Ibid., 396.

Orthodox needed to loosen up a bit and break with the literalism that the term son carries with it and to adopt a more metaphorical usage of language more in the spirit of Scripture itself, by allowing for a greater "latitude of signification." Generally the title Son of God is used metaphorically, and "it must be remembered that metaphors have as real a meaning as literal language; and they often convey their meaning more strikingly, than any other expressions could."[45] On this basis we may conclude that while the titles Christ and Son of God are not synonymous, they do mean substantially the same thing. But for Woods the title Son of God applies more to the office than to the nature of Christ, more to the incarnate Word than to the eternal relation that Christ has to the Father as the Second Person of the Trinity. He acknowledges with "modesty and diffidence" that this is "a subject on which I differ somewhat from so many great and good men" (including his colleague Moses Stuart), but what he did not recognize was that with this admission one of the cornerstones of his own Christology was weakened. While he did acknowledge the metaphorical nature of language and the distinction between literal and metaphorical usage of words, Woods was not ready or willing to carry this insight further into a new theory of language that might have recast his Christology. His Christology is essentially a sustained polemic against Arianism in which he seeks on the one side to protect the genuine humanity of Christ over against what he perceived to be a pallid and fleshless Christ of the Arians, and on the other side to protect the genuine divinity of Christ against its denial by the Arians. The Christ who emerges from the pages of Woods's theology is a figure who is now human and now divine, but that he is a figure who is at once genuinely divine and human is not clear.

---

45 Ibid., 400.

# Chapter IV

# CHARLES HODGE: CHRIST AS DIVINE AND HUMAN

At Princeton Seminary the faith once delivered to the saints was carefully guarded and passed on by Charles Hodge (1797–1878), the school's distinguished professor of systematic theology, who presided over this citadel of Presbyterian orthodoxy for over four decades. Through his lectures to more than three thousand students who passed through his classroom, through his editorship of the scholarly *Biblical Repertory and Princeton Review*, through his involvement in Presbyterian denominational affairs, and perhaps most especially through his widely used *Systematic Theology*, Hodge exerted an enormous influence within and beyond the bounds of Old School Calvinism of which he stood as the chief representative.[1]

The subject of the person of Christ did not of course escape Hodge's detailed notice, for this was after all according to him

---

1 The standard biography of Charles Hodge is by his son Archibald Alexander Hodge, *The Life of Charles Hodge* (New York: Scribner's Sons, 1881, reprinted 1969); see also Mark A. Noll, ed., *The Princeton Theology 1812–1921: Scripture, Science and Theological Method from Archibald Alexander to Benjamin Warfield* (Grand Rapids: Wm. Eerdmans Publishing Co., 1983); "Charles Hodge," in *Reformed Theology in America: A History of its Modern Development*, ed., David Wells (Grand Rapids: Wm. Eerdmans Publishing Co., 1985), 36–59; Leonard Trinterud, "Charles Hodge: Theology Didactic and Polemical," in *Sons of the Prophets: Leaders in Protestantism from Princeton Seminary*, ed. Hugh T. Kerr (Princeton: Princeton University Press, 1963), 22–38; and John Oliver Nelson, "Charles Hodge: Nestor of Orthodoxy," in *The Lives of Eighteen from Princeton*, ed. Willard Thorp (Princeton: Princeton University Press, 1946), 192–211.

"the great theme of the sacred writers."[2] With his customary thoroughness and self-assurance, Hodge approaches Christology with the conviction that like every branch of theology, the doctrine of the person of Christ can be set in order by appropriately assembling and arranging the "facts" of Scripture into a coherent whole. The task of the systematic theologian is to collect the scattered truths of revelation in the Old and New Testaments and properly arrange and relate them to each other, thereby attaining "a higher knowledge" that exhibits more clearly the grandeur and harmony of the sacred writ. Admittedly, this process of collecting and collating the facts of Scripture is a struggle, and in the area of Christology "it cost the church centuries of study and controversy to solve the problem concerning the person of Christ, that is, to adjust and bring into harmonious arrangement all the facts which the Bible teaches on that subject."[3] At long last however these necessary adjustments have been made and the proper arrangement of scriptural evidence has been achieved, and there is really little if any need now for further discussion. The truths of revelation arranged and harmonized by the science of theology are now in place, and the final product is a thing of beauty. The objective facts of Scripture and the subjective realities of religious experience finally have been united in one complete system of theology, which Hodge has placed in the reader's hands.

The preliminary order of business in constructing a Christology is then to assemble the biblical facts about Christ and to begin putting them in order. The process starts with an examination of the testimony of the Old Testament, from which Hodge compiles numerous passages testifying to the divinity of Christ. He fixes for example on "the angel of Jehovah" in Genesis who appears as a distinct person, is referred to as "the Son of God," and who comes intermittently to the people of Israel in the course of their long history. This angel of course was none other than Christ, the angel of God who led the Israelites through the wilderness and who then dwelt in the temple at Jerusalem. To the satisfaction of

---

2 Charles Hodge, *Systematic Theology*, (Grand Rapids: Wm. Eerdmans Publishing Co., 1981 reprint), vol. 1, 483.
3 Ibid., 2.

Hodge's mind it is the progressive character of biblical revelation that makes this particular interpretation eminently clear and persuasive. But if further evidence not only of the presence but also of the divinity of Christ in the Old Testament is necessary, then even a casual survey of the royal Psalms (notably Ps. 45, 72 and 100), and of the the prophets (notably Isa. 6, Mic. 5:1–5, Joel 2:23, Jer. 23, Zech. 1–6 and Mal. 3:1–4) should dispell any doubt regarding both the presence and the divinity of Christ under the old covenant.

But of course the capstone of biblical revelation is found in the New Testament, where the first proof of Christ's divinity is evidenced in the title Lord or God, as Jehovah is called in the Old Testament. Precisely this same title is applied to Christ in the New Testament. Not only that, as if to make the point perfectly clear, Christ is even called "Lord of Lords," thereby denoting not the mere supremacy of one creature over another but testifying to his genuine divinity. As such, Christ is the proper object of the believer's affection and worship, certainly not as a mere creature but as God manifest in the flesh. And finally, in the New Testament witness to the authority of Christ as teacher one may discern further evidence for the genuine divinity of Christ, because unlike the authority of the prophets and the apostles who spoke in the name of God, Christ spoke as God. But at this point Hodge is only warming to the subject of the divinity of Christ, and this after all is not the appropriate place in his system to launch a full-scale investigation into the person of Christ. His rather lengthy preliminary survey of proof texts for the divinity of Christ is therefore labeled as "imperfect and unsatisfactory," and he moves on to other issues with the passing note that after all "it seems to be a work of supererogation to prove to Christians the divinity of their Redeemer."[4]

It is rather in the second volume of his *Systematic Theology* in the third major section on soteriology that Hodge finally focuses on the person of Christ and outlines his Christology with some detail. Here the focus of his interest is primarily on a defense of the Christology of the Westminster Confession, according to which "two whole, perfect, distinct natures, the

---

4 Ibid., 283.

Godhead and manhood, were inseparably joined together in one person, without conversion, composition or confusion. Which person is very God and very man, yet one Christ, the only mediator between God and man." Against the detractors of this formulation who argue that it ends up splitting the personality of Christ in two, Hodge argues that both the useful but imperfect analogy of the union of the soul and body in one self as well as the fixed facts of Scripture establish beyond question the unity of Christ's person. And he does not find the slightest evidence that either the argument from the analogy of the self or the argument from Scripture yields up a twofold personality of Christ; two natures do not at all necessarily result in two persons. Just as the union of soul and body is a personal union without mixture or confusion of spirit and matter that results in a genuine communion of the attributes of both soul and body, so from the union of the body and the soul in one person we may discern by analogy the union of the divine and human natures in the one person of Christ.

To this human analogy are to be added the scriptural facts concerning the person of Christ, namely that Christ was truly a man with a genuine human body and a rational soul and that he was truly God with all the divine attributes. These two natures of true humanity and true divinity are nevertheless united in one person, for which Hodge is more than willing to supply copious scriptural references including John 1:1–14, 1 John 1:1–3, Rom. 1:2–5, 1 Tim. 3:16, Phil. 2:6–11 and Heb. 2:14, in support of the plain truth that Christ is God and man in one person. There is but one Christ, whose one personality unites the natures of humanity and divinity, and what appears to be "conflicting representations" is in fact "the key to the whole Bible . . . God manifest in the flesh is the distinguishing doctrine of the religion of the Bible, without which it is a cold and lifeless corpse."[5] Because it is so clearly stated in Scripture the whole subject of the person of Christ might well

---

[5] Charles Hodge, *Systematic Theology*, vol. 2, 384. For The Westminster Confession of Faith see John H. Leith, ed., *Creeds of the Churches: A Reader in Christian Doctrine from the Bible to the Present,* 3rd. ed. (Atlanta: John Knox Press, 1982), 203–204. Hodge also cites with approval the Second Helvetic Confession of 1556, which may be found in chapter 11 of Philip Schaff's *Creeds of Christendom* (New York: Harper Brothers, 1931).

be left alone at this point, except for the fact that in every age there are those who deny the truth concerning Christ's divine nature, question the integrity of his human nature, or reject the unity of the two natures in one person. Consequently, the task of the theologian is to call the church back again and again to what the Bible teaches.

For Hodge what the Bible teaches regarding the person of Christ is the unequivocal truth, which can be grasped easily by even the simplest minds—that the two natures of humanity and divinity are united but not confounded in the one person of Christ. Further, what the Bible has to say about the person of Christ is in line with generally agreed upon axiomatic principles concerning the relation between substance and attributes. In this case, the union of the two distinct natures of humanity and divinity in Christ does not yield a third nature or substance, any more than the union of the two natures results in the transfer of attributes of one nature to the other. The union of the two natures in the one person of Christ is a personal "hypostatic union" that protects the distinctness and genuineness of both Christ's humanity and his divinity while at the same time ensuring the oneness of his person. Such a union is "not a mere indwelling of the divine nature analogous to the indwelling of the Spirit of God in his people. Much less is it a mere moral or sympathetic union; or a temporary and mutable relation between the two."[6] The person of Christ is the union of humanity and divinity from all eternity in the Godhead, and it was therefore "a divine person, not merely a divine nature, that assumed humanity, or became incarnate. Hence it follows that the human nature of Christ, separately considered, is impersonal. The Son of God did not unite Himself with a human person, but with human nature."[7]

Several consequences flow from this doctrine of the hypostatic or personal union of divinity and humanity in Christ, including for example the "communion of attributes," which simply means that the one person of Christ partakes of both natures and that what is true of either nature is true of his person. There is therefore no problem in asserting that Christ

---

6 Hodge, *Systematic Theology*, vol. 2, 390.
7 Ibid., 391.

is both finite and infinite, both less than and equal to God, that he existed from eternity and was born in time, and so on. This same principle carries over into the acts of Christ of which some are purely divine, others are purely human, and some are "theanthropic" or those acts in which both the divine and human natures concur. Hodge concludes that the personal or hypostatic union of two natures in one person is a teaching of both Scripture and the creeds of the church that protects at once against the twin errors of merging the humanity of Christ in his Godhead and of merging his Godhead in his humanity.

It should however come as no surprise from even a casual review of the history of doctrine that on the subject of the person of Christ, despite the plainess of Scripture teaching, there has been a wide range of error and heresy in the church resulting from theological speculation. Fortunately the faith of the church is not determined by the formulations of theologians, who are inevitably the victims of whatever the philosophy of their time and place happens to be. Rather, the faith once delivered to the saints is in the safekeeping of common people who cling to the word of God and whose doctrinal awareness fortunately is shaped more by such things as liturgy and hymnody than by the speculations of theologians. Hodge then launches, for the benefit of his readers, a survey of the doctrinal wreckage of the past resulting from the incurable curiosity of theologians concerning the "how" of the hypostatic union in the person of Christ. His historical survey begins with the Ebionites, who held what amounts to a humanitarian view of Christ as a mere man, and proceeds to the other extreme of certain Gnostics (including the Docetists), who denied the true humanity of Christ altogether. Less objectionable but no more acceptable were the attempts of the Apollinarians, who struggled with the question of Christ's person but finally rejected the perfect humanity of Christ by denying that he possessed a rational spirit or mind. Two other christological heresies of the past merit attention, including first the Nestorians, who labored over the relation between the divine and the human in Christ but ended up implying the division of Christ into a twofold personality while at the same time compromising the genuine divinity of Christ. Finally, there were the Eutychians, who compromised the humanity of Christ by absorbing it into the divine, transmuting Christ's earthly life into an illusion or an empty show. Of course the opposite extreme of losing the divine in the human and ending up with a merely human savior is equally unacceptable. Between these two extremes is a third equally objectionable notion of some theanthropic combination of humanity and divinity by which the person of Christ ends up being neither God nor man.

For his own part, Hodge was well satisfied that these ancient heresies had long since been definitively addressed by the Council of Chalcedon, whose definition had laid to rest the risks of truncating Christ's genuine humanity (Apollarianism), of endangering the unity of Christ's person (Nestorianism) and of absorbing Christ's humanity into his divinity (Eutychianism). According to "The Definition of Chalcedon" with which Hodge was so enamored, Christ "is perfect both in deity and also in human-ness; the selfsame one is also actually God and actually man, with a rational soul and body. He is of the same reality as God as far as his deity is concerned and of the same reality as we are ourselves as far as his human-ness is concerned; thus like us in all respects, sin only excepted." Further, Christ is apprehended "in two natures; and we do this without confusing the two natures, without transmuting one nature into the other, without dividing them into separate categories, without contrasting them according to area or function. The distinctiveness of each nature is not nullified by the union. Instead, the properties of each nature are conserved and both natures concur in one person and in one *hypostasis*."[8]

Since not much of anything of theological significance occurred between the Council of Chalcedon in 451 and the Reformation of the sixteenth century, Hodge passes quickly over the Middle Ages directly to his brief discussion of the person of Christ in the Reformed churches. The tradition of Calvin and Zwingli is pronounced doctrinally clean and in line with the formulation of Chalcedon, as echoed in the Second Helvetic Confession as well as in "the beautifully clear and precise statement of the Westminster Confession." As for the Lutheran doctrine of the person of Christ, it comes in for some rather lengthy and harsh criticism from Hodge for being both

---

8 See Leith, *Creeds of the Church,* 35–36.

confused and unsettled. Especially troublesome are the issues of the *communio idiomatum* or the teaching "that whatever is true of either nature is true of the person" of Christ, and beyond this the *communicatio naturarum* whereby the divine essence is communicated to the human (but not vice versa). The Lutherans therefore end up in a position of making the human nature of Christ divine, and this Hodge finds unacceptable on the ground that "there is such an essential difference between the divine and human natures that the one could not become the other, and that the one was not capable of receiving the attributes of the other."[9] Unlike the Lutheran formulation, the communion of attributes according to the Reformed tradition "concerned only the person and not the natures of Christ," and in this way God remains God and man remains man. Lutherans on the other hand have been led by the *communio idiomatum* to the notion that the attributes of the divine nature were communicated to the human person, and therefore whatever is true of either nature is true of the person. This creates an unnecessary christological complexity that has no foundation in the simple truths of the gospel regarding the person of Christ. Finally, by making the capacity of human nature for receiving divinity the centerpiece of their Christology, the Lutheran doctrine loses touch with the real humanity of Christ by merging it into divinity, "and he becomes not God and man, but simply God, and we have lost our Saviour, the Jesus of the Bible."[10] Hodge finds the whole of Lutheran Christology so filled with subtleties and speculation that he exits the discussion by simply referring his reader to Isaac Dorner's massive *The Person of Christ* and Charles P. Krauth's *The Conservative Reformation and its Theology*.

The Princeton professor's survey of post-Reformation Christologies includes brief analyses of the thought of Socinus, Swedenborg and Isaac Watts among others. But it is "the modern forms of the doctrine" that concern Hodge the most. He is especially troubled with what he identifies as the "pantheistical Christology" of German theology, which insists

---

9 Hodge, *Systematic Theology*, vol. 2, 409.

10 Ibid., 417. Hodge further suspected that the Lutheran doctrine of the person of Christ was being driven by eucharistic theology, and being no great admirer of sacramentalism he was quick to distance himself from Lutheran Christology on this ground also.

on making the notion that God and man are one the centerpiece of Christology and a fundamental of Christianity. His survey of German theologians leads Hodge to the uneasy conclusion that in each instance the doctrine of the two natures of Christ has been rejected, which is a significant departure from the faith of the church. Of special concern to him is the work of Friedrich Schleiermacher, who Hodge finds "the most interesting as well as the most influential theologian of modern times." He identifies Moravian piety, pantheism and rationalism as the operative intellectual influences on Schleiermacher's Christology, the combination of which results, as might be expected, in the loss of the "historical Christ" or at least of "the ordinary historical basis for faith in Christ." According to Hodge, Schleiermacher was determined "to construct a Christology and a whole system of Christian theology from within; to weave it out."[11] Naturally, a theological program predicated on the basis of subjective experience to the exclusion of the objective facts of Scripture was not going to pass by Princeton unnoticed and uncriticized, and as might be expected Schleiermacher does not fare well in the hands of Hodge.

Schleiermacher's portrait of Christ as the ideal man or the *Urmench* "in whom the idea of humanity is fully realized because his God-consciousness was developed perfectly" and who therefore is the source of God-consciousness for others was not an image of Christ with which Hodge could rest comfortably. As the Princeton professor became further acquainted with Schleiermacher's Christ as the one who "awakens the dormant God-consciousness in men, and gives it ascendency over the sensibility, or sensuous element of our nature, so that believers come to be, in the same sense, although ever in a less degree, what Christ was, God manifest in the flesh,"[12] Hodge was convinced that he had wandered into a christological never-never land, and he set to work on a trenchant rebuttal. He was not about to stand idly by and watch the Westminster standards on the person of Christ be

---

11 Ibid., 441. Schleiermacher's Christology is developed in his *The Christian Faith*, ed. H. R. Mackintosh and J. S. Stewart (Edinburgh: T. & T. Clark, 1928), 374–475.

12 Hodge, *Systematic Theology*, vol. 2, 442.

trampled by German idealism—never mind that Schleiermacher is a pleasant enough person; his theology is an abomination.

Naturally, Hodge's primary objection to Schleiermacher's Christology is that "it is not and does not pretend to be Biblical," but is rather a system "founded on what Christians now find in the contents of their own consciousness."[13] An unbiblical theology grounded in human consciousness is in effect no theology at all. But Hodge is far from finished, because second, while Schleiermacher's theology purports to be free and clear of philosophical speculation, in fact his whole system and not just its Christology is shot through with philosophical speculation from beginning to end. But after all, what else is to be expected from the Germans, who habitually ground theology in the authority of reason and not in the witness of revelation. Third, Schleiermacher has fallen victim to German pantheism and is guilty of collapsing God into the world by conjoining the natural and the supernatural. The result is that he ends up denying any proper dualism between God and the world and therefore "he does not admit the existence of a personal, extramundane God."[14] This is a serious charge with profound consequences for the whole of systematic theology and especially for Christology, because by denying the difference between the natural and the supernatural and thereby not admitting to the existence of an extramundane God, Schleiermacher ends up rejecting the doctrine of the Trinity. A God with no extramundane activities is not the trinitarian God of the Christian faith who is three persons in one from eternity, including the person of the preexistent Son of God. The result of all Schleiermacher's theological tinkering is that Christ has been made into a mere man who in the end possesses only a human nature, because Schleiermacher, intoxicated by German idealism, has lost the dualism of the natural and the supernatural. God and man, divinity and humanity have been rolled into one by the assumption of idealism that divinity is the completed development of humanity. Even if Schleiermacher does call Christ divine it means very little in a system in which the

---

13 Ibid., 443.
14 Ibid., 444.

divine is human and the human is divine. It is bad enough that this christological horror show of Christ as the *Urmench* or the ideal man is playing in Berlin, but it has made its way to the American shore and is now appearing regularly in the pages of *The Mercersburg Review.*

Schleiermacher's Christology has been further corrupted, Hodge thought, by a faulty anthropology that overturns the biblical view of human nature and displaces it with an organic or developmental view of human nature. Try as he may, Hodge cannot muster any enthusiasm or sympathy for developmental theories of human nature, according to which "there is an infinite, absolute, and universal something, spirit, life, life-power, substance, God, Urwesen, or whatever it may be called, which develops itself by an inward force, in all the forms of existence."[15] His assessment is caustic and his patience runs thin with romantic notions of the unfolding or self-evolution of the spirit in nature or history, which allow "no room for special intervention, or creative acts," all of which effectively undercuts the heart of the biblical witness. Schleiermacher does admit that at the time of creation there was a "special intervention," but the problem according to Hodge's analysis of the German theologian's position is that the quantum of life or spirit or whatever was issued to man at the time of creation is simply insufficient to carry humankind through the entire evolutionary process to perfection without some infusion of new life along the way. This boost to the organic development of nature and history then becomes the explanation for the necessity of the person of Christ, who comes on the evolutionary scene as a new creative force giving a much needed shot in the arm to the otherwise faltering progress of humanity. According to Schleiermacher, after the arrival of Christ in history the evolutionary process goes on again unfolding itself, this time in the church. The church thereby becomes the embodiment in time of the spirit or the "principle of life," which in turn is passed over from Christ to individual believers who are made divine or one with God by a process of organic development. Hodge simply cannot contain his disdain for all of this unscriptural organicism and romanticism that

---

15 Ibid., 448.

subsumes the supernatural in the natural and transforms Christ into an ideal man whose spirit is now developing as an inward force in the life of the church. Despite all of its seductive attractiveness Schleiermacher's Christology, which is grounded in a pantheistic blending of God and man, is unscriptural and untenable.

But for Hodge the saddest result of all this pantheistic German theologizing is that Schleiermacher's Christology distorts the scriptural plan of salvation and disrupts in turn the doctrines of the atonement, of regeneration, of justification and of sanctification by injecting into each a Christ who "saves us not by what he teaches, or by what he does, but by what he is." According to Schleiermacher's plan Christ is the one through whom a new influx of life is infused into the world and the church, thereby stimulating the ongoing historical development of humankind toward its goal of perfection. But, complains Hodge, there is no place in all of this for the supernatural, and the whole is a mess of naturalism or of mysticism. Christ and his work have been transformed into a natural process through which it is the character and influence of Christ that bring salvation, which bears little or no resemblance to the biblical plan of salvation. Hodge was determined to keep the Reformed tradition in which he stood faithful to the heritage of Chalcedon and Westminster and to the doctrine of two natures in one person. This he would do by fending off the Christology of Schleiermacher and his American disciples, of whom he concludes that they "are as much out of reach, and out of contact with the sympathies and religious life of the people, as men in a balloon are out of relation to those they leave behind."[16] This was not the first nor would it be the last time that Hodge accused certain theologians of having their heads in the air, while at the same time assuring the faithful that Princeton had and would keep its feet planted firmly in the solid ground of Scripture and in the common sense of ordinary Christians.

16 Ibid., 539.

# Chapter V

# JOHN W. NEVIN: CHRIST AS THE CENTER OF NATURE AND HISTORY

John Williamson Nevin (1803–86) was born in Franklin County, Pennsylvania, and reared within the context of a rather strict Scotch-Irish Presbyterian family. At the tender age of fourteen he was sent off to Union College in New York where he was caught up in the religious excitement at the college and professed conversion during a revival meeting conducted by the popular Asahel Nettleton. Some years later he renounced this conversion experience as "all subjective," but the young Nevin nonetheless left Union spiritually and intellectually prepared to set off for the seminary at Princeton, "the theological Athens of the Presbyterian Church." Upon his graduation from Princeton he remained at the seminary for an additional two years to fill the post temporarily vacated by his teacher Charles Hodge, who was on a sojourn to Europe.

At the age of twenty-seven Nevin was appointed to the position of professor of biblical literature at Western Theological Seminary in Allegheny, Pennsylvania, where he took up his duties instructing young ministerial candidates for Presbyterian pulpits on the frontier. In his very readable and instructive autobiography, entitled *My Own Life: The Early Years*, which covers the years up to 1840, Nevin casts a critical eye back on his own intellectual development and notes that its most serious shortcoming was "an utter want of proper historical culture in all my thinking at this time."[1] He

---

1 John W. Nevin, *My Own Life: The Early Years,* Papers of the Eastern Chapter, Historical Society of the Evangelical and Reformed Church, no. 1 (Lancaster, 1964), 40. The standard biography of Nevinis by Theodore Appel, *The Life and Work of John Williamson Nevin* (Philadelphia: Reformed Church Publication House, 1889; reprinted 1969); see also

complains without reproach about his historical training under Samuel Miller at Princeton, about his reading of "the pietistically feeble" Joseph Milner, "the dreary sense of reading Mosheim," and in general about the prevailing view of history as "a system only of dread outward facts." The study of church history at Princeton was a lifeless exercise in scoring denominational points rather than the more vital and exciting study of "the onward moving presence of the Christian life itself, reaching age after age toward its appropriate end."[2]

Nevin was rescued from his historical naivete by the reading of August Neander, which became for him "an actual awakening of the soul" to a new consciousness of what history properly means and to a new awareness of the historical element in all human existence. Nevin moved to Mercersburg, Pennsylvania, in 1840 to accept a rather unexpected call by the German Reformed Church in the United States to become professor of theology in the fledgling denominational seminary there. In 1844 he was joined on the Mercersburg faculty by Philip Schaff, who was appointed as professor of ecclesiastical history, and together the two men formed one of the most unusual and creative combinations in the history of American theological education. It was the influence of Schaff more than any other single source that freed Nevin from a rather stilted view of church history that posited a golden age of the church during the time of the apostles, followed by a lengthy and dreary course of decline into "a sort of devil's millennium" that was finally checked by Luther and the age of the Reformation, a view that ends up finding little or no hope in the present for the church apart from "the eschatological dream of Christ's second coming." His liberation from the shackles of this historical parochialism came through Schaff's influence and the discovery "that Christianity is a new and living creation in itself that can be enlarged properly speaking only from within, and not at all from without. Not by mechanical accumulation

---

James Hastings Nichols, *Romanticism in American Theology: Nevin and Schaff at Mercersburg* (Chicago: University of Chicago Press, 1961); Luther J. Binkley, *The Mercersburg Theology* (Lancaster: Franklin and Marshall College, 1953).

2 Ibid., 43.

or accretion can it be said to grow, but only by the way of organic development."[3]

Indeed, it was this shift from the mechanical to the organic that marked a major turning point in Nevin's thinking, and from this point on the idea of the organic becomes a crucial operative principle in his thought. The relation between the natural and the supernatural is not one of mechanical fixation but of historical development, of life and growth, which need to be unfolded in the dynamics of the divine-human encounter. Revelation is historical and "must house itself in the actual life of humanity itself, and not float over it only in an apparitional magical manner."[4] With this new perception of the nature of history Nevin came to a new understanding not only of the church but of Christology as well. The key to this new way of seeing is the incarnation, through which the divine has become incorporated in a living way into the actual human life of the world, and "this, of itself, does away with the common error of seeing in revelation a system of thought and words only, committed to writing in the Bible; and causes it to be apprehended as being, what it is in truth, a system of supernatural *facts*, a series of actual doings or deeds on the part of God, by which He entered always more and more deeply, since the fall, into the onward movement of the world's religious life."[5] The divine has become incorporated into the human life of the world concretely through the person of Christ, who is no apparition or magician but chief among the supernatural facts or actual doings by means of which God has entered more deeply into the onward movement of the church's and thereby the individual's religious life.

In his keynote sermon, entitled "Catholic Unity," preached before the joint convention of Reformed Dutch and German churches in Harrisburg in August 1844, Nevin stressed the importance of understanding that the person as well as the work of Christ are not merely outward or forensic matters. Rather, a new nature is organically imparted to the believer

3 John W. Nevin, introduction and appendix to *The Principles of Protestantism* by Philip Schaff, ed. Bard Thompson and George H. Bricker (Philadelphia: United Church Press, 1964), 44.

4 Ibid., 49.

5 Ibid., 50.

"by an actual communication of the Saviour's life over into his person. In his regeneration, he is inwardly united to Christ, by the power of the Holy Ghost . . . [and] a divine seed is implanted in him, the germ of a new existence, which is destined gradually to grow and gather strength, till the whole man shall be at last fully transformed into his image."[6] This transformation or regeneration of the believer is furthermore not just a matter of copying the excellencies of Christ as a moral example, but rather "the very life of the Lord Jesus is found reaching over into his person, and gradually transforming it with its own heavenly force."[7] This "mystical union" with Christ therefore "is not simply moral, the harmony of purpose, thought and feeling, but substantial and real, involving the oneness of nature." And by this "inward union," as it turns out, "the whole humanity of Christ, soul and body, is carried over by the process of Christian salvation into the person of the believer."[8] The nature of Christ thereby becomes one with the nature of the believer, transforming the believer's nature into Christ's nature, the believer's person into Christ's person.

But beyond the person of the individual believer is the community of believers, wherein the real presence of Christ joins the church into an organic union with its head and its many parts. The church is not a mere aggregation or collection of different individuals drawn together by similarity of interests and needs; it is not simply an abstraction of some kind "by which the common in the midst of such multifarious distinctions is separated and put together under a single general term."[9] Just as Adam was not a man but the man "who comprehended in himself all that has since appeared in other men," so too Christ, as the second Adam, is not merely a man "but the man, emphatically, the Son of Man, comprising in his person the new creation or humanity recovered and redeemed as

---

6 John W. Nevin, "Catholic Unity," a sermon delivered before the joint convention of the Reformed Dutch and the German Reformed Churches at Harrisburg on August 8, 1844, in *The Mercersburg Theology*, ed., James Hastings Nichols, Library of Protestant Thought (New York: Oxford University Press, 1964), 37, 38.

7 Ibid., 38.

8 Ibid., 39.

9 Ibid., 40.

a whole."[10] Little wonder that Charles Hodge at Princeton grew increasingly restive about what his former student was teaching at Mercersburg concerning the "mystical union," because he did not recognize in Nevin's organic Christology the Christ of either Chalcedon or Westminster. But Nevin was far from finished.

In 1846 Nevin wrote what was to become his most famous and enduring contribution to theology in America, a book entitled *The Mystical Presence*, which grew out of a controversy within the German Reformed Church over the subject of the Lord's Supper. It is the Lord's Supper that, according to Nevin, "must condition and rule in the end our view of Christ's person and the conception we form of the church. It must influence, at the same time, very materially, our whole system of theology, as well as our ideas of ecclesiastical history."[11] The root of Nevin's dissatisfaction with sacramental developments on the American ecclesiastical scene was what he perceived to be an overly rationalistic and ahistorical mind-set that had seized theology and in turn eroded the very foundations of Christianity itself. Regarding this foundation of Christianity, Nevin assured his readers that "no higher wrong can be done to it than to call in question its true historical character; for this is in fact to turn it into a phantasm, and to overthrow the solid factual basis on which its foundations eternally rest."[12] The historical nature of Christianity is obviously visible and tangible in the person of Christ and in the form of the church and will remain so to the end of time because "a religion without externals must ever be fantastic and false." However, the twin acids of rationalism and ahistoricism had eaten away at the foundations of the Christian faith so that little more than "fantastic and false" religion with an equally fantastic and false Christ was left. And one of the most devastating consequences to the American church of this process of christological and sacramental erosion was a clearly discernible antisacerdotal bias, against which Nevin was now

---

10 Ibid., 40.

11 John W. Nevin, *The Mystical Presence*, ed. Bard Thompson and George H. Bricker (Philadelphia: United Church Press, 1966), 23.

12 Ibid., 25.

prepared to hurl the full force of his rather considerable theological talent.

It needs to be made clear from the start, according to Nevin, that forms are constitutive of Christianity and therefore that a purely invisible church is an anachronism: "the outward and inward in the church can never be divorced, without peril to all that is most precious in the Christian faith." Therefore it should come as no real surprise that "the incarnation of the Son of God, as it is the principle, forms also the measure and rest of all sound Christianity."[13] Christianity that has lost touch with the incarnation and does not "form" itself is no Christianity at all, and Christ is the incarnate form of the divine. By its very nature therefore Christianity is christocentric because the incarnation is the organic conjoining of the natural and the supernatural; it is in other words the clear evidence that "nature and revelation, the world and Christianity, as springing from the same Divine Mind, are not two different systems joined together in a merely outward way. They form a single whole, harmonious with itself in all its parts."[14] The incarnation is "the great central fact of the world" because Christ is the center of nature, of history and of humanity. Just as nature strives and bends ever upward toward a fuller realization of itself and reaches its fullest development in human consciousness, so too history is a developmental process carrying forward the seeds within itself of the ideal union of nature with the supernatural or of humanity with divinity. The upwardly bound organic movements of nature and history are reflected in the struggles of humanity toward the realization of its perfection, which in fact has occurred in the person of Christ, who is the true union of humanity and divinity. The person of Christ is the focal point of nature, history and humanity through which the rays of each are refracted and in light of which the meaning of each is illuminated. As the one in whose person humanity and divinity are united, Christ "is the proper completion of humanity. Christ is the true ideal man."[15] Paganism and

---

13 Ibid., 25, 26.
14 Ibid., 201.
15 Ibid., 203.

Judaism both served as preludes to this union of the two natures of humanity and divinity in the one person of Christ, playing their appropriate parts in the progressive upward movement toward that moment in time when humanity and divinity were conjoined, at which point each of these two older forms yielded to the fuller realization of the new form of the divine introduced by the incarnation. The person of Christ as the union of humanity and divinity discloses the full sense of nature, history and humanity because Christ is the life-giving organic principle of each.

Nevin clarified further his thinking on the above points in a remarkable article in *The Mercersburg Review* entitled "Wilberforce on the Incarnation." He issued a sharp attack on both Orthodox and Unitarian views of Christ, arguing that each side has been and continues to be too fixed on the work of Christ in the atonement to the neglect of the person of Christ or Christology. Accordingly, Christ may be viewed as

> a mere prophet in the Unitarian sense, who saves by his excellent doctrine and holy example; or he may be allowed to be far more than this, a Saviour possessed of truly divine powers, according to the orthodox faith by the mystery of the Incarnation, who takes away sin by suffering the penalty of it in his own person; but still, in either case, the thing done has its proper seat and substance in the relation of the parties concerned by itself considered, which Christ as the doer of it stands always, as it were, on the outside of the transaction, in the character comparatively of an instrument or servant to his own glorious work.[16]

In effect Nevin is crying a plague on the christological houses of Orthodox and Unitarians alike, because in each case the person of Christ is not organically related to the work of Christ; for both, who Christ is and what Christ does have little bearing on each other. Both sides lack a genuinely incarnational theology, and as a result the person of Christ has become an observer to the work of Christ; Christology and the atonement

---

16 John W. Nevin, "Wilberforce on the Incarnation," *The Mercersburg Review*, 2 (March, 1850). Reprinted in Nichols, *Mercersburg Theology*, 79.

have gone their separate ways. The person of Christ has been lost in the fog and smoke of the atonement in American Protestant theology, and this has resulted in turning theology on its head. Christology needs to be restored to its rightful place within the theological enterprise, for "the mediation of Christ, we say, holds primarily and fundamentally in the constitution of his person. His Incarnation is not to be regarded as a device *in order* to his mediation, the needful preliminary and condition of this merely as an independent and separate work; it is itself the Mediatorial Fact, in all its height and depth, and length and breadth."[17] American Protestantism therefore needs to be drawn back to the person of Christ and to reestablish a firm christological foundation for the work of Christ.

Nevin placed this "Mediatorial Fact" of the person of Christ at the center of his thought and never let go of it, making it clear throughout that the person of Christ was no mere instrument inserted into the world to serve as a convenient device for the work of Christ through which the law is honored and divine justice is satisfied. All of this objectivity, this ahistoricism, this mechanicalism of the Orthodox and the Unitarians alike lacks vitality, warmth and breadth; in short it lacks the life that only a genuine incarnation can give. Both parties have failed to see in the person of Christ that "the power which belongs to him to make reconciliation and atonement, lies in the fact than the parties between whom he mediates are in truth united first of all in the constitution of his own life."[18] Theology begins and ends with the person of Christ, and that something so basic and obvious should need to be pointed out is a source of irritation and sadness to Nevin.

Equally disconcerting to Nevin were those guilty of displacing Christology and the centrality of the person of Christ with "bibliolatry." He has some harsh words for those who displace Christ with the Bible as the central principle of Christianity and notes that "however grating it may sound to some ears, the truth needs to be loudly and constantly repeated: the Bible is not the principle of Christianity, neither its origin,

---

17 Ibid., 79.
18 Ibid., 80.

nor its fountain, nor its foundation."[19] Rather it is the incarnate Christ whose person unites divinity and humanity who is the principle of Christianity, and a theology founded on anything other than this christological basis is a theology founded on sand rather than rock. It is the organic and historical continuity between the life of Christ or the incarnation and the life of the world that must be kept in constant and full view. Only a genuinely incarnational theology can in the end hold together the tension between the humanity and the divinity of Christ, because only a genuinely incarnational theology recognizes in Christ a "strict organic and historical continuity and unity with the life of the human world as a whole."[20] To miss this point is to miss everything.

Nevin was genuinely discomforted by views of history and of Christ that posited a too severe disjuncture between Christianity and the world, therefore disallowing any genuine union between the divine and the human. Christ is no mere fantasy or some kind of a disruptive theophany who enters the world as a foreign element and was never really incorporated into nature or history. Christ is not some kind of natural or historical aberration, because the union of the divine and the human in the person of Christ in truth "forms no violent rupture, either with nature or history. It fulfills, and in doing so interprets, the inmost sense of both."[21] Between the Gnostic error of losing the humanity of Christ to his divinity and the Ebionite error of losing the divinity of Christ to his humanity stands "the new creation," which unites the human and the divine in one person. In Christ the supernatural is not above or beyond but now truly incorporated with both nature and history. And the effect of this new creation in Christ who unites humanity and divinity in one person is not simply to provide "a new order of thought and character" because that kind of moralism is both simplistic and unbiblical. The person of Christ and the Christology that seeks properly to understand and express it is not intended to present us with moralism. Properly understood, the person of Christ as the new creation uniting humanity and divinity introduces "a new

---

19 Ibid., 81.

20 Ibid., 82.

21 Nevin, *The Mystical Presence,* 208.

divine force" into the heart of both nature and history as the actualization of the former and the meaning of the latter. Christ is "the revelation of God *in* man and not simply to him," and Christology is the faithful search for understanding of what it means that in nature and history humanity and divinity have come into perfect union in one person.

In another remarkable piece from *The Mercersburg Review* entitled "The New Creation in Christ," Nevin responded to charges that his views of the person of Christ smacked of transcendentalism because of his emphasis on the union between Christ and the believer. In defense of his position, Nevin replies that he is only reading St. John and St. Paul as they were meant to be read, and not as others are reading them through the lenses of rationalism or moralism. The true biblical image of Christ that is formed in the hearts of believers is not of some wooden outward model but "the power of his own life continuing itself over organically into their person . . . as its principle and fontal spring; the whole flows forth really from his person."[22] If this understanding of the person of Christ is transcendentalism then so be it, and Nevin will gladly number himself among the transcendentalists. He is however, utterly convinced that his is a faithful reading not only of the New Testament but also of the historical creeds as well as the writings of the early church fathers, and that therefore his christocentrism and not transcendentalism best reflects the whole spirit of the Bible and early Christianity. Seeking to discredit his Christology with the charge that it is transcendentalism simply will not work, for there are many widely accepted doctrines with far less biblical and historical warrant than his teaching of the mystical presence—so why the fuss? If those who object so strongly to his Christology would only take their New Testaments in hand they would discover there the simple truth that the person of Christ "repeats itself in believers; then salvation is carried forward by a mystical reproduction in them of the grand facts of his history: he is born in them, suffers in them, dies in them, rises in them from the dead, and ascends with them to the right

---

22 John W. Nevin, "The New Creation in Christ," *Mercersburg Review* 2 (January, 1850), 5.

hand of God in heaven."[23] The "grand facts" of the history of Christ are repeated in the lives of believers by being made over into them through "the mystical presence" of the person of Christ. To remove Christ from the process of history is to lose both Christ and Christianity, which is precisely what happens in the rationalism of the Orthodox and the moralism of the Unitarians, both of which are only the prelude to real transcendentalism. But Nevin's Christology is just the opposite of transcendentalism and serves instead as a bulwark against it, for rather than removing Christ from history he has restored Christ to his rightful place in history. Christ is "the form in which the sense of all previous history came finally to its magnificent outlet . . . the grand terminus towards which it was urged from the beginning."[24] Indeed, rationalism, Unitarianism and transcendentalism in America had few more trenchant critics than John Williamson Nevin.

The Mercersburg professor of theology labored to define and to defend right doctrine against what he perceived to be any and all threats to it, and perhaps this was nowhere more true than in his defense of the doctrine of the two natures in one person of Christ. Nevin was widely read in the history of Christian doctrine, especially in patristics and in Reformation figures. He was also remarkably familiar with the history of New England theology from Jonathan Edwards to Edwards Amasa Park, a tradition with which he was never very comfortable because of its lack of an ecclesiastical sense. He was thoroughly acquainted with the Princeton theology in which he was trained but of which he grew increasingly critical and distant. He knew modern German theology, which was introduced to him by his colleague Philip Schaff, and which became and remained an enduring influence on him. And last, he was well read in the theology of Horace Bushnell, whose work Nevin admired and adopted, but never uncritically. Nevin stands as a solitary figure through whom these several theological strands, both European and American, flow into a confluence that produces a unique synthesis. It should come then as no surprise that Nevin's Christology reflects the

23 Ibid., 5.
24 Ibid., 7, 8.

influence of these several theological strands, which are woven into a creative portrait of the person of Christ.

Yet for all of his interest in the formulation of right doctrine, Nevin did not allow doctrine to displace life as the primary category for the understanding of Christianity. He opposed rationalism and moralism in their several guises and sought instead to offer Christ as a new creation to the mind and to the heart, not as a truth for the intellect only or as a holy example for morality only. It is ultimately not right doctrine that brings the believer to God, "but only by being made to participate in the Divine Nature itself; and this participation is made possible to us only through the person of Christ."[25] Nevin develops this theme in a sermon on "The Knowledge of God Through Christ Alone," preached in September 1869, where he notes that self-consciousness is complemented by a God-consciousness universal to all persons. But this universal God-consciousness needs an exemplification or manifestation in some outward form, which is answered to in the person of Christ. The doctrine of Christ's person does not and cannot contain the reality of Christ's person, which "is deeper than anything purely intellectual. It involves a common life and fellowship of existence."[26] And the context of this "fellowship of existence" where the new life in Christ takes place is not in the inner religious life of the individual but in the communal life of the church. It is at this point that Nevin separates himself from and is most critical of the mainstream of evangelical Protestantism in America. It has failed to get the person of Christ beyond the subjective religious experience of the individual and into the common life and fellowship of the church. American evangelical Protestantism in general and the New England theology in particular have failed to make the necessary linkage between Christology and ecclesiology.

Nevin's reviews of several contemporary works on the subject of Christology reflect his criticisms of the theological failures of evangelical Protestantism. This criticism is most evident in his review of Ernest Sartorius's *The Person and Work of Christ,*

---

25 Nevin, *The Mystical Presence,* 219.

26 John W. Nevin, "The Knowledge of God through Christ Alone," preached September 25, 1869; in *College Chapel Sermons,* ed. Henry Keiffer (Philadelphia: Reformed Church Publications, 1891), 144.

which appeared in the *Reformed Quarterly Review* for March 1849. Nevin was perfectly ruthless in his criticism of the Rev. Oakman S. Stearn's translation of Sartorius, describing the translation as "neither elegant, nor intelligent, nor edifying," and noting that it was "a most lame, clumsy performance throughout," a "miserable travesty" and a "bungling attempt" that ends up leaving the original work in ruins.[27] The Rev. Mr. Stean's incompentencies as a translator are compounded by his Baptist christological biases, which prevent him from ever understanding correctly what the Lutheran Sartorius is saying in the first place. The root of the problem is that Stearns shares in the general New England mind-set in which the person of Christ becomes an outward instrument in the machinery of the atonement. The work of Christ, "which was required to take away sin, needed a conjunction of divinity with humanity in Christ, to qualify him for the execution; but once executed it carries with it an independent and separate value in the divine mind, and may be set to the account of men as a mere abstraction in this way, apart from Christ's life altogether."[28] As a result, the work of Christ has eclipsed the person of Christ in the New England tradition to such a degree that what is left under this arrangement is hardly recognizable as the genuine incarnation of a real person. Despite all protests to the contrary, this imbalance of atonement and Christology has resulted in the abandonment of the hypostatical union of two natures in the one person of Christ. The person of Christ has been effectively lost to the work of Christ, and "the deep rich overwhelming sense of the living *fact*, is not understood or felt." The domino effect of this theological imbalance is evident in the sad neglect of the doctrine of the church and in turn of the importance of sacramental life within the community of faith. Regretfully, Stearns is but one example, according to Nevin, of "the general Puritan and Methodistic tendency" away from the genuinely orthodox Protestant understanding of the church, away from the sacraments, and finally away from the true doctrine of the person of Christ.

---

27 John W. Nevin, "Review of Ernest Sartorius on the Person and Work of Christ," in *Reformed Quarterly Review* (March, 1849), 146f.
28 Ibid., 161.

To add insult to injury, it has taken a German Reformed theologian from Mercersburg to rescue Martin Luther from his American torturers. With something more than a tinge of sarcasm, Nevin notes that a review of Sartorius in the *Lutheran Observer* fell far short of adequately defending Luther here in evangelical America, where "the whole sacramental dream of the sixteenth century" has become antiquated. "The sympathies of this organ of Lutheranism fit it for making love ecclesiastically to the Cumberland Presbyterians, and other such sects, much more than for coming up to the help of its own proper faith in the hour of distress and danger. Could there well be, however, a more grinning irony on our existing sect system, than is presented to us in such a spectacle—the creed of Luther, the faith of the Augsburg Confession, thus mortally wounded, in favor of the Baptists, and in the house of its own professed friends!"[29] Once the sects begin defining the person of Christ and the nature of the church apart from the historical creeds of the Reformed and Lutheran traditions then real theological trouble will follow. Nevin was sounding the alarm to alert both of these faith communities to the necessity of holding firmly to the traditional formulations of the faith in the face of the threat of the "sect system."

In his *Concio ad Clerum* preached in Pittsburgh in November 1863, Nevin reminded his fellow clerics that christologies that transform Christ into "a man only, or some higher created intelligence in human form, empowered and enabled to make known the divine will"[30] are simply inadequate. In Christ are conjoined as they never have been before or will be again both the natural and the supernatural. Returning to his favorite theme of the incarnation, Nevin reminds his fellow clerics that it is the incarnation that incorporates the power of God's own life into the world. Thus Christ becomes the center and the principle within the world of a new creation that is at once both human and divine. Consequently, the incarnation is the center from which all goes out and to which all returns, and any doctrines that are "torn from their living, organic union with

---

29 Ibid., 168.

30 John W. Nevin, "Christ and Him Crucified: A *Concio ad Clerum*," preached in Grace Church, Pittsburgh, November, 18, 1863 (Pittsburgh: J. McMillin, 1863), 5.

this divine constitution become no better than hollow abstractions, and acquire in truth a positively false and anti-Christian character."[31] Christ is the midpoint of nature, history and humanity where life and doctrine flow together, and any Christology that substitutes a dry theory for living piety is misguided and guilty of doing far more harm than good. Life and doctrine go hand in hand, and "if the life and practice of Christianity are felt by any to be something independent of its doctrine, in their necessary Christological order and connection, we may be very sure that it is because they have not yet learned at all what the Christian life means, and that their practical Christianity therefore is not proper Christianity at all, but only a bastard imitation of it, made to stand in its place."[32] Christology is then the key to both Christian life and Christian thought, and no theologian in nineteenth-century America labored harder to ground both doctrine and practice in Christology than did John W. Nevin. He even suggested that because it made more of the person of Christ than any other nineteenth-century American Protestant theology, the Mercersburg theology thereby came closer to capturing the faith of the apostles and the church fathers.

Late in his career Nevin surveyed the course of theology in America over the previous fifty years and noted with some satisfaction that whereas once "the very terms Christological and Christocentric, as applied to theology, were viewed by many with grave apprehension and distrust," but now "the era of Christological theology has set in with a force which may be said, so far at least as profession goes, to carry all before it."[33] He took some measure of satisfaction that his own christocentric theology had to some degree served as a bulwark against the inroads of the "life of Jesus" movement by presenting a more comprehensive portrait of the person of Christ. The objective of the life of Jesus movement to reduce the history of Christ to the plane of other history was, in Nevin's opinion, a "flat miscarriage" in theology, demonstrating the impossibility of reducing the mystery of the incarnation to a

---

31 Ibid., 15.

32 Ibid., 20.

33 John W. Nevin, "Christ the Inspiration of His Own Word," *Reformed Quarterly Review* (Jan., 1882), 5, 6.

commonplace. Among those who moved with Nevin into "the era of Christological theology" was Horace Bushnell, whose *Nature and the Supernatural* elicited a prompt and for the most part favorable review by Nevin in the the pages of the *Mercersburg Review.* Nevin did have some rather critical reservations about Bushnell's understanding of the place and nature of creeds in Christendom and about his lack of an adequately developed conception of the church. From Nevin's vantage point Bushnell simply lacked an "ecclesiastical feeling;" he possessed an "unchurchly spirit" in no small part because he was the victim of "the stereotyped Puritanic way of thinking in regard to the historical church of past ages, by which it is made to be from the beginning, a systematic falling away from the proper sense of the Gospel."[34] Bushnell's lack of a proper view of the church catholic and his rather distorted sense of church history represent serious flaws in what Nevin finds otherwise to be a truly commendable effort to do theology from a christocentric vantage point.

Nevin was particularly impressed with this "distinguished author's" efforts to stem the tide of a rationalism that transforms the gospel into myth and poetry and also with Bushnell's attempt to return the supernatural to its rightful place within "the one system of God." Bushnell's treatise is especially persuasive because its "argument for the supernatural is made to rest centrally upon the person of Jesus Christ," and he along with Schleiermacher is to be credited with breaking "the melancholy reign of Rationalism." Bushnell is applauded for recognizing in Christ "the presence of a new supernatural life in the world, an order of existence which was not in it before" and which brings both nature and history to their respective fulfillments. Nevin was quick to express his approval of Bushnell's description of the incarnation as the unifying principle of the natural with the supernatural, and he rejoiced to find in Bushnell a fellow traveler who recognized in Christ

---

34 John W. Nevin, "Nature and the Supernatural," a review of Horace Bushnell's *Nature and the Supernatural, as together constituting the One System of God,* in *Mercersburg Review* 11 (April, 1859), 176f.

> an advent answerable to the glorious mystery of his person; such as shall bring with it the full presence of a new creation, and yet serve to set him really and truly in the bosom of the old creation. He must have a mission commensurate with his nature. He must be at once perfectly human and yet no less perfectly divine, in all his teachings and doings. He must be in the world, as being all the time above it, and as comprising in himself the power of a life destined to triumph over it at last through all ages.[35]

This merely reflects what Nevin had written a number of years earlier in response to Orestes Brownson when he observed that "in Christ, most literally and truly, the supernatural order came to a living and perpetual marriage with the order of nature; which it could not have done, if the constitution of one had not been of like sort with that of the other . . . so as to admit and require such union as the last and only perfect expression of the world's life."[36] In the end, for Nevin, Christ was "the last and only perfect expression of the world's life."

---

[35] Ibid., 194.

[36] John W. Nevin, "Brownson's Quarterly Review," in *Mercersburg Review* 2 (Jan., 1850), 65.

# Chapter VI

## HORACE BUSHNELL: CHRIST AS GOD'S LAST METAPHOR

Many of the clerics in attendance at the annual commencement of Yale College in August 1848 left the exercises somewhat stunned by the discourse of the commencement speaker, Horace Bushnell. The pastor of the First Congregational Church of Hartford, Connecticut, had just spoken *concio ad clerum* on "The Divinity of Christ," a subject over which he had been brooding for some time and about which he now had delivered himself with candor and creativity. The address not only left his Yale audience abuzz, it also created for Bushnell no little criticism and grief in the months ahead.[1]

Bushnell plunged into his discourse by noting that the divinity of Christ was a given of revelation, but that in New England this basic Christian teaching was threatened on the one side by dogmatizing about Christ's humanity and obscured on the other side by metaphysical speculations about the nature of the Trinity. Of these two, the more serious threat was posed by continuing unbridled speculation about the doctrine of the Trinity, behind which the divinity of Christ has been all but lost. Only as the person of Christ is rescued from this metaphysical jungle called the Orthodox doctrine of the Trinity will his true divinity be preserved. The doctrine of the Trinity in its current New England form only ends up

---

1 For biographical information on Horace Bushnell see especially Mary Cheney Bushnell, *Life and Letters of Horace Bushnell* (New York: Harper Brothers, 1880); Theodore T. Munger, *Horace Bushnell: Preacher and Theologian* (Boston: Houghton Mifflin Publishers, 1899); Barbara Cross, *Horace Bushnell: Minister to Changing America* (Chicago: University of Chicago Press, 1948); and Robert L. Edwards, *Of Singular Genius, of Singular Grace* (Cleveland: The Pilgrim Press, 1992), especially 95–135.

subordinating Christ and turning the Godhead into a speculative nightmare, or even worse turning it into a virtual tritheism. At stake is the relationship between Christology or the person of Christ and the doctrine of the Trinity, and the chief difficulty is that of maintaining the strict unity of God without at the same time compromising the divinity of Christ, and to do this in a way that will "justify the language of Scripture and be clear of any real absurdity." [2] Here then is the problem stated in its most basic terms, and the task is to see how Bushnell sets about solving it in a way that to his satisfaction is faithful to the demands of both Scripture and reason.

The point of attack is on the doctrine of the Trinity, of which Bushnell is convinced that until this pile of doctrinal rubble is cleared the divinity of Christ will remain at best obscured and confused. The real motivation for a fresh look at and reconstruction of the doctrine of the Trinity is his concern to recover the true divinity of Christ. He is keenly aware of several obstacles, including that of language, along the way toward a doctrine of the Trinity that will show forth and not eclipse the divinity of Christ. Doctrinal precision is an elusive goal because neither the Trinity nor Christology are matters that can be apprehended by direct inspection or expressed in direct terms. The infinite finds expression within the finite "molds of language and discursive thought. And in whatever thing He appears, or is revealed, there will be something that misrepresents, as well as something that represents Him."[3] The central problem all along with the doctrine of the Trinity has been with those thinkers who have treated words as though they could be trundled about as absolute representations for things, when in fact the knowledge of God is not given in quite so simple and direct a manner. What is known of God does not come through direct disclosure but by way of antagonisms, contradictions, paradoxes and relativities, which taken together constitute our knowledge of the divine. And to miss this distinction between the "something" that misrepresents

---

2 Horace Bushnell, *God in Christ* (Hartford: Brown and Parson, 1849), 136.

3 Ibid., 140.

and the "something" that represents in language and thought has been the source of no little mischief in theology.

The consequence of New England's theological word processing is that the person of Christ now lies buried beneath formulas that are lifelessly transported from mind to mind under the illusion that what is being pass along is the true knowledge of God in Christ. But nothing could be further from the truth. The knowledge of God in Christ always carries with it obscurity and mystery, contrarieties and relativities, representations and misrepresentations. This is so simply because these are the means by which humans are carried to the Absolute. The limitations of language cannot be wished away or laundered out and replaced by what we think are absolute representations of things. The forms in that God finds expression outwardly are always finite forms that are adapted to human limitations and needs, and therefore they are at best earthen vessels containing divine things. The person of Christ is just such a finite relativity, for Christ is "the form of God," the Logos, or the outward representation of God in and to the finite. Christology is possible only as we recognize the misrepresentations within the representations and as we resist the temptation to transform Christ into something that he is not by seeking to capture completely his person in theological formulas.

As the self-expression of the divine nature to humankind, Christ cannot be held captive by outdated metaphysics or fixed in place by dogmas, for Christ is rather God's gift to the imagination. Christ is not given to the human mind to be received by logic and subsumed by thought and language without remainder. Christ is given instead to the human imagination, which leaves plenty of room for mystery and free play. As the form of God, Christ conforms to human language, not by way of thought and logic, but by way of the imagination and poetry, which reflect more faithfully the vitality of biblical language. Bushnell is not at this point issuing an open invitation to the theologian to abandon all reason and to engage in willful obscurantism. He is rather issuing an important reminder that we need to recognize the nature of revelation and to acknowledge the limitations of both our finite apprehensions and expressions of the same through language.

That God in the person of Christ has chosen to enter "into the biographic history of the world" reflects the divine will to express itself more fully and worthily. And because "the human person will express more of God than the whole created universe beside,"[4] the advent of Christ is therefore to be viewed as an exhibition of the fullness of the life of God in history. This fact of revelation is in turn an invitation to reassess in a new light the troublesome issue of the relationship between the human and the divine in Christ. As the form of God in time, Christ is not just a good or even perfect man but the very image of God and as such is "the hinge of the gospel." God in Christ takes on the human as the form of divine self-expression, and the person of Christ is "an organ or type of the Infinite" that truly unites humanity and divinity. Bushnell is therefore not much impressed with the rather desperate attempts of some to doctor up the unity of the two natures of Christ by simply adding a divine soul onto the human soul of Jesus. This kind of theological sleight of hand solves nothing and creates other difficulties, including the danger of making the divine nature a spectator of the human nature in the work of redemption. Rather than probing the interior nature of Christ, of which Bushnell notes that "we perhaps know nothing," or trying to piggyback the human nature on the divine, it is better simply to acknowledge that "the reality of Christ is what he expresses of God, not what he is in his physical conditions, or under his human limitations."[5] The key to Bushnell's Christology is in many ways to be found in the phrase "what Christ expresses of God."

Christ is here to communicate the divine life, to "graft himself historically" onto humankind. The larger question regarding the person of Christ and the relationship between the human and the divine natures is always "What is here expressed?" On this point it is better to cease all theological inquiries into the two natures of Christ and to acknowledge rather that in the person of Christ we encounter mystery, paradox, contradiction and something that cannot be reached

4 Ibid., 149.

5 Ibid., 156.

but is rather to be received in faith. The simple truth of Christ as the form of God's self-expression is missed by those who are preoccupied either by logic chopping or by psychologizing. The person of Christ is not addressed to human intellect through metaphysics or to human consciousness through psychology, but to the human imagination through antagonisms, contradictions and paradox. In short, regarding the relation of the two natures in Christ, Bushnell rather tersely concludes that "as to any metaphysical or speculative difficulties involved in the union of the divine and the human, I dismiss them all, by observing that Christ is not here for the sake of something accomplished in his metaphysical or psychological interior, but for that which appears and is outwardly signified in his life. And it is certainly competent for God to work out the expression of His own feeling, and His union to the race in that way which most approves itself to Him."[6]

Not unlike Channing, Bushnell turned increasing away from the nature of Christ as lodged in the formulations of classical Christology to the character of Christ as the self-expression of God. Christology is not the internal mystery and mix of the two natures of Christ whereby his doings are credited to a ledger, some to his human and others to his divine nature. Christ is "the organific union" of God with human history, and as such the incarnation is "the crowning result of a grand, systematic, orderly work, which God has been forwarding in the history and heart of the race, ever since the world began."[7] It is not the transcendence of God but the immanence of God communicated to the imagination and human experience that is primary, and Christ is the form of God's self-revelation communicating the

---

6 Ibid., 163. See also Claude Welch's discussion of Bushnell in *Protestant Thought in the Nineteenth Century* (New Haven: Yale University Press, 1972), 258–268, where he notes that Bushnell refused to investigate the mystery of Christ's person in the categories of divine and human subsistences, persons, souls and natures, and sought to speak of a full self-expression of God in Christ whereby the life and love of God is communicated.

7 Ibid., 166. The unfolding of this organic and orderly work was to receive detailed attention in Bushnell's *Nature and the Supernatural.* On the relation between human character and divine character and their importance in Bushnell's thought see David L. Smith, *Symbolism and Growth: The Religious Thought of Horace Bushnell* (Chico, Calif.: Scholar's Press, 1981), introduction and chapter 1.

divine character to humankind. Christ is the expression of God who leaves an impression on the imagination of the individual, making for the development of character. The character of Christ as the expression of the character of God is the transforming power communicated not by logic to the mind but by symbols to the imagination, leading to moral and spiritual growth in the life of the individual.

As "the impersonation of God in time," Christ expresses the character, feeling and truth of God toward us by bringing to expression *ad extra* the warmth and the vitality of the *ad intra* relations of the persons of the Trinity. Behind and prior to the incarnation is a unity of Christ as the Logos of God for the believer and a unity of Christ as the Spirit of God with the believer. This warmth and vitality of the inner-trinitarian relations of Father, Son, and Spirit cannot possibly find expression in metaphysical abstractions regarding the Trinity, but these are rather relations that come to expression in and through human experiences made possible by the instrumentality of the Trinity and the work of each person in and through it. The same holds true of the two natures in one person of Christ: it is a matter of external expression only and not open for internal investigation. Here Bushnell is content with an "instrumental trinity" that functions as "a vitalizing element" through which the three persons "each and all together dramatize and bring forth into life about us that Infinite One."[8] Likewise, it might be said that Bushnell is perfectly content to stick with an "instrumental Christology," emphasizing Christ as the expression of God and refusing to investigate the inner mystery of his person.

But there is a greater warmth in the mystery and paradox of the Trinity and the person of Christ than in the imagined precision of dogmas about the same, and we are elevated to proximity with God more by mystery and paradox than by logic and dogma. The result is that the vitality and warmth of the divine finds expression as God struggles "into the measures of human knowledge, revealing Himself through the petty modes and molds of our finite nature. . . . He comes into the human itself, and melts into the history of man through agonies,

---

[8] Ibid., 173. It was his notion of an "instrumental trinity" that brought the charge of Sabellianism against Bushnell.

sorrows, and tears."[9] Bushnell boldly concludes his Yale discourse by noting that his views of the person of Christ and the Trinity differ in some respects from those that are commonly held, "but I hope the difference will not disturb you."

The year 1848 was a busy and important one in Bushnell's career, for in addition to the Yale commencement address he also delivered "A Discourse on the Atonement" at Harvard and a discourse entitled "Dogma and Spirit" at Andover. The problem of language loomed large in each of these and forced Bushnell into a sustained reflection on the nature of language resulting in his "Preliminary Dissertation on Language," which was published along with the above three discourses as *God in Christ*. The preliminary dissertation has been widely acknowledged as the centerpiece of Bushnell's thought, or in the words of his daughter, Mary Bushnell Cheney: "Here. . . is the key to Horace Bushnell, to the whole scheme of his thought, to that peculiar manner of expression which marked his individuality--in a word to the man."[10] His struggle to speak meaningfully of the divinity of Christ, among other things, forced him to reflect more carefully on the power and capacity of words "taken as vehicles of thought and of spiritual truth." To speak of the person of Christ we must know the appropriate language, which of course is the language of the Bible. But it is precisely this language that has been lost, and the task of theology is to recover the vitality of biblical language and to reform itself in the light of this recovery.

Bushnell was critical of the prevailing view of language as a precise instrument of thought in which words are carefully defined abstractions used according to logical method. But beyond the mere sound of words is the "language of intelligence," and here the difficulty begins as we move from outward sound to inward meaning. This is especially true in matters of religious expression, where the physical or literal usage of language to provide names for objects that are not observable is inappropriate. This is true simply because the inner experiences of thought, sentiments and religious awareness do not take on sensory or physical form. The language of religion is symbolic and therefore points in a

---

[9] Ibid., 180–81.

[10] Mary Bushnell Cheney, *The Life and Letters of Horace Bushnell*, 203.

different direction, toward "the vast analogy in things which prepares them, as forms, to be signs or figures of thought, and thus bases or types of words."[11] As they come from the outer sensory world into the world of inner consciousness and religious awareness words are transformed from being denotative to being expressive; they change from literal to symbolic usage. It is important therefore to recognize and to understand that "all the terms in language which are devoted to spiritual and intellectual uses have a physical or outward sign underlying their import" and that therefore "the outer world is the vast dictionary and grammar of thought . . . an organ throughout of Intelligence."[12]

If then theology is to speak meaningfully of the person of Christ it must not forget that the language that it uses is not denotative or literal but expressive or symbolic, and try as we may we cannot get rid of the element of ambiguity that accompanies all symbols, or as Bushnell says "the misrepresentation in the representation." Christ cannot be contained in the denotative language of theological definitions and formulas, and all attempts of theology to do this are simply misguided. Christ after all does not literally denote God, but the person of Christ is the symbolic expression of God. Christ communicates the divine character and reproduces this character in the believer by shaping him or her into its image. The source of much of the present confusion in theology is the penchant for making words over into "absolute measures and equivalents of truth," conveniently overlooking the basic distinction between the physical/literal and the spiritual/analogical usage of words. And while this distinction may be easily enough drawn in theory, in practice it is not all that simple because, as already noted, language devoted to spiritual or religious usage already has an underlying physical base and import. In other words, the symbolic always carries with it a tinge of the literal that reflects the misrepresentation in the representation.

---

11 Horace Bushnell, "Preliminary Dissertation on Language," in *God in Christ: Three Discourses delivered at New Haven, Cambridge and Andover, with a Preliminary Dissertation on Language* (Hartford: Brown and Parsons, 1848). Reprinted in H. Shelton Smith, ed., *Horace Bushnell* (New York: Oxford University Press, 1956), 76.

12 Ibid., 81.

It is the function of symbols to point beyond themselves, and rightly understood and handled they are a powerful means of communicating religions truth and of expressing the world of inner experience. The language of symbols is not propositional or informational, for the meaning and power of a symbol lies in the effect it has not so much on the intellect as on the imagination and in turn on the inner life. Regretfully the habit of carrying words around as if they were the "absolute measures and equivalents of truth" has become the albatross of theology from which it must be freed by a new theory of language that understands that words "are legitimately used as the signs of thoughts to be expressed. They do not literally convey or pass over a thought out of one mind into another.[13] Theology has not been well served by its attempts to eliminate metaphor and symbol and to deal only in the language of the literal and the truth of reference. Theology needs to incorporate into itself the language of the figurative and the truth of the expressive also. Alongside the rational, theology needs to discover the intuitive; alongside the intellect, it needs to discover the power of the imagination.

The task then is to free theology from the chains of literalism by means of a theory of language that understands words as "signs of thoughts to be expressed," as hints or images rather than as logically filtered propositions that are piled up into a ponderous volume "of formulas, filled up, rolled about, inverted, crossed and twisted—a grand, stupendous, convoluted sophism."[14] Freed from its bondage to the physical/literal side of language, theology may now recognize the poetical and metaphorical richness of language, especially of biblical language, and instead of trying to destroy paradox and contradiction it can now follow them to their appointed ends. Above all it needs to be remembered that "words are not given to imprison souls, but to express them," and therefore the basic task of Christology is to free Christ from the prison of literal language that insists on presenting him to the mind through

---

13 Ibid., 91.

14 Ibid., 96. For further discussion of Bushnell on language see Donald A. Crosby, *Horace Bushnell's Theory of Language, in the Context of Other Nineteenth-Century Philosophies of Language* (The Hague: Mouton, 1975).

lifeless formulas and to present Christ to the imagination through poetry and metaphor. Metaphysics after all does not have an exclusive handle on the truth, for the "most rounded view of any truth" must be approached and expressed in several different forms, including the forms of metaphor and symbol. Nowhere is this need for a more rounded view more pressing than in the understanding of biblical language, which if approached only by logic and literalism yields boundless absurdities. But if read with all its paradoxes, contradictions and repugnances of language intact, the Bible will yield truths far exceeding any expectations. It is in the interplay, the struggle and the tension of these antagonisms and paradoxes of the Bible that the truth finds expression.

For all the feats of theology and despite the impressive structures of its numerous systems, theology must be declared a failure because dogmatics violates the essentially poetic nature of scriptural language. The Christ of the Bible is connoted by symbol and metaphor and not denoted by logic and dogma, and the truth of Christ is therefore kept fresh by means of the former and not the latter. If then the comprehensive truth for which systematic theology so desperately yearns is to be achieved it will not be through treating words as "beasts of burden" and by way of "a few propositions, so intensely significant and true, as to dispense with all besides," but rather by way of"[15] An unexamined theory of language fueling the notion of "the possibility of reasoning out religion" was working like a fate in New England theology, driving it into ever greater obscurity and irrelevance. The time is now at hand to create a new theological method driven by a new theory of language that will usher out "the stern, iron-limbed speculative logic of our New England theology" and usher in a new age of theological vitality and comprehensiveness. The task of theology generally and of Christology in particular is to comprehend all the antagonisms, to bring together the many shadows and figures that are necessary to represent the truth of Christ. As Bushnell noted in another of his important addresses of 1848: "In nothing did Christ prove his superhuman

[15] Ibid., 99. See also Williston Walker, "Dr. Bushnell as a Religious Leader," in *Bushnell Centenary: 193rd Annual Meeting of the General Association of Connecticut* (Hartford: Hartford Press, 1902), 15–34.

quality more convincingly, than by the comprehensiveness of his spirit and his doctrine. . . . It is by this singular comprehensiveness, in the spirit of Christ, that the grandeur of his life and doctrine is most of all conspicuous."[16] The time is at hand to "take down the drapery of language" and by means of symbols and metaphors to get at the warmth of living truth. The plague of partiality that has kept theology shackled to the past is now being overcome as the antagonistic and repugnant forms of truth are being unveiled and united in a comprehensive Christianity.

Bushnell was genuinely disappointed and even hurt that all three of his 1848 addresses were either misunderstood or misrepresented, and he came to his own defense before the Hartford Central Ministerial Association in a volume entitled *Christ in Theology*. Rather than backing down from his earlier views on either the nature of language or the person of Christ, Bushnell reiterated even more strongly his position that to really see and hear what God is expressing in the truths of revelation theology needs to give up "the extempore clatter of logical judgment" in favor of the power of symbols and the method of analogy. The trick is "to read God's eternal language . . . for I cannot but suspect that there is an eternal and necessary connection between the forms God has wrought into things—thus into language—and the contents, on the one hand, of his own mind, and the principles, on the other, of all created mind."[17] As the form of God, Christ is the Logos or content of God's mind who has been "worded forth" to the human mind. As the form of God, Christ is also the living expression of the character of God, which is apprehended by metaphor or the principle of analogy. The connecting link between the mind and

---

[16] Horace Bushnell, "Christian Comprehensiveness," *New Englander* 6 (January 1848): 83. See also the article by Irving H. Bartlett, "Bushnell, Cousin, and Comprehensive Christianity," *Journal of Religion* 37 (April 1957): 99–104.

[17] Horace Bushnell, *Christ in Theology: Being the Answer of the Author before the Hartford Central Association of Ministers, October, 1949, for the Doctrines of the Book entitled "God in Christ"*(Hartford: Brown and Parsons, 1851), 31. See also Bushnell's essay on "Revelation: A Discourse Delivered before the Porter Rhetorical Society," September 13, 1839; excerpts in David L. Smith, ed., *Horace Bushnell: Selected Writings on Language, Religion, and American Culture* (Chico, Calif.: Scholar's Press, 1984).

character of God and the mind and character of the individual is language. It is not however the language of logic, by which Christ is rendered into a lifeless corpse, but the language of metaphor, through which Christ as "God's last metaphor" becomes a living presence.

Bushnell reassures his critics that he is not out to create a new language much less a new Christ; the language and the Christ of the Bible are just fine. The problem is that the Christ of the Bible has been eclipsed by a misunderstanding of the language of the Bible, and the forms in which the truth is revealed have become confused with the truth itself. Unless and until it is understood that all religious truth is presented under the form of symbol this confusion in theology about the nature of language will persist. Theology must come to recognize that what words carry into the heart and bring to expression by metaphor is something quite different from that which words carry into the mind and bring to representation by logic. Theology is guilty of looking in all the wrong ways and in all the wrong places for what it is that words do: they are not the means of a divine calculus that is thought out, but the means of divine expression that is simply to be received. Such is the nature of revelation that it contains both forms as the outward bodies of truth as well as intelligent beings who can read these forms and discover the truth in them. Christology in the past has generally agreed that Christ is the form of the truth, but the reading of this form to discover the truth in it has been a source of error and confusion. Reading the form of Christ through the lens of metaphor instead of the lens of logic yields a Christ whose person and work is more compatible with the vitality of biblical language.

Bushnell likewise reassures his critics that he is not playing footloose with the truth but that he is earnestly seeking to open new vistas on the truth of Christ as it finds living expression under God's own forms. He strengthens his stand by several illustrations from the history of Christian doctrine and cites a number of supporting sources, including August Neander and Richard Baxter. He argues that theology will remain in its present gridlock until it recognizes that "the principle difficulty we have with language now is, that it will not put into the theoretic understanding what the imagination only can receive, and will not open to the head what the heart only can interpret."[18] Further, this theory of language is one at which Bushnell has arrived only after many years of reflection, and what he is proposing as the analogy between things visible and invisible is not really all that radical. He is simply asking that theology look directly into the face of those words by which God is expressed and separate out the form from the spiritual significance thay contain, a process that is carried out not so much by thought as by intuition and insight. A Christ who is "thought out" is not the Christ of the Bible; on the other hand a Christ who is received by the imagination as the expression of God is the Christ of the Bible, who should in turn become the Christ of theology and of faith.

Despite his trenchant criticism of theology, Bushnell further reassures his critics that he is not interested in dispensing with it altogether. Quite the contrary, the theological task is one of receiving the truth of revelation in the forms by which it comes to us, and the responsibility of the theologian is to put this truth into language that meaningfully expresses it to others. The task of uncovering the forms that underlie all religious language and to discover the truth contained in the forms is an ongoing task, and therefore the necessity of theology is ensured. We cannot do away with these forms and therefore the theologian, knowing "that we have no properly literal terms for the expression of spiritual ideas," will be especially sensitive to the presence and types of forms and figures that make their way into the inner life through the imagination and come to expression in the language of faith. Each and every revelation, including the Trinity, the person of Christ and the atonement, needs to be subjected to this kind of patient and careful screening in light of this new theory of language. This task of moving the foundation of theology from logic to metaphor essentially defines the life and work of Horace Bushnell.

Theology needs a new, truer and simpler method of doing business, a method that thinks less and intuits more and that is less aggressive and more receptive. In short, theology needs a method that allows for the organific power of truth to come to expression not just in doctrine but also in life. Bushnell notes

---

18 Horace Bushnell, *Christ in Theology*, 33.

that over against Catholicism, it is a fundamental principle of Protestantism that the church is not organized around sacerdotalism or the priesthood, but in and by theological formulas "taken as being the very essence and literal being of the truth." But he questions the organizing power of dogmatism and of theological systems, which have at best a limited duration. There are limitations to this Protestant principle of dogmatic organization, not the least of which is that it tends to fix in time those things that are really not given to be frozen in systems of dogma, including the doctrine of the person of Christ. But the process of system building among Protestants goes on apace, and "having gotten a few forms of words mortised together by the carpentry of logic, it offers them to the world as another and better account of the Infinite Material, that is, of God and divine government. And so it comes to pass that, while there is but one truth, we have many theologies—little finite universes all, soap-bubble worlds rising by their own levity, whirled away by all cross winds of philosophy and Providential history, bursting in tiny collisions, or without collisions, by the mere thinness of their films, and not leaving moisture enough, at the point where they vanish, to show where they were."[19]

Beyond the sacerdotalism of Catholicism and the dogmatism of Protestantism is "the true organific principle of Christianity," and that is God: "The Divine Nature incarnate outwardly, and so inserted inwardly in human faith and consciousness."[20] Christology is not a matter of sacerdotal reception of Christ at the hands of a priest, nor is it a matter of dogmatically thinking our way through to Christ and of organizing our thoughts and theories about him into "sound doctrine." Christology is a matter of both of these and more, and a comprehensive Christology will not confuse the forms of sacerdotalism or dogmatism with the truth of Christ. Christ is in the sacrament and Christ is in theology, but Christ is not the sacrament nor is Christ theology. Christ is rather the living cell who cannot be contained in the crustacea of theology, for he is always breaking free of those forms that tend to imprison him in order that he may be to us "the Life of God in the soul of

---

19 Ibid., 72–73.
20 Ibid., 74.

man." Theology, and perhaps Christology in particular, must carry with it this experiential component, beginning at the point of a "living consciousness" of God in Christ as "the true organific principle of Christianity" and moving from there to expound the person of Christ and "to find a place for faith that is freer and more simple, and just as much more intelligent."[21] All the more reason then to proceed with this "modest and practical" program of theological reconstruction based on a new understanding of the power of words to produce an impression of Christ in us rather than a theory of Christ from us.

His essay "The Person of Christ" in *Christ in Theology* demonstrates that Bushnell refused to be badgered by his critics into giving ground on his Christology. He looks again at the question "Who is Christ?" in light of his new understanding of the nature of language and reiterates his basic conviction that Christ "is not given as a riddle to our curiosity, or that we may set ourselves to reason out his mystery, but simply that God may thus express his own feeling and draw himself into union with us, by an act of accommodation to our human sympathies and capacities."[22] Christ expresses or communicates God by humanizing the conception of God and serving as a vehicle for the communication of the divine character. The study of the person of Christ should focus on him as the manifestation of the "Life of God," and not on questions about the internal composition of his person and whether for example he has a human soul and will. The question for example of Christ's human soul is an idle distraction, one of many that leads us into unnecessary speculation and away from the principle issue of Christ as nothing less than the image and life of God under the human type. For Christology to take up with the task of probing the interior nature of Christ's person is a dead end because it is a topic closed to investigation. Christology is not an investigation of Christ's psychological makeup; it is rather a simple and faithful acceptance of the miracle of the union of the divine and the human in one person as the expression of God. Christology needs to stay focused on Christ as the external expression and to forget about probing into all kinds of perfectly useless and indeed unscriptural issues relating to his

---

21 Ibid., 91.

22 Ibid., 93.

inner nature. Christology is not psychology any more than it is metaphysics; Christology has to do with Christ as God's last metaphor, not with Christ as God's last personality or as God's last puzzle in logic.

Concerning the classical christological formula of two natures in one person, the temptation has been one of endless speculation rather than of simply accepting what is here externally expressed. The result is that Christology ends up expressing everything except the life of God in Christ. The two natures in one person formula is perfectly capable of bringing to us a sense of God and of union with God, which in truth is its intention. But instead this classical formulation gets treated as a scientific problem and its power to bring God in Christ to expression is siphoned off in the pursuit of countless theological impossibilities and irrelevancies. The result of this process is that certain activities are assigned to the human nature and other activities to the divine nature of Christ, which ends up "running the two natures into two persons," which of course is exactly the opposite of what the formulation intended in the first place.

On this point Bushnell argues that he in fact is more orthodox than the Orthodoxy of New England precisely because he holds to the two natures in one person formula more faithfully than they do. It is the Orthodox who have split Christ in two and are guilty of rendering asunder the unity of his person and endangering the genuineness of the incarnation. Again it is a simple matter of taking what is given rather than making up what is not, of accepting what has been revealed and not wishing to know more than Scripture teaches. By sticking to the instrumental, the exterior, and the practical, the unity of Christ's person will prevail and Christology will thereby operate within proper boundries. The two natures in one person of Christ is a classic example of the paradox and contradiction that are "instrumentally necessary to the right conception of it" about which Bushnell has been talking all along. It is in this paradox of the unity of humanity with divinity that we see in the person of Christ not two but one, not God with a human soul added on, but the Word made flesh. He stands firm in the conviction that his refusal to speculate on the interior nature of Christ's humanity means that he denies the real humanity of

Christ. Neither is he guilty of denying the eternity of Christ's human person or of what is sometimes referred to as his "glorified humanity," although he confesses to some difficulty with this phrase and does not want to press the language beyond what it can bear.

Christology should be content with "an instrumental duality" and leave behind all questions about the interior nature of the relation between the human and the divine in the person of Christ. Christology should start from below and work up, rather than starting from on high and working down. There is no limit to the christological absurdities that get passed on in the name of the gospel, when for example attempts are made to determine whether it is the human or the divine nature of Christ that suffers. Better rather to accept the mystery and the paradox of the God-man, that "when he suffers, it is only a part of the mystery that he is man, and his form contradicts the deity of his nature as radically as his suffering does the divine impassibility."[23] This short discourse in *Christ in Theology* on the person of Christ is vintage Bushnell—relishing paradox, reveling in contradiction, and from them seeking to draw out a deeper meaning and a higher comprehensiveness. Above all it is the work of a man who has "seen the gospel" and who writes with the confidence of a thinker who is not going to depart from his theological convictions.

1

The discourses on the person of Christ in both *God in Christ* and *Christ in Theology* contain more or less the theoretical statement of Bushnell's Christology. However, Bushnell saw himself primarily as a preacher and not a theologian, and any discussion of his Christology must include his sermons if we are to see how theory translates into practice. For example, in a sermon entitled "The Gospel of the Face" he begins by delivering one of his characteristic blasts against the distortion of the gospel that has resulted from "a huge milling process of construction—by much theologizing, propositionizing, schematizing and abstractisizing," all of which have put "the gospel too generally out of its proper divine form, into our own

---

23 Ibid., 103.

human form."[24] This "milling process" has ended up putting the gospel on its head, for its truth lies not in theology and propositions but "in sentiment wholly, in what goes to make impression by expression." And the person of Christ is the expression of God, "God's own formulization of himself, i.e., not the statement but the image of himself. What less than a very bold irreverence then can it be to substitute the revelation-form or face of God, by any so prosy thing as a formula in words. And the more evidently is this true, that all that Christ was and did is summed up in character and feeling."[25] It is in the face of Christ, in the "revelation-form" of the gospel that we see the glory of God, and it is the task of the preacher through words to bring his listener face to face with God, not to give them "a mere pile of bricks" in the form of theology, propositions, schemes or abstractions. The person of Christ is the gospel of the face and Christ is "the truth beheld in living expression." Christ enters the soul as life and not as a proposition, and all too much Christology of the past has been misguided into dissecting the human and the divine natures of Christ into the part that does and the part that does not suffer, the part that increases in knowledge and the part that does not, and so forth. This has made the person of Christ into "a kind of double personation," when "exactly contrary to this he is to be two poles in unity, a solidly concrete, impenetrable, unsolvable person—God's full beauty and love in the human type or face, the Word made flesh."[26]

Bushnell never tired of reminding his congregation that Christ was an antidote to abstraction, that God entered history not as a proposition but as "a concrete personation." The Word has a human face, even as words themselves have a human face in the form of symbol and metaphor. Through the faces of words not as propositions but as symbols and metaphors we can be brought face to face with the Word. Faces carry expressions, which in turn make impressions on the soul. So too, words have faces that carry expressions in the form of symbol and metaphor, which in turn are capable of making impressions on

---

24 Horace Bushnell, *Sermons on Living Subjects* (New York: Scribner, Armstrong & Co, 1872), 74.

25 Ibid., 75.

26 Ibid., 79.

the soul, thereby shaping the character of the believer. But so long as theology treats words as faceless and lifeless blocks that are piled into propositions it will miss the true nature and power of language. The believer must rather have the courage to look words in the face so that his or her soul may be re-inspired and restored through the symbolic and metaphorical power of language. At stake is "God's indwelling life itself," which comes to the believer through "a living gospel worded to our feeling, in the face of Jesus and the concrete matter of his life." And the gospel is "worded to our feeling" not by means of propositional truths to which ascent is given, but through a living faith that is relational and not propositional. The gospel is a dramatic enactment, it is the Word becoming flesh in history and in turn becoming the life of God in the soul of the believer. Where the dynamics of the living Word are displaced by the stasis of lifeless propositions, there Christology has killed Christ. The gospel can be killed by dissection and analysis; Christ can be crucified by propositional language just as he can be made to live by metaphorical language.

In a sermon entitled "The Putting On of Christ," Bushnell attacks what he calls "the fig-leaf stitching" of religion, its wordiness and busyness by which the spiritual nakedness of the time is covered. As the expression of God, Christ impresses the character of God on the character of the believer and becomes the dress of the soul. Character is the form or figure of the soul, and it is Christ that the believer puts on in the formation of character; believers are not clothed by makeshift religious garments of their own stitched out of theological propositions and pretexts. Christ alone is the garment fitted to human nature (that is the point of the incarnation), for he "humanizes God to us, or brings out into the human molds of feeling, conduct and expression, the infinite perfection, otherwise inappropriable and very nearly inconceivable. Since we are finite, God must needs take the finite in all revelation. . . . In the man-wise form only can we put him on."[27] In Christ the infinite perfections of God are cast in finite molds and "are

---

[27] Horace Bushnell, "The Putting On of Christ," in *Christ and His Salvation: In Sermons Variously Related Thereto* (New York: Charles Scribner, 1865), 421.

ready to have them even upon ourselves." As the garment of God that believers are to put on, Christ is not a loose or shoddy fit but perfectly tailored "in the exactest fit of our humanity." The individual is thereby "infolded" by the perfections of God, and invested with this new dress of the seamless robe of Christ the soul is "new charactered" in time and for eternity by "the holy texture" of Christ's character. Christology has very much to do with the character of Christ and with the formation of character in the believer, and very little to do with the person of Christ and manner of the relationship between the human and the divine natures.

Bushnell continued to focus on Christ as the central biblical symbol and to show an increased interest in and preoccupation with christological issues. As we have seen, his objective was not merely to tinker with christological formulations of the past but to raise fundamental concerns about the very possibility of doing Christology. This christocentrism is reflected in a sermon entitled "Heaven Opened," in which Christ is presented as the one who opens in each person an otherwise dormant sense of things supernatural. The argument is simply that humans have lost touch with the supernatural, that the original state of "a full, free commerce" with God has been suppressed or shut up within, leaving the self preoccupied with itself and isolated from God. The complement of immediate self-consciousness or self-knowledge is the consciousness or knowledge of God, a higher sense opening to the supernatural but which has been lost and now needs to be retrieved. The problem is that the aspirations and gropings of the soul after the supernatural, its "supernatural sense" or the suppressed longings for God cannot be restored by self-cultivation. It is Christ alone who can revivify the soul, opening it to the spiritual and supernatural things of God, which is what faith is: "Nothing but the opening of the supernatural sense of the soul on the supernatural being to be apprehended."[28]

It is Christ who welds heaven and earth together, in whom nature and the supernatural unite so that "supernatural event and character are built in solidly thus, into the world's history, to be an integral part of it. Mere nature is no longer all, and

---

[28] Horace Bushnell, "Heaven Opened," in *Christ and His Salvation,* 443.

never can be again. The very world has another world interfused and working jointly with it."[29] The wall between the natural and the supernatural, between the finite and the infinite has been broken down and brought under "a common headship" in the person of Christ, the same Christ who awakens our dormant sense of things supernatural and opens the soul to heaven. Christ has come then not to seek approval before the tribunal of human logic but to awaken the supernatural sentiments of the human soul, restoring the integrity of the self as a unity of both natural and supernatural faculties. Christologies that do not deliver to us this living Christ of human experience who opens up the supernatural to us are guilty of "taking away our Lord." Only in this case Bushnell was perfectly convinced that he knew exactly where they had laid him—among the ruins of theological dogma.

In a sermon entitled "The Completing of the Soul," Bushnell reminds his listeners that the soul is always in the process of growth and development, moving toward completion and unfolding in the direction of that for which it has been made. Created as finite, the soul has natural aspirations and longings for the infinite, the possession of which alone brings it to completion. Only as the properties and perfections of infinity flow through the soul, only as it is empowered by the Infinite Life is the soul brought to fulfillment; anything short of this and the soul remains incomplete. In the character of Christ "we have the exact figure in our feeling of what requires to be fashioned and completed in us . . . . Christ is the mirror that glasses God's image before us, and the Spirit is the plastic force within us, that transfers and photographs that image; and so, beholding as in a glass the glory of the Lord, we are changed into the same image."[30] Christ is therefore "copied into us," transforming our character and our relations by drawing us forward into the "principle intents and highest summits of our nature." The struggle of human growth needs the objective reference of Christ and not the subjectivism of self-culture. No matter how much Emerson and his followers may protest to the

---

29 Ibid., 449.

30 Horace Bushnell, "The Completing of the Soul," in *Sermons on Living Subjects*, 107–108. See also Conrad Cherry, introduction to *Horace Bushnell: Sermons* (New York: Paulist Press, 1985), 1–23.

contrary, it is Christ alone and not self-culture or education that completes the soul.

In February 1848, after a period of intellectual struggle and personal trials, Bushnell reached a quiet but decisive turning point in his life. When asked by his wife what had occurred he replied simply, "I have seen the gospel." The sermon following on this experience is entitled "Christ the Form of the Soul," and in it Bushnell develops his definition of character as "the form of the spirit." Christ as the form or image of God expresses the character of God and at the same time restores in us the lost image of God, which has been de-formed by sin. "Being in the form of God, the eternal Word assumes humanity, that he may bring into humanity the form of a divine character."[31] The "sublime reality" is that in the one person of Christ the two natures of humanity and divinity have been united, and the aim is to have this union completed in the believer through Christ as the form of the soul. Again, this is the work of grace and not of self-culture, because the forming of Christ in the soul moves from him to the individual. What then can be done to contribute to this forming of Christ in the soul? The answer is to "present yourselves to Christ in just that way that will most facilitate his power over you and in you," which means emptying the soul so that Christ may take form in it. Through him believers become partakers of the divine life as their character is "Christed." In short, "the great design of God in the incarnation of his Son is to form a divine life in you. It is to produce a Christ in the image of your soul, and to set you on the footing of a brother with the divine Word himself. . . . He will raise the human even to the divine, for it is only in the pure divine that God can have complacence and hold communion."[32] For all of his occasional protestations against mysticism, there is a genuine mystical strain in Bushnell's Christology, for the great design of salvation is "the divine occupancy of Christ" as the form of God in the soul and the character of believers.

---

31 Horace Bushnell, "Christ the Form of the Soul," in *The Spirit in Man* (New York: Charles Scribner's Sons, 1903). Reprinted in *Horace Bushnell: Sermons*, ed. by Conrad Cherry, 55.

32 Ibid., 60.

In a sermon entitled "Christ as Separate from the World," Bushnell struggles to bring the oneness of the person and the duality of the natures of Christ into focus by setting the incarnation and the eternal sonship alongside each other. There is a danger in making Christ too familiar and an equal danger in making Christ too distant; the oneness of Christ with us must be balanced by the separateness of Christ from us. Christ is the one in whom the balance of oneness and separateness, of humanity and divinity is perfectly struck, for Christ is the one who lived out in the molds of human conduct and feeling the perfections of God. To the one side Bushnell asserts that "Christ rose up out of humanity or the human level into deity and the separate order of uncreated life, by the mere force of his manner and character, and achieved, as man, the sense of a divine excellence, before his personal order as the Son of God was conceived."[33] This rather puzzling statement might serve to quiet Bushnell's critics who accused him of not taking the humanity of Christ seriously, but almost immediately to the other side he softens its effect by noting that regarding the person of Christ "the great and principal lesson derivable from this subject is, that Christianity is a regenerative power upon the world, only as it comes into the world in a separated character, as a revelation, or sacred importation of holiness."[34]

This separateness of Christ provides yet another occasion for Bushnell to launch a rather caustic attack on salvation by self-culture or voluntary activism, both of which promulgate the notion that the salvation of humankind is promoted by a simple appeal to the development of goodness within human nature. Christianity however operates quite otherwise, for Christ "brings to men what is not in them, what is opposite to them, the separated glory, the holiness of God." Notions of redemption within history by the forces of history are not at all convincing, and Bushnell finds that the millennial schemes of self-culture advocates, the hip-pocket plans of social reformers and the activism of philanthropists are collectively little more than "a toy-shop apparatus." Redemption is by a power brought into the world that is not of the world, and it is

---

33 Horace Bushnell, "Christ as Separate from the World," in *Sermons for the New Life* (New York: Charles Scribner, 1858), 447.
34 Ibid., 450.

the person of Christ who fits this description. Here then is "the desolating error of our times," and that is the failure of Christianity to be less in conformity with and more separate from the world, trying to make an impression on the world by being homogeneous with it rather than in the manner of Christ by separateness from it.

Bushnell was equally sharp in his criticism of millennialists who were yearning for and calculating the time of the bodily second coming of Christ. We do not need the physical and localized Christ of millennialism but the spiritual and universal Christ of the Bible. Christ is to be seen by faith and not by sight, and nothing would be such "a dead loss" as a Christ who is "locally descended and permanently visible." Only a faulty Christology would make of Christ "a bodily resident Saviour," when in truth Christ is present through the Spirit "in a way more immediate, and blessed, and evident, and as such more beneficial."[35] The Spirit is the inward impression of what Christ outwardly expressed, and it is through the work of the Spirit that "a divine testimony flows into human impression" and comes to consciousness as God in Christ. Indeed, such a present relationship with Christ in the Spirit as our "friend, consoler and glorious illuminator" is even preferable to the outward company of the incarnate Christ, for in his present relations with his followers Christ "comes up from within, through our personal consciousness itself, we are raised in dignity, and have him as the sense of a new and nobler self unfolded in us."[36] This is Christology from below to above rather than from above to below, and doctrinal knowledge or "notional furniture" may be necessary and useful in the believer's spiritual odyssey, but it is at best second rate compared to the immediate knowledge of God in Christ. Neither God-consciouness nor self-consciousness that comes up from within is a matter of sudden inspiration or revivalistic surges, but of growth and development. And further, lest we think that the immediate experience of God-consciousness, which gives "the sense of a new and nobler self," is designed to waft the believer away into some abyss of mystical

---

35 Horace Bushnell, "Present Relations of Christ and His Followers," in *Christ and His Salvation*, 337.

36 Ibid., 343.

contemplation, "we simply let the Son of Man be God in our feeling, and fashion us in the molds of his own humanly divine excellence."[37]

In a sermon entitled "In and by Things Temporal are Given Things Eternal" Bushnell explored further the person of Christ as the expression and communication of the character of God. There is a transparency to things temporal whereby looking through them we may discern an image of the eternal. Nowhere is the relation of time and eternity more evident than in the incarnation, through which the temporal enshrines the eternal. Just as it is by looking through and not at the telescope that we discover greater things, so too it is by looking through and not at things temporal that we discern in them signs or images of things eternal—the expression of God. The eternal is made visible as "poems for the eyes" in and through things temporal, "so that all the growth of knowledge is a kind of spiritualizing of the world; that is, a finding of the eternal in the temporal. For God will not let us get lodged in the temporal, but is always shoving us on to what is beyond."[38] It is Christ who comes "to re-reveal and re-empower the eternals we have ceased to see," those forgotten or pent up voices of eternity within us that await reawakening through the person of Christ "whose office it is to bring the great eternals near and keep them in power." The "theologic Christ" who lies buried beneath the rubble of dogma cannot do this; only the living Christ who has been rescued by symbol and metaphor can be expected to "re-reveal and re-empower" the eternal within each soul.

The relationship between the temporal and the eternal and the image of Christ as the prism of time and eternity fascinated Bushnell up to the very end, as reflected in the last sermon that he preached to his Hartford congregation. The sermon contains heavy doctrinal fare to which his congregation had grown accustomed over the years, as here he focuses once again on the christological implications of the doctrine of the Trinity. Reiterating his long-held conviction that the doctrine of the Trinity is "the best that human language permits" to

---

37 Ibid., 345.

38 Horace Bushnell, "In and by Things Temporal are Given Things Eternal," in *Sermons on Living Subjects* (New York, 1883), 279.

express at once the personality as well as the magnitude of God, Bushnell basically reminds his listeners that Christology needs to be rooted and grounded in the Trinity. Once it slips off its trinitarian base, as has happened in much of New England theology, Christology loses its sure footing and is subject to every whim of the time. Much of nineteenth-century Jesusology and the fanciful expectation of a relation to Jesus in heaven in the future life is the result of a Christology inadequately grounded in and developed from a trinitarian basis. The person of Christ before, during and after the incarnation is grounded in the Trinity as the everlasting prerequisite and fact of revelation. The relations of believers to Christ in the future life are then not to a heavenly Jesus but to the eternal Son, "to God in Christ, and never to Jesus in Christ. . . . Christ will remain, because the Eternal Son is in him, but the Jesus, the human part, will be made subject, or taken away, because all that he could do for us in the revelation of God is done."[39] Christ is at once the preincarnate Son of God and the incarnate Son of man, and he is in history what he is in eternity as both the form of God and the form of a servant. Christ is not divided as the Son of God who is in the Trinity and as the Son of man who is out of the Trinity, for it is precisely this trinitarian basis that holds the two natures in on person of Christ together. Christ is everlastingly centered in the Trinity, and Christology that does not begin and end with the Trinity results in pious Jesusology on the one hand or Unitarianism on the other.

The primary task of Christology is not then to explore the interior composition of Christ's person, but to accept him as the trinitarian medium of God's self-expression to the world. Here is "the beauty and glory of Christ," that he goes before and never behind his flock, "that he does not drive them on before, as a herd of unwilling disciples, but goes before himself, leading them into paths that he has trod, and dangers he has met, and sacrifices he has borne himself, calling them after him and to be only followers."[40] In all of this Christ renders God more approachable, and the point of doing Christology is

---

39 Horace Bushnell, "Our Relations to Christ in the Future Life," in *Sermons on Living Subjects*, 452.

40 Horace Bushnell, "The Personal Love and Lead of Christ," in *Sermons for the New Life*, 133.

to illuminate the nature of the relationship between God and humanity and to demonstrate the approachability of God.

2

In the often reprinted chapter on "The Character of Jesus Forbidding His Possible Classification with Men" from his *Nature and the Supernatural,* Bushnell drives home the point that Christ is not a social reformer, a literary gentlemen, a philanthropist or an example of a good man. But precisely because his character cannot be thus classified with men, the "organific power" of the God-man can transform human consciousness and "new-create" the human race, restoring it to God. Christ is the one who has come out from God and broken into the world as an expression of God, and therefore "Christ and his all-quickening life are in the world, as fixed elements, and will be to the end of time; for Christianity is not so much the advent of a better doctrine, as of a perfect character."[41] The rediscovery and recovery of the person of Christ will come not through resurrecting and reformulating old christological formulas and propositions, but through first accepting what comes to expression in Christ as symbol and metaphor, and then allowing these symbols and metaphors to speak in their own language in the formation of character.

The time has come then to take down the drapery of language to disclose the figure of Christ who has been given to our imagination to be received as the expression of God and interpreted by faith. The person of Christ cannot be reached other than by symbols and by metaphors, for Christ is given not to be formed into doctrines but into character. Speculations on the derivation and composition of Christ's person are largely a waste, and Christology must be led into the way of metaphor if Christ is to be found. "So when we come to the person of Christ; what he is to the imagination, as the express image of God, God thus manifest in the flesh, is everything; what he is in his

---

41 Horace Bushnell, "The Character of Jesus: Forbidding His Possible Classification with Men," in *Nature and the Supernatural as Together Constituting the One System of God* (New York, 1858), 344. This chapter from *Nature and the Supernatural* was reprinted numerous times between 1860 and 1917, a total of fifty-seven years during which it circulated as part of the popular piety of American Protestantism.

merely human personality, and how that personality is related to and unified with the divine nature, is nothing. All is easy when we take him for what of God is expressed in him; but when we raise our psychologic problem in his person, insisting on finding exactly what and how much is in it, and how it is compacted, we are out of our limit, and our speculation is only profane jangling."[42] The imagination is the inlet through which the poetry of the Bible pours, and it is the power by which the truths of God's own images are discerned. The gospel is then truly "a gift to the imagination," and the task of Christology is one of finding the metaphoric meanings of Christ.

42 Horace Bushnell, "Our Gospel a Gift to the Imagination," *Building Eras in Religion* (New York: Charles Scribner's Sons, 1881), 280. This essay originally appearing in the magazine *Hours at Home* 10 (December 1869): 159–72.

# CONCLUSION

The foregoing survey is at best a selective account of the changing conceptions of the person of Christ in American Protestant thought from Jonathan Edwards to Horace Bushnell. No attempt has been made to be comprehensive, but every effort has been made to provide a representative selection of major figures and parties within the period under consideration. It cannot be argued that Christology was the centerpiece of New England theology, and Christology drifted to the edge as the doctrines of sin and human nature, of the atonement, and of the work of the Spirit in regeneration occupied the center. But the question of the person of Christ would not go away, and as the nineteenth century wore on christological interests and concerns did come to play an increasingly important role not only within New England theology but especially beyond it. It was increasingly recognized that the question of the person of Christ, never an idle one for faith, could not be put off and that Christology would have to regain a more prominent position within the theological spectrum. The old formulas no longer served to define the person of Christ, and there were those who refused to be held hostage by them and who were more than willing simply to bypass ancient creeds on their way to new definitions of who Christ is. On the other hand there were those who found solace and assurance in the historical creeds and confessions of the church and held all the more firmly to them as reliable sources upon which to draw in establishing the person of Christ. The divisions were sharp and real and much was at stake as it became increasingly clear that the answer to who Christ is determines to a large extent the nature of Christianity. The identity of Christ surfaced as a decisive and divisive issue, and the christological debates were sharp and impassioned.

All of the participants turned to the same Scripture, but depending on the principles of interpretation employed, not one but many Christs appeared from Scripture. What many turned to as a hoped-for source of unity turned out to be a source of the opposite. All of the participants pleaded for rationality and reasonableness, but again the reason of one became the absurdity of another and as a result not one but many Christs were produced. All of the participants appealed to "common sense" as a reliable resource in the interpretation of Scripture and the formulation of doctrine, but once again common sense was not so kindly in yielding up a unified perception of the person of Christ. All of the participants with varying degrees of enthusiasm and success sought support for their respective positions from the writings of the early church fathers, and again the same patristic sources could yield antithetical results. As a result, in many instances the person of Christ fades behind arguments over who was more faithful to Scripture, reason, common sense and the church fathers.

Christology is integrally related to the doctrines of the Trinity and the incarnation to the one side and to the doctrine of the atonement and justification to the other. For some the person of Christ could not possibly be defined apart from his participation in the Godhead and his relation to the First and Third Person of the Trinity. The trinitarian foundations of Christology were therefore absolutely essential to the task at hand. To the other side were those equally convinced that the person of Christ could never be properly identified unless it was cut loose from the Trinity, and so long as Christology was tied to such an irrational and unscriptural teaching the Christ of the New Testament would never be recovered. The christological implications of the doctrine of the Trinity were therefore a source of dispute and wrangling, and equally troublesome on the other side was the relation of the person of Christ to the doctrine of the atonement. If the question is shifted from who Christ is to what Christ does, then the latter will help to define the former. If the work of Christ is to satisfy divine justice then the Christ who fulfills this task is one thing. But if the work of Christ is the reformation of character, then the Christ who fulfills this function will be something quite different. For much of the period under consideration, the work of Christ or what he does served to drive the definition of the person of Christ or who he is.

Christology was overshadowed by the atonement, and it might be argued even further during this same period that theologically the work of Christ was overshadowed by the work of the Spirit in regeneration. Christology needed then to be rescued from its dependence on the atonement, and this came especially in the work of John Nevin and also Horace Bushnell. In short, questions regarding the incarnation and how eternity enters and relates to time were less pressing and interesting than questions regarding the atonement and how justice relates to mercy. Bringing time and eternity, nature and the supernatural, humanity and divinity into relation with each other is not easy under any circumstance.

# INDEX

# ABOUT THE AUTHOR

Bruce M. Stephens earned his undergraduate degree in philosophy and religion at Allegheny College and the Master of Divinity and a doctorate in church history at Drew University. Dr. Stephens has been a member of the Religious Studies faculty at the Delaware County Campus of The Pennsylvania State University since 1970. He is the author of two books on American Protestant thought, *God's Last Metaphor: The Doctrine of the Trinity from Jonathan Edwards to Horace Bushnell* (1982) and *The Holy Spirit in American Protestant Thought 1750–1850* (1992). He has published numerous journal articles on themes related to religion in American culture.